ATTITUDES TO THE BODY IN WESTERN CHRISTENDOM

Attitudes to the Body
in Western Christendom

FRANK BOTTOMLEY, MA, PhD

LEPUS BOOKS

LONDON

© Lepus Books 1979
An associate company of Henry Kimpton Ltd
7 Leighton Place, Leighton Road, London NW5 2QL

British Library Cataloguing in Publication Data

Bottomley, Frank, b. 1920
  Attitudes to the body in Western Christendom.
  1. Body, Human (in religion, folk-lore, etc.)
  —History
  I. Title
  233   BR115.B/

ISBN 0-86019-032-3

Typesetting by Malvern Typesetting Services Ltd
Printed in Great Britain at the
University Press, Cambridge

CONTENTS

PREFACE

Attitudes towards the body reflect social pressure and intellectual concerns and, equally, express themselves in a variety of forms varying from games and recreations to art and literature. This book, which treats both the positive and negative sources of the Western tradition in regard to the body, should consequently be of interest and perhaps of concern to those involved with physical education in all its aspects, to sociologists, general and cultural historians, theologians and concerned Christians, as well as the general public.

An attempt has been made to trace and assess the influence and teaching of the Western Church from its beginnings to the disintegration of the Reformation and its aftermath, with some consideration of the widespread effects both of its apparent failures and successes. An extensive bibliography and full notes allow the interested student both to assess the thesis and to pursue some matters beyond the necessarily restricted confines of the present work, which is believed to be the first attempt to consider the subject in this particular way.

It is my thesis that Christianity brought into the world a new concept of the relationship of the creation to the Creator, a new concept of man and a new respect for the flesh which, as its cardinal belief, it proclaimed has been joined eternally to the nature of God Himself. As a historical religion, the message of Christianity was affected both positively and negatively by the thought forms and intellectual assumptions of its environment. It inherited Jewish notions and came into the Graeco-Roman world; subsequently it had to survive the collapse of the world into which it had entered and endure the long night of the Dark Ages before, with the return of law and order, it was able to show something of its broader possibilities and implications with the dawn of the Middle Ages.

In attitudes towards the body, as in practically everything else, the mediaeval period was struggling towards a synthesis, a balance and an order. This order was crowned and assured by the omnipotence of God, but man occupied a central position for his nature and destiny involved the enfleshment of God and the restoration of the cosmos. Thus the grand themes of the early Middle Ages were the Kingdom of God and the eschatological topics of Death, of a Judgment, Heaven and Hell, but with an increasing delight in the lesser things of life and an awed interest in the wonders of the whole creation of which man was both a summary and a symbol. Not only his own body, but the body of all things exercised an increasing fascination. This development was perhaps less obvious in the literary arts[1] than in the plastic and graphic ones where there was an increasing portrayal of the immediately experienced, the sensible and the particular.

Organic life, which after the end of the ancient world had lost all meaning and value, once more comes to be honoured, and the individual things of experienced reality are henceforth made the subjects of art without requiring some supernatural, other-worldly justification. There is no better illustration of this development than the words of St Thomas (Aquinas), 'God enjoys all things, for each accords with His essence'.[2] They are a complete epitome of the theological justification of naturalism. Everything real, however slight and ephemeral, has an immediate relationship to God: everything expressed the divine nature in its own way and so has its own value and meaning for art too[3] . . . the ideal that no stratum of being, however lowly, is quite without significance or spark of divinity, and so none unworthy to be portrayed in art, marks a new epoch. (Hauser, 1962, I, 210f.)

This assertion of the goodness of the whole of creation and its hierarchical continuity in a 'great chain of being' would obviously tend to blur any sharp dualism of body and spirit. Furthermore, the fact that this respect for nature and for the human body was rooted in theology meant that there was no room for the sort of naturalism that reduces the whole of reality to a mere sum of sense impressions nor for that kind of sentimental romanticism associated with the name of Rousseau. Similarly, the theological grounding meant that the psychosomatic unity of man would be respected and neither male nor female would be reduced to a body object or their sexual nature exploited under the guise of liberation.[4]

The notion that all things, however different, are linked together effects a subtler modification of the previous sharp distinction between the conventional male and female attributes. Not only in thought, but in action, in social structures as well as in literature, physical beauty and intelligence, gentleness and power are increasingly seen as attributes of the individual and not of the sex. This interchange of the highest qualities of humanity and their separation from sexual typology can be seen as a feminisation of the age or of a cyclic triumph of 'matrism' over 'patrism' but it seems better understood as a characteristically mediaeval tensioned balance which, among other things, raises woman to new heights and places her in a position so novel and unexpected as to seem, at first sight, quite incomprehensible.

The same period also produced a new concept of love which is viewed as 'a sovereign principle of education, an ethical power and channel of the deepest experience of life'. In these words, Hauser (1962, I, 191) is speaking specifically of the poetry of chivalry, but this 'romantic' expression is peripheral rather than central. The Middle Ages not only restored and refined the love between man and man, as expressed by 'friendship' and 'comradeship', but it also nourished the tender aspects of such affection without the suspicion of homosexuality. Perhaps an even greater achievement was its transference of this kind of love to the relations between man and woman to allow the fullest kind of reciprocal and equal relationship, whether or not it was accompanied by sexual union. This love was of the kind which could and would give its all for the beloved, whether that beloved was man, woman or God. Its mediaeval preacher was St Bernard of Clairvaux, but its original exemplar was Christ Himself as portrayed in the Gospel of St John. It was a love in the Body which would sacrifice even the Body in its divine cause. This theme is most graphically and movingly represented in the hagiographical accounts of 'spiritual friendships' e.g. in St Ailred of Rievaulx's treatise *On Friendship* and, in the plastic arts, by the carvings of the group *Jesus and the Beloved Disciple*.[5]

This total mediaeval synthesis which embraced the body in its strengths and weaknesses, but without self-consciousness or disorder, grew until its flowering in the cultural explosion which is usually called the Renaissance. Here, something of the potentiality of a balanced and reverent view of the body can be observed until the unstable order collapses under internal and external pressures. The most serious of these latter, from the point of view of ecclesiastical attitudes to the body, is the Reformation which, from a theological point of view, manifests that unbalanced emphasis of a partial truth which is usually described as heresy.

After the breakup of Western Christendom, occasioned by the Reformation, it seems illogical to talk of the Church's attitudes to the body, though what might be called sectarian points of view persist with greater or lesser strength. At this point it seemed rational to bring the study to a conclusion by pointing out what seem to be some of the consequences of the loss of the balanced development which had been founded in the Fathers, survived through the Dark Ages and was showing increasing promise in the late Middle Ages and the associated Renaissance.

I offer this introductory survey with apologies and some misgivings. The subject is of obvious importance and interest, yet I know of no extended treatment of it. It was my original intention to examine the ideas of Christian leaders in the West (the West was taken as more central and also to limit the subject), particularly theologians, and to supplement their expressions with that of

Christian art, especially painting and sculpture. Even this purpose has had to be severely limited because of economic situations, and exploration of the area has constantly revealed new sources of information and contingent areas which are not without relevance. One would have liked hundreds of illustrations – not merely from the plastic arts, but from the history of costume, from architecture and portraiture, because such areas show the 'received teaching' as distinct from the 'transmitted teaching', and also because the witness of art is no less germane than that of the theologian. If one confines oneself to the written 'evidence' one is aware of vast tracts that are unexplored: sermons, romances and novels – all of which show something of the reception of Christian teaching by the laity who are, after all, the Church. A complete treatment would have had to include the performing arts plus dance and the possible source of them both: the liturgical worship of the Church with its sacralisation of time and space and movement. The great Easter liturgy is particularly important in this connection.

Attitudes towards the body extend to its use and abuse, from the penal codes and forms of corporal punishment to attitudes towards sex and marriage: very largely, much of this material has also had to be omitted or cursorily treated. I would particularly have liked to attempt a 'theology of the body' as a concluding chapter with some indications of fruitful development and criticism of what seem to me, at any rate, to be false assumptions, such as seeing sex primarily from a productive angle. But this would perhaps be another book.

In apology for the present book, I must show not only my awareness of its omissions but also, perhaps, explain some of its inclusions. In the earlier part, in particular, I have inserted verbatim material frequently because this is not always easily accessible to the enquirer. Some material may appear to be at the best peripheral and at the worst irrelevant, but I hope its purpose becomes clearer as the reader continues. Attitudes to the human body are not only complex but affected by a variety of influences, some of which might be surprising. It is a paradox that though our body lies in the area of our most intimate knowledge it is intrinsically very mysterious, particularly in the relationship between the knower and the known. Body-concepts are affected by social and cultural assumptions as much as by individual ones. Similarly, theological assumptions (even for the believer) hover in a kind of limbo between the heaven of Revelation and the hell of the sociology of knowledge. The fundamental task of the theologian is to disentangle the *philosophia perennis* from its local habitation and temporal name. I have spent a comparatively long time on the background and first beginnings of the Church's attitudes to the body because I believe that this is fundamental to the later development. How far that development is faithful to the original and how far it has been corrupted and when, if ever, it reached expression is for the reader to decide. This book is an attempt to identify the development.

1

THE GRAECO-ROMAN
BACKGROUND

Christianity was born into the late classical world, a cultural amalgam mainly of Greek and Roman elements but not without trace elements from the East.[1] In order to see and understand the influence of this new religion on ideas of the body, or anything else, some treatment of this background is necessary and we will do so under the headings of religion, philosophy and practice.

Religion
The religion of late antiquity was syncretistic, open and generally tolerant; though there were exceptions to this tolerance when the safety of the State was thought to be involved. Consequently, at the beginning of the Christian era there is a confusing variety of survivals and new arrivals in the religious sphere. Prehistoric notions of life after death continue, whether this survival is conceived as corporeal in another world or as spirits to be placated in this world. Primitive gods from Rome's beginnings are remembered as, for example, Vulcan who seems to have been conceived as a kind of archetype of the tough, practical Roman craftsman. Even the established 'high gods' were ill-defined both in function and attributes, and this vagueness was increased by the Roman habit of assimilating them to the chief gods of other peoples, especially the Greeks, whose Zeus, Hera and Athene became more or less identified with Jupiter, Juno and Minerva.

If the principal gods of the ancient world were ill-defined, the confusion becomes more confounded as we penetrate further into the Roman heaven with its increased insubstantiality and proliferation of gods, of whom some are little more than names associated with a particular gate (as Janus) or a specific stone (as Terminus).[2] These lesser gods were almost innumerable and were related to nearly every conceivable situation, action or predicament,[3] and their worshippers were sometimes in doubt as to whether they were to be addressed as male or female and often covered their uncertainties by erecting altars 'to the unknown god'.[4]

Religion and magic were almost indistinguishable. Ritual instructions required the exclusion of strangers or 'the profane', the secrecy of the words used in the ritual and the necessity for the whole being repeated if the minutest error was made in either word or ceremonial act. Omens were seen everywhere, charms were provided for all occasions and many hallowed ceremonies perpetuated ideas and taboos which were unknown to their contemporary practitioners. The lifeless conventionality and moral meaninglessness of traditional Roman religion would have led to its extinction if it had not been for its association with the State and for the Roman veneration of the past. The State cult served to maintain the nature and persistence of Rome: it identified with *Romanitas*, with civic loyalty and it had little, if anything, to do with the relation between the individual and the Divine.

The political changes that followed the end of the Republic (*c.* 30 B.C.) were accompanied by religious change as the Roman citizens became increasingly familiar with the religions and philosophies of other nations and peoples. Some of these elements were brought within the State cult either by assimilation or addition, but others were to provide expression for a personal religion. The importation of Eastern cults had begun earlier and is exemplified in the critical situation of 205 B.C. when the Asiatic 'Great Mother' Cybele was translated from Galatia to Rome.[5] With Cybele was associated the cult of Attis and the orgiastic ceremonies of self-castrated priests which Roman citizens were forbidden to attend when the Senate belatedly discovered this association. Twenty years later, the orgies of the Bacchanalia[6] also caused alarm and the Senate forbade the worship of Bacchus in Rome. But, in spite of the efforts of the authorities, the dams were breached and the Eastern flood would continue until it brought both Judaism and Christianity into the very heart of Rome. Assimilation would continue also: one of the forms of the Great Mother goddess of the Orient was represented in the famous cult-statue at Ephesus, the many-breasted manifestation of fecundity. She became identified with the Greek Artemis and the Roman Diana and her enormous and splendid temple was one of the seven wonders of the ancient world. Her devotees and dependents were to bring the Christian missionary, Paul, into danger of life and limb in the first century of the new era.[7]

The conjunction of Roman deities to their Greek counterparts led not only to the appropriation and universalisation of Greek legend and myth, but it also turned the minds of some Roman citizens to the Greek philosophy which was to become a substitute religion for thoughtful aristocrats. Ordinary men (and women) might find in Eastern emotionalism the release and relief they sought in the 'mystery religions' (of Isis, Dionysius, etc.), but the educated Roman who had lost faith in his own religion was little attracted (at least in the Early Empire) to the frenzy and emotion of Asiatic novelties and, instead, he turned for his comfort to Greek philosophy.

Philosophy

Heracleitus and Democritus apart, Greek philosophy tended to focus on the concept of 'mind' – so that Anexagoras of Miletus was even nicknamed 'mind'. Plato had been much concerned with mind and its relation to the absolute world of ideas, but both he and his great pupil, Aristotle, seemed less relevant in the contemporary world. They had both believed that the 'good life' involved active participation in political life, i.e. in the affairs of the city-state or *polis*. These human-sized units had been swept away by Alexander's creation of a multi-racial society, centrally administered, which the Romans had inherited and developed. Political change was accompanied by a shift in philosophical interest: from metaphysics to ethics and from society to the individual. By the middle of the first century B.C., Cicero considers philosphy to be 'the art or guide of life' and concerned with the 'training or healing of the soul' while Plutarch, over a century later, was to describe it as 'the only medicine for spiritual diseases'.

When St Paul visited Athens in A.D. 59,[8] it was with the Epicureans and Stoics that he disputed, for these philosophical schools had become the chief influences in the intellectual formation of the upper classes throughout the Roman Empire since they seemed able to meet the spiritual questions of the individual at a time when society was in a state of flux. Epicurus' approach to the problems of life was rationalistic, voluntarist and resigned. Man has reason, free will and is involved in a natural process with which the gods have nothing to do. Even if gods exist, they are irrelevant since they are remote from and utterly unconcerned with man: from this it follows that concepts of hell or of divine retribution are sheer folly, nor is there any heavenly life beyond the grave. Thus, this life is all we have and 'therefore Death, the king of terrors, is nothing to us, because as long as we exist Death is not present, and when Death is come we are no more'. The great enemies of this rational approach to life (and death) were superstition on the one hand and scientific determinism on the other. Indeed, of the two, the latter is the greater folly: 'It were better to follow the fairy-tales of the gods than to be a slave to the determinism of the scientists. The one does suggest a hope of appeasing the gods by reverencing them, but the other implies a necessity which is implacable.' The result of this approach was an almost Eastern resignation. The true Epicurean would concentrate on the attainment of *ataraxia* (peace and quiet, untroubled tranquillity) and to this end would avoid public life, passion and matrimony. The removal of the fear of death, the knowledge that this life was all and that the gods were non-existent could provide for the noble-minded a self-reliant guide to a detached and contemplative life. The same principles, however, could also offer a rational basis for a life of self-indulgence to less lofty souls. Epicureanism reached Rome at a time when materialism and sensual excess were making great inroads, particularly among the young, and the Romans, by and large, took from it what they wanted. Generally, they degraded and perverted Epicurus' teaching and gave the word 'epicurean' the sense it commonly bears, though Horace, Lucretius and Virgil remained close to the original doctrine.

Stoicism originated with a contemporary of Epicurus, the Semitic Zeno (c. 335–264 B.C.) who had an uncompromising belief in eternal order and a consequent intolerance of the imperfect. In his developed teaching there was nothing fortuitous about the universe which was governed by an immutable law whose transgression was the source of all evil. The true philosopher is the man who can tell evil from good and act accordingly. The ultimate physical reality is fire which Zeno associated with reason or God and the pregnant originality of his system lay in his identification of the intellectual 'logos' or 'reason' of the Socratics with the material 'logos' of Heracleitus. Thus, the reason which rules the universe becomes identified with the reason that indwells man and should rule his life. The law of the universe is also the law of human nature which we can realise only by conforming to the divine purpose and thus find our own freedom in service to the cosmic law.

Stoicism was more fortunate in its transmission to Rome than Epicureanism had been, for its first teacher there was the outstanding Panaetius who not only knew his subject but the kind of people he was trying to teach. The disciplined and practical Roman mind would naturally be attracted by the idea of the universal rule of law, but Panaetius increased this sympathy by emphasising Stoicism's relevance to political theory and to the duties of the ordinary citizen as well as to the necessity of living in accordance with nature. Nevertheless, Stoicism remains a chilly doctrine[9] associated with endurance, duty, self-discipline and a generally puritanical cast of mind. It had little to offer to the emotions and indeed required the suppression of their outward manifestations if not their total annihilation, yet, in spite of this deficiency, it inspired a philosopher (Seneca), a slave (Epictetus) and an emperor (Marcus Aurelius).

In ideas, as in architecture, the Romans were great borrowers of useful inventions and they were not obsessed either by purity of style or of doctrine. Another element in their eclectic world of thought was provided by Pythagoras, the mathematician and mystic (sixth century B.C.), whose ideas included belief in a future life, in the transmigration of souls, and the notion that this life needed to be purged by asceticism in preparation for another to come. Plato was said to have consulted Pythagoras about the immortality of the soul, but his ideas lay dormant until the early first century when they were revived in Rome by Posidonius who continued Panaetius' work of making philosophy digestible to the Romans. Zeno's passion for unity had produced a pantheistic doctrine which admitted of no distinction between earth and heaven or soul and body and left no place for a transcendent god. Panaetius' modifications had included an injection of Platonic-Aristotelian psychology which tended towards a dualistic concept of soul and body and thus opened up a way for new ideas in a society which had abandoned burial for cremation and given up the notion of a prolongation of human life in a shadowy existence beneath the earth. Posidonius continued this tendency and, in Warde Fowler's (Fowler, 1974) words, 'at once gave mysticism – or transcendentalism if we choose so to call it – its chance. For in such a dualistic psychology *it is the soul that gains and the body that loses*'. (Our italics.)[10]

This neo-Pythagorism was the source of Cicero's transcendentalism and he eulogised the Pythagoreans in his influential *Tusculan Disputations* (64 B.C.). It is Posidonius' teaching, almost as much as Plato's, which underlies *The Republic* begun ten years later. The most famous part of this work is its conclusion – 'The dream of Scipio' which would, sixteen centuries later, affect European art and thought. The 'Dream' is concerned with the paradisal reward of those that 'have done the state some service', but we must limit ourselves to the answer to the Younger Scipio's question about life after death. He is told that they 'are indeed all alive who have escaped from the bondage of the body as from a prison; but that life of yours which men so call is really death'. His father also tells him that he cannot join the blissful state 'unless that God whose temple is everything that you see has freed you from the prison of the body', but if the son loves justice and duty then 'such a life is the road to the skies, to that gathering of those who have completed their earthly lives and have been relieved of the body and who live in yonder place you now see . . . and which you on earth, borrowing a Greek term, call the Galaxy'. The last words in this book are given to young Scipio's grandfather: 'Strive on, indeed and be sure that it is not you who are mortal, but only this body . . . the spirit is your true self, not that physical figure. Know, then, that you are a god, if a god is that which lives, feels, remembers and foresees and which rules the body over which it is set just as the supreme God above us rules the universe', and he concludes with a reminder that the Great First Cause is itself a Spirit – 'the only force which moves itself, it surely has no beginning and is immortal'.[11]

Practice

The above kinds of philosophical and religious ideas obviously affected only a small proportion of the population, generally those endowed with education, leisure and wealth. What of the rest? The poor and ordinary do not make history because their records are scanty: they do not leave records themselves and the general is rarely news. We can, however, catch a glimpse of more common attitudes through literature, archeology and passing references, to some of which we will now turn.

We have already noticed the vulgarisation of Epicurean ideas when they are transmitted to the Romans, and we might briefly consider some of their more popular (and debased) expressions. In all decadent societies, including our own, there is a tendency to demand instant pleasure at the expense of delayed gratification, and the Romans were no exception to this principle. Since the body affords more direct, immediate and easy pleasure than the mind, there was a natural (or unnatural?) urge to gratify it. Even the genial and balanced poet Horace[12] advised his audience to cut down their distant hopes and to confine their expectations within a narrow and realistic compass 'since, even while we talk, death draws near and therefore we must take all that each day offers'. This, to Horace, was largely summed up in good talk, conviviality, wine, women and song. A generation earlier, Catullus had pursued and celebrated the pleasures of the flesh, equating life with love, and seeking thousands of embraces since man's short day is followed by the perpetual sleep of death which devours everything from men to sparrows.[13] Yet he was fastidious in his Epicureanism and well aware of the existence and use of male toiletries (cf. Ovid's advice to lovers in *Ars Amatoria*, tr. Moore, 1965, 37f., 93–9).

This gathering of rosebuds (and lesser blooms) was not confined to a bored upper class, the dilettante men-about-town, who had the leisure for such pleasures. It is not usually realised that, at the height of the Empire in Rome, nearly one day in two was a public holiday and that it was a matter of high politics that suitable mass entertainments should be provided to entertain the rabble upon these days. The free shows and spectacles which filled the theatre, amphitheatre or circus established a salutary contact between the exalted emperor and the mob 'which prevented him on the one hand from shutting himself off in dangerous isolation and prevented them on their part from forgetting the august presence of the Caesar' (Carcopino, 1956, 211). The historian, Fronto, said of his model Emperor Trajan that 'his wisdom never failed to pay attention to the stars of the theatre, the circus or the arena, for he well knew that the excellence of a government is shown no less in its care for the amusements of the people than in serious matters, and that although the distribution of corn and money may satisfy the individual, spectacles are necessary for the contentment of the masses' (cited Carcopino, 1956, 213). Subsequent tyrants and totalitarian governments have learned well from Trajan and even 'democracies' have recently paid more attention to the cultivation and provision of distractions and leisure activities deprived of implications beyond themselves than to those which might involve the stimulation of thought about the purpose and end of human existence.

The games, *par excellence*, were the chariot-races (*circenses*) and the largest stadium for this purpose, the Circus Maximus, seated 150,000 spectators at their ease and possibly provided over a quarter of a million places in all. The attraction of these races was increased by acrobatic tricks, foul play and, above all, gambling. To maintain the tension and/or interest, on at least some occasions, the boredom of the intervals between the races was lessened by crucifixions or similarly barbarous executions so that the crowds would never lack entertainment.[14] The popular esteem lavishly given to the charioteers who starred in these races far exceeded that of pop-stars and professional footballers combined in present-day culture. This veneration was apparently based on the physical and psychological qualities of these heroes: their strength, imposing presence, agility and coolness, the expertise resulting from severe and prolonged training, together with their cavalier disregard for the real and frequent danger of death or serious injury. The driver or charioteer was hired at enormous cost to serve a particular colour or faction which not only had its own staff and mindless supporters but also professional cheer-leaders.[15] Interest in the teams was a substitute for political or other human concerns and, like all pseudo-sports, it was strongly underpinned by gambling. The mania for winning unearned money held the crowd in its grip, and various means of spending money in physical pleasure was provided in or near the course.

All Rome today is at the circus:
Such sights are for the young, whom it behoves
To shout and make rash wagers with a smart wench by their side.[16]

In the days of the Republic, the theatre had been even more popular than the circus and now, though its popularity had declined, it still flourished in magnificent buildings.[17] The performances had declined from the majestic tragedies of the Greeks to third-rate musicals and worse. The dedication of a team of actors working in a quasi-religious activity had been replaced by a decadent 'star' system where the supporting cast of actors, musicians and dancers were nameless satellites around the solo actor or 'pantomime'.[18]

It was the soloist alone who filled the stage with his movement and
the theatre with his voice. He alone incarnated the entire action,
whether singing, miming or dancing. He prolonged his youth and
preserved his slimness by a strict diet which banned all acid food
and drinks and which called for emetics and purgatives the
moment his waistline was threatened. Faithful to the most severe
training, he exercised unremittingly to preserve the tone of his
muscles, the suppleness of his joints, and the volume and charm of
his voice. Skilled in personifying every human type, in
representing every human situation, he became 'the pantomine'
par excellence, whose imitations embraced the whole of nature,
and who created a second nature with his fantasy. (Carcopino,
1956, 227).

These stars became the 'personalities' of their day, the darling of the
women, and their petty rivalries were a threat to public order. The
Empress Domitia gave herself to the pantomime Paris; an earlier
star, Pylades, filled Augustan Rome with gossip about himself; under
Tiberius a squabble between fans of rival show-biz personalities
provoked the death of a tribune, a centurion and several soldiers who
were trying to restore order.

These pantomimes were not only actor-managers but total dic-
tators of the matter and manner of the productions in which they
appeared and, naturally, they aimed at catching the eye and
titillating other senses rather than touching the heart or reaching the
mind. Their shows were frankly sensational, centring on violence and
sex. Not only was perverse sexual activity enacted on the stage but
the violence, too, was often real and condemned criminals were
hurled to their death, had their tongues cut out or were otherwise
maimed to add more than a touch of verisimilitude to an otherwise
bald and unconvincing narrative. One play concluded with a man
tortured to death and another combined crucifixion with mauling by
an enraged bear, and in neither was there anything imaginary or
illusory. That the masses were not sickened by such atrocities was not
unrelated to the fact that the ghastly butcheries of the State-
supported amphitheatres had long since debased their feelings and
perverted their instincts in regard to the human body.

It is an incredible, and admonitory, fact that the Romans, so
admirable in many ways, made human sacrifice into a festival
celebrated by the whole city and that they preferred, above all other
entertainments, the spectacle of men killing and being killed for
their delight. The emperors pandered to this murderous lust and
practically monopolised gladiatorial shows because of their
usefulness as an instrument of political power. It is perhaps

significant that the Flavian amphitheatre, or Colosseum, became the dominant building in Rome. It is a triumph of architecture and of functional building – an edifice most apt for its purpose. It is estimated that it provided seats for 45,000 and standing room for a further 5,000 and it is provided with a most ingenious system of easy, undisputed and ordered access, providing each division of citizen with a well-planned progression to his numbered seat while avoiding any contact with inferior or superior social classes.

Not only the building itself, but all its facilities were a triumph of practical civil engineering. The audience was well-protected against rampaging beasts (either human or animal) by a metal grille, and from the hot sun by a vast awning that could be pulled over the entire building. Provision was made for colonnaded walks, foyers where the crowds could idle before the show and between the acts, stalls for food and drink, promenades for the ladies of easy virtue, and *vomitoria* where patrons could be sick – not because of the sights they had witnessed but through the overindulgence of their bellies. There was a system for flooding the arena with water for real naval battles and a complex array of ramps and hoists by which animals could be driven or launched on to the stage.

The gladiators were highly organised and expertly trained, so that they could fight with murderous efficiency either on land or water, and were housed in special barracks built by the emperors. The wild and exotic animals, which were so painfully and wantonly destroyed, were kept until required in the emperor's menagerie when they arrived as political presents from subject provinces or client kings. In a show, which usually lasted from dawn to dusk and which, on special occasions, might be prolonged into the night, it was important to prevent the crowd from suffering a moment's boredom. This was usually done by constantly varying the forms and instruments of death, though there were some acts which were little more than impressive circus turns: panthers drawing chariots, lions releasing at command a newly-caught live hare, tigers docilely licking a hand which had just ceased whipping them, elephants doing obeisance to the imperial box and tracing with their trunks Latin words in the sand. These animal acts may have temporarily amused the Romans, but their full involvement required blood: either strangely matched pairs of maddened animals fighting to the death or men facing large and ferocious beasts and deliberately increasing their danger, or flaunting their skill, by feats of daring. These deadly animal performances were called *venationes* (hunts) and could be viewed as an exaggerated representation of ancient hunting were it not for the incredible number of kills, for example 5,000 in one day at Titus' inauguration of the Colosseum in A.D. 80.

More sinister and germane to our purpose were the gladiatorial shows proper, where men fought against men, differently armed to give variety: 'Samnite' v. 'Thracian', *murmillio* v. *retiarius*. Sometimes the entertainment began with a mimic battle using blunted weapons as a kind of aperitif to the *munus* (offering) where pairs fought either simultaneously or in sequence and where the only hope of avoiding death was to deal it first to one's opponent. Before this munus, the combatants were treated to a lavish banquet to which the ghoulish public were admitted so that they could see the various attitudes with which the gladiators partook of their last supper. Some would abandon themselves to the pleasures of the moment and eat gluttonously; some, more prudently, would try to improve their chances of survival by eating and drinking in moderation; others would lament their fate, commend their dependants to the onlookers and make their wills.

The munus itself began with a ceremonial deployment where the gladiators in parade dress, covered with a purple and gold chlamys, were driven in chariots from their barracks to the amphitheatre. Here they alighted and, with batmen carrying their arms, they marched at ease to halt before the imperial box and salute the emperor with the words, 'Hail Caesar, we who are about to die, greet you!'. Then the parade uniform was exchanged for battle-dress, the weapons checked to ensure that they were lethal and then redistributed before the duellists were grouped in twos by lot so as to produce either pairs with matching arms or grotesque combinations such as not only Thracian v. Samnite, but Negro v. Negro or dwarf v. woman. The fighting opened to an instrumental accompaniment of flutes, trumpets, horns and even a hydraulic organ and the spectators settled down to enjoy the sport, giving it added zest by betting on *parmularius*, *retiarius*, or whatever they fancied. To prevent any arranged fights or lack of murderous enthusiasm, an instructor stood by each pair, supported by 'whippers-in' who drove. the fighters to a homicidal frenzy by screamed encouragement or bloody blows. In this task they were aided by the screaming of the enthusiastic crowd and their yells of 'That's got him!', 'He's had it!', and the like.

As soon as a combatant fell mortally wounded, other attendants, costumed to represent Charon or Hermes Psychopompus – the personages who escorted souls across the river of death – smote the prostrate gladiator on the forehead with a mallet to ensure his death, after which the corpse was removed on a stretcher or dragged out with a meat-hook, and the sand was raked over so that the next blood would be more conspicuous. Sometimes both combatants died, sometimes both survived without the strength to strike another blow even under the impulse of savagely applied whips: in such cases a draw was declared. Most frequently, the prostrate figure was only temporarily stunned or incapacitated by wounds and he appealed for quarter to his victorious opponent who would renounce his rights in the presence of the emperor. The crowd, according to their judgment of the loser's performance, would hoarsely indicate their view of whether the fallen man deserved to live or die. The emperor, if present, would give his verdict by an up- or down-turned thumb and perhaps the loser would survive until the next Roman holiday. Carcopino (1956, 242) mentions the case of a gladiator subsequently slain by an adversary that he had once spared and his tombstone records this fiercely practical advice: 'Take warning from my fate: the victor should always kill the loser!'

The winner was lavishly rewarded on the spot, given the palm-wreath of victory and immediately joined the ranks of popular idols, together with the pantomimes and charioteers. The successful criminal was lionised by men and avidly sought after by women, even those from the highest social classes. If he was ruthless enough, adequately adept at killing, and very lucky indeed, he might even be given the wooden sword which signified his freedom and retirement from the socially approved game of inhuman butchery. It was, however, not unknown for a successful gladiator to decline this relief if he found the rewards of successful slaughter too attractive: the luxurious life of the barracks, the surrender of women,[19] the plaudits of the crowd and the thrill of danger.

Some notion of the scale of human victims can be gained from the fact that a single *munus* in A.D. 202 lasted nearly seventeen weeks and involved almost 5,000 pairs. It is a significant social comment that such highly regarded characters as Cicero and the Younger Pliny tolerated such abominable events because they encouraged bravery and contempt for pain and death. Excess breeds excess and, as sensitivity became blunted, atrocity had to be piled on atrocity to hold the mob enthralled. Combats were devised where the fallen was replaced by another gladiator until the entire body of combatants, save one, was exterminated. As a means of spicing the noon intermission, condemned criminals were paired, one armed and the other defenceless, and, as soon as the latter had been despatched, his slayer was disarmed to be the defenceless one of the next pair and so the grisly alternation continued until the last body was hooked away.[20] The pleasure of watching helpless victims must have had a special appeal, for after Augustus' reign the criminal penalty of *ad bestias* was introduced and alleged felons of both sexes and all ages provided a matinee performance in the arena where they were mauled to death by enraged wild animals prodded from their cages in the basement. There was a special titillation if the victims were attractive virgins.

The Romans clearly loved to see the human body bloodily mangled and dismembered, and indeed its contemptuous and sadistic ill-treatment seems to have provided the greatest possible pleasure in a world which had seen men crucified in thousands. But there were other pleasures to be derived from the body: banquets and orgies, spiced with music and Syrian dancing-girls – though these, because of their expense, were distractions of the rich and notable expressions of the principle of conspicuous expenditure as a proof of social status. Food was valued in such circles for its rarity, its abundance, its novelty and, above all, for its costliness. The body was not only satiated with extravagant and exotic foods and drinks but, increasingly, private houses and public places were provided with *vomitoria* so that the gorged could disgorge in order to gorge again. Not unsurprisingly, because of its association with sadism and excess, unbridled sexual licence affected all classes from the highest to the lowest.

About A.D. 50, the time that St Peter and St Paul came to Rome, Messalina, wife of the Emperor Claudius, used to wait until her husband was asleep and then, according to Juvenal, would leave the palace clad in a cloak and attended by a single slave. She was on her way to take her position in the special cell reserved for her use in the public brothels where she would spend the rest of the night, open to all comers, in service as a common prostitute.

> There she stood with nipples bare and gilded . . . here she graciously received all comers, asking from each his fee; and when, at last, the brothel-keeper dismissed his girls, she remained to the very last before closing her cell and, with passion still raging hot within her, went sorrowfully away. Then, exhausted by men but still unsatisfied, with soiled cheeks and begrimed with the smoke of the lamps, she took back to the imperial pillow all the odours of the stews.[21]

We do not know what Messalina charged for her services, but there is a wall notice outside a whorehouse in Pompeii which reads: 'I am yours for two *asses* cash' – the price of a mediocre bottle of wine. An expense account from the same place lists 'three *asses* for wine' and 'eight for women'. Another wall inscription shows provincial life aping the metropolis as best it could by advertising the imminent arrival of a show involving thirty pairs of gladiators and 'a full card of wild beast combats and awnings for the spectators'.[22]

Within the context of using the body for gain, we might mention Trimalchio's boast that it was through his indifferent service of both his master and his mistress that he got the means for his own start in life.[23] The body of a slave was generally considered as no more than a living machine to serve its owner's every need and whim,[24] though there were protests, like this from Juvenal:

> Does the paterfamilias believe that the bodies and souls of slaves are made of the same stuff as his own? Or is he inculcating cruelty in his family, never happy until he has summoned a torturer and he can brand someone with a hot iron for stealing a couple of towels? What advice is a father giving his son when he revels in the clanking of a chain and takes wondrous pleasure in branded slaves, in prisons and in his country bridewell?[25]

The same author tells of a woman who crucified slaves at a whim and that so much iron was used for chains that there was a danger of shortages for other uses.[26] It was not until the reign of Hadrian (A.D. 117–38) that masters were forbidden to kill their slaves, sell them to procurers, or commit them to the wild-beast shows or into training at the gladiatorial schools.

These aberrations do not imply that some Romans did not care for the body: their military hospitals were probably unsurpassed until the nineteenth century and the practical art of medicine was included in Celsus' early first-century encyclopedia along with agriculture, warfare, rhetoric, philosophy and jurisprudence, although its practice was apparently confined to Greeks and Orientals according to the testimony of Pliny.[27] Perhaps the most outstanding institution of the Romans was the public baths which had special rights of water-supply, their detailed operations being covered by law.[28] These establishments functioned not only in some of the largest buildings of Rome itself, but occupied humbler premises in such places as Portuguese mining villages where the entrance fees were legally fixed at half an *as* for men and one *as* for women.[29] Some baths were privately owned and a wall-notice in Pompeii offers the lease of 'the élite Venus baths' while others were State establishments bearing the name of an emperor. The entrance fee was always comparatively small and certain classes of people (including soldiers and minors) were granted free admission. All were built and furnished to the full extent of available resources and they provided community, recreation and social centres in every municipality (Pliny mentions that even the village to which he retreated from the city had three public bathing establishments). The city ones were grandiose and sumptuous, real 'people's palaces', finished in a variety of expensive marbles, adorned with statues of the gods of health and hygiene and providing within their walls libraries, art galleries and facilities for sport. They also provided massage, depillation, snacks and refreshment and produced so much noise that they made poor neighbours.[30] They also offered places for assignment, sexual stimulation[31] and opportunities to satisfy the desires thus whetted either on the premises or very near.[32] A description of Rome, composed about the middle of the fourth century A.D., lists not only eleven palatial buildings for public bathing but also includes more than 300 smaller establishments with the same function.

SUMMARY

The Roman world into which the Church came was decadent in both philosophy and life. The former was increasingly emphasising a dichotomy between body and soul, and abstract thought tended to denigrate the body in order to free the soul for the contemplation of higher things on earth and to facilitate its ascent, when disburdened of the body, to the realms above. Philosophy was very much a minority interest and the majority indulged their own bodies when they could, mostly at the expense of the bodies of others, and there seems no evidence of its consideration as a temporary tenement of the soul. Immediate gratification, already facile enough for a fallen nature, was positively encouraged by the State on the principle that a satiated body will leave the mind little energy for the pursuit of disturbing truth. The economic combined with the political environment to encourage the abuse and exploitation of human bodies, and the fullest use was made of the drives of hunger, sex and sadism.

The most barbarous recreations were spectator-sports, salted by extensive gambling and auxiliary indulgences, to whose amenities the fullest resources of a most efficient technology had been applied. Not only were bodies bought and sold in thousands but many, including gladiators, pantomimes and prostitutes, seem to have been eager to sell themselves or to remain in this state because of its compensations. The State not only participated in this traffic, but positively encouraged it as a displacement of attention which emphasised superficial, physical, crowd and sensational elements at the expense of the profound, human, individual and contemplative elements. The mere survival of the citizens of the Roman world was assured by bread and other doles, while his contentment was gained by holidays filled with mind-destroying entertainments. 'Bread and circuses' were enough for him whose individual resources had been eroded or stultified by client relationships and a standard of living resting on the exploitation of both individuals and races.

The same tendencies were developed by a multitude of public holidays, State and individual benevolences which provided him with both a leisure and uses for it which cost little in money or mental effort. The body had no dignity and its care was either a military necessity in the hospitals or an indulgence in the baths. There seems no hint anywhere that man was a psychosomatic entity whose physical and psychological needs enmeshed and interacted. The thoughtful found meaning either in service of the state or life of the mind, while the thoughtless lost themselves in others' torments or their own physical satiety.

2
IDEAS OF THE BODY IN THE OLD TESTAMENT

The Acts of the Apostles portrays the shift of the Christian centre from Jerusalem to Rome as a Jewish sect became a Catholic church. Nevertheless, its roots were in Jewry, its founder was brought up in the Jewish religion and He presupposed certain ideas in the minds of His first hearers: in particular, notions about the nature of God and man. The Hebrews considered man to be basically a unity, though their use of language does not always make this quite clear.

Basic elements in Hebrew anthropology

The Old Testament – the teaching that the new Church inherited – presents us with a single psychosomatic entity made up of two elements represented by the Hebrew words *nephesh* and *basar*. [1]

The former is usually translated 'soul', but this single English word does scant justice to a very complex concept. [2] The basic meaning of nephesh is 'throat' and thus Jonah cries to God from the bottom of the sea that 'the waters have closed in over my nephesh' (Jonah ii, 5; cf. Wolff, 1975, 11–14). By metonymy, the meaning shifts from the gate of breath to breath and the act of breathing. A further extension embraces the meanings of 'desire' or 'appetite' (Wolff, 1975, 15–17) and we are told, for example, that 'a righteous man considers the nephesh [appetite] of his beast, but the mercy of the wicked is cruel' (Prov. xii, 10) and, in the same book, that 'the nephesh of the treacherous is for violence' (Prov. xiii, 2). Gelin (1968, 14) comments that there is always a pathetic note in the word 'nephesh' and Wolff (1975, 10) heads his study of this word 'needy man'. The final connotation is to express the centre of the human personality or of any living organism – its very being (Wolff, 1975, 18–22). This seems to be its meaning in a number of Psalms, e.g. 'Bless the Lord, O my nephesh' (ciii, 1). 'My nephesh longs, yea faints, for the courts of the Lord' (lxxxiv, 2). The description of the love between David and Jonathan tells how 'the nephesh of Jonathan was knit to the nephesh of David, and Jonathan loved him as his own nephesh' (I Sam. xviii, 1); and the story of the Creation concludes: 'Then the Lord God formed man out of the dust of the ground and breathed into his nostrils the breath of life; and man became a nephesh [a living being]. (Gen. ii, 7).

The word sometimes means 'person' as in Gen. xii, 5 where

Abraham, journeying to Canaan, is described as having with him some nephesh, i.e. some people, some persons. It means 'soul' in the sense that 'the ship sank with a loss of thirty souls', it is 'soul' almost in the Thomist/Aristotelian sense of 'life-principle' except that the Old Testament tells us that the nephesh continues in the underworld of Sheol where man is enfeebled and a mere shadow of himself (Num. vi, 6), but this nephesh is, paradoxically, described as 'dead'. Gelin's conclusion (1968, 15) is that 'my nephesh' could almost be rendered by the personal pronoun reinforced by 'self' – 'myself'.

The second basic element in Hebrew anthropology is represented by the word *basar*, usually translated 'body' or 'flesh', which may indicate infirmity (Wolff, 1975, 26–31), but lacks any pejorative sense or association for the unitative approach sees the basar as the concrete manifestation of the nephesh (Gelin, 1968, 15). Soul and flesh might be distinguished as in Isaiah x, 18, but not as two fundamentally different forms of existence (Richardson, 1950, 83). Soul is more than flesh, but flesh is a perfectly proper manifestation of soul (cf. Gen. ii, 7). Job (xxi, 6) can say: 'horror taketh hold on my flesh' because 'flesh' means the entire human being. 'All flesh' means the visible community of mankind and to be 'of one flesh' by kinship, or, specially, by marriage means to have community of soul. The nephesh is known through the basar and a number of texts seem to regard various parts of the body almost as 'faculties' which relate to and recapitulate the nephesh (Gelin, 1968, 15f), so that in Psalm xvi, 9f. 'heart', 'glory', 'soul' and 'flesh' all refer to the whole man in different manifestations. Thus the 'heart' can be almost the equivalent of the nephesh incarnate.[3] God requires it to be not 'a heart of stone' but a heart of flesh which can be penetrated (Ezek. xxxvi, 26) and Jeremiah speaks of the 'circumcision of the heart' (iv, 4), the inner reality of the covenant marked by the outward sign in the flesh. If the heart is the seat of reason and conscience, then the kidneys seem to be the seat of desire and will and Jeremiah sees God as testing both kidneys and heart (xi, 20). Basic emotions, such as grief and anger, seem to have been associated with the liver (Lam. ii, 11, but cf. Wolff, 1975, 64). However, this usage is to some extent metaphorical or at most represents aspects of the whole man so the Psalmist can thank the Lord because 'in the night my *kidneys* instruct me . . . therefore my *heart* is glad and my *bowels* rejoice, my *flesh* also shall dwell in safety' (ps. xvi, 7, 9, cf. lxxxiv, 2). Similarly, Psalm xxxv, 9–10 parallels 'My *soul* shall be joyful in the Lord' with 'All my *bones* shall say: Lord, who is like thee?'

In the Old Testament, flesh and soul only seem to be in contrast or any sort of opposition[4] when the former is used of man as a whole and the latter of God: 'In God I have put my trust, I will not be afraid;

what can flesh do unto me? (Ps. lvi, 4). 'Now the Egyptians are men and not God; and their horses flesh and not spirit' (Isa. xxxi, 3).

There is another Hebrew word *ruah*, usually translated 'spirit', which should be considered in this context.[5] Originally, it seems to have meant 'wind' – the invisible gust of air that could be beneficient or destructive (e.g. I Kgs xviii, 45; Ps. ciii, 16; Jer. iv, 11) which is sometimes conceived as an instrument of the equally unseen God (Gen. viii, 1; Num. xi, 31; Amos iv, 13; Isa. xi, 15). In view of our earlier referral to the Stoics, it might be worth mentioning that they spoke of a warm Air or Spirit as the source and goal of all things.[6]

This original meaning was soon associated with respiration, with the air that gives and is life. In Genesis i, 2 the creative breath of God moves over the face of the primal waters and in ii, 7 we have God breathing or emitting a ruah into the clay which He will shape into man. This 'breath of God' is the essence of life as the mother of the Maccabean martyrs, 'stirring up her womanish thoughts with a manly *stomach*', declares to her heroic sons: 'I cannot tell you how ye came into my womb; for I neither gave you breath nor life, neither was it I that formed the members of everyone of you; but doubtless the Creator of the world, who formed the generation of man . . . will also of His own mercy give you breath and life again, as you now regard not your own selves for His laws' sake.' (II Macc. vii, 22f). Conversely, to 'expire' or to 'give up the ruah' is to die, as in the speech of the ungodly in Wisdom ii, 2f:

> For we are born at all adventure; and we shall be hereafter as though we had never been; for the breath in our nostrils is as smoke and reason a little spark in the motion of our heart; which, being extinguished, our body shall be turned to ashes and our spirit shall vanish as the soft air.' (cf. II Macc. xiv, 45f).

Thus, even in its connotation of 'breath', the word ruah and its equivalents carries with it overtones of God's dynamic, creative activity (Richardson, 1950, 234). Gelin (1968, 17) goes rather further than this and sees the ruah as 'the source of the nephesh-basar composite'. The ruah can be conceived as a life-force, coming from above, which keeps the living being in existence and, in the story of the creation of man, it is this ruah which gives consistency to the living nephesh formed of moulded clay. Consonant with this idea is the Biblical presentation of sickness as a manifestation of loss of ruah: when we become ill, dynamic life more or less departs from us. Sickness is a kind of decomposition, of loss of wholeness,[7] while the recovery of health implies that god 'recharges' us with breath, His breath which is the source of all life.

In Hebrew thought, it is only a question of degree between sickness and death, sickness is the beginning of dissolution, whereas death is the almost total loss of ruah, the exhausting of the nephesh so that it can hardly stand. There is still life in Sheol, but it is very feeble and very attenuated. The tidal energy is almost drained away and only the most shadowy of existences is left. Sleep, also, is thought of as a loss of ruah and Psalm civ describes how, when living creatures – men or animals – go to sleep, their 'ruah' leaves them temporarily but, in the morning, Yahweh sends forth His ruah upon all living things and they then rise to their feet and stand up once more.

Though we have tried to distinguish the meanings of nephesh, basar and ruah, they are closely connected and indeed overlap. In the post-Exilic period, ruah became almost a synonym for 'soul' and 'heart' (Richardson, 1950, 234), the seat of intelligence and emotion in man (cf. Job xx, 3; xxxii, 18; Isa. lvii, 15; Dan. v. 20). Human characteristics are described in terms of ruah: 'poor and contrite spirit' (Isa. lxvi, 2), 'grieved in spirit' (ibid. liv, 6, cf. Wisd. v, 3) and it is used of energy, conscience and force of character (e.g. Hag. i, 14).[8] God not only creates and controls heaven and earth by his ruah and inspires prophets by sending His ruah upon them (Isa. lxi, 1, etc.), but he forms the inner life of man by a sharing of His personality or spirit[9] (Zech. xii, 1; cf. II Macc. vii, 22) and thus by this link of ruah can be called 'the God of the spirits of all flesh' (Num. xvi, 22; xxvii, 16, cf. II Macc. iii, 22).

Such ideas are related to the Old Testament notion of resurrection which seems to have found its first literary expression in the Book of Daniel, probably written c. 165 B.C. under the threat of martyrdom – a situation similar to that which produced the Book of Maccabees. Its author asserts that the martyrs will be restored to life through God sending His ruah which will enable them to stand upright in His Kingdom. Because of the persistence, even in a weakened state, of the nephesh, the shades of Sheol can be recharged with the Spirit of God and raised back to life. To summarise, the ruah is the source of physical life, of moral life and of resurrection: the energy which renews both body and soul (cf. Ezek. xxxvi, 27; Ps. li, 11) and there are obvious implications for the care of the body.

External influences on Judaic thought

Besides the internal development of the Hebraic concept of man, some attention should be given to external influences on Judaic thought, particularly to those emanating from the city of Alexandria. This great Hellenistic city, founded by Alexander the Great towards the end of the fourth century B.C., was perhaps the most thriving commercial and intellectual centre of its time. As well as spacious harbours and a famous lighthouse, it possessed a university (the Museion) and an associated library said to contain half a million volumes. In addition to its active social, athletic and religious life, the city was indefatigable in scholarship: research, grammar and literary criticism, the production of dictionaries, memoirs, editions of the great Greek tragedies, and much besides. In the midst of this Hellenistic culture dwelt a great colony of Jews (estimated at 100,000) who lived in their own quarter, a city within the city surrounded by walls and gates of its own. Here, in the second and third centuries B.C., the Hebrew Scriptures were rendered into Greek (the version known as the Septuagint because of the tradition of its seventy unanimous translators) and here, too, as part of the great missionary effort of these outward-looking Jews, was produced the Book of Wisdom. It seems to have been written between 100 and 50 B.C., a time when anthologies were very popular, and it appears that its author knew of the works of Plato, especially *Phaedo* – the dialogue that treats of the immortality of the soul – through such collections. Wisdom deals with the purpose of life and the kind of living which is consonant with that purpose. It belongs to the so-called Sapiential group of Old Testament writings, which includes Proverbs, Ecclesiastes and Ecclesiasticus, but Wisdom represents a development of this genre where folk-sayings and prudential advice have been assimilated to higher concepts, including some from Greek philosophy which do not correspond exactly to traditional Jewish ideas. It is a book in praise of wisdom which is hypostasised, almost personalised, and which has some affinities with the Platonic 'Logos' (e.g. Wisd. xviii, 15). It recapitulates the salvation-history of Israel, but includes elements which seem to belong to an extra-canonical tradition. It presents Wisdom as, so to speak, the genius of Israel who guides, delivers, preserves and re-creates this people, undoing the effects of Adam's Fall. Wisdom leads the patriarchs, effects the deliverance from Egypt and inspires the prophets.

All this, and the ironic and caustic attacks on polytheism and idolatry, is essentially Jewish, but some commentators have identified non-Jewish ingredients apart from the Platonic ones already mentioned. The famous passage (ibid. vii, 22–27) describing the 'spirit of understanding' which 'pervades and penetrates all things' does not seem far from the Stoic doctrine of a 'world-soul' or 'logos' which was immanent in all things. Similarly, in the prayer for wisdom which is the substance of chapter viii, the following words occur: 'For the thoughts of mortal men are miserable, and our devices are but uncertain. For the *corruptible body presseth down the soul*, and the *earthly tabernacle weigheth down the mind* that museth upon many things.' (viii, 14f). This seems akin to some of the Orphic doctrines that influenced Plato and other philosophers – the notion that the body is a tomb,[10] a limiting environment which the soul had to escape in order to rise to the higher world. Here we are close to a dichotomy between body and soul whose union is only extrinsic and temporary (as a horseman is joined to his horse). The beginning of chapter vii has also been judged to possess alien, Stoic, affinities through its assertion of the common lot of men, their equality in birth and death (1–6) and its assertion that it is only the degree of their love of wisdom (philo-sophia) that distinguishes men from each other.

Some critics have found the resolution of this tension between Jewish and Greek thought in the closing verses of chapter viii: 'For as a child I was well endowed [i.e. well formed in the physical sense] and a good soul fell to my lot. Yea rather, being good, I came into a body which was undefiled.' It almost seems as if the 'I' is first associated with a body to which a soul is attached and then the writer corrects himself and emphasises the primacy of the soul to which a fitting body is added, but in either case there is an implicit dichotomy and dualistic anthropology.

Besides direct literary references, there are other sources which throw light on Jewish attitudes towards the body. First, there is the practice of circumcision, a rite which was part of the Mosaic Law. Its significance seems to have lain in its association with the origin of life and the shedding of blood which was believed to be entailed in fertilisation.[11] The Jews believed that the 'life of the flesh is in the blood' and that blood was suitably offered to the Author of life.[12] Circumcision was the outward mark of belonging to the people of God and only the circumcised were allowed to partake of the Passover meal which commemorated God's deliverance of His people (Exod. xii, 44, 48). It became such an essential mark of Jewishness that, in the Hellenistic period, Jews who wished to adopt the Greek way of life (including naked athletics, Greek manners and fashions) resorted to painful surgery in order to rid themselves of this tell-tale sign in the flesh of the separatist religion.

Another distinction from the Gentiles lay in the obligation of ritual purity which, if strictly observed, imposed an almost intolerable burden on Jews, particularly if they lived in a non-Jewish environment. This requirement of 'cleanliness' was originally made of the priests who officiated in the sanctuary. Its extension to the entire people was probably due to more developed notions of religion and the idea of 'a holy people', but its practice implied either constant ablutions or reduction to a state which rendered one unfit for religious exercises. Contact with Gentiles, or with the dead,[13] or with certain diseases, or involvement in any sexual process or with a person who had contracted uncleanness, were all defilements. There were various degrees of uncleanness according to the nature of the object touched and six kinds of water were denominated for these different degrees. In addition to the general dietary regulations, food had to be protected against defilement which meant, in practice, that it could not be handled by Gentiles (Orchard, 1953, 731).

In the past, anthropologists have viewed such regulations as an aberrant system of hygiene, but they are better seen as manifestations of particular thought-systems whose underlying assumptions are of special importance in understanding the culture of which they are a part. The sociologist, Mary Douglas, has pursued this approach in her *Purity and Danger* of which the third chapter is entitled 'The abominations of Leviticus'. Its conclusion is worth quoting:

> If the proposed interpretation of the forbidden animals is correct, the dietary laws would have been like signs which at every turn inspired meditation on the oneness, purity and completeness of God. By rules of avoidance *holiness was given a physical expression* in every encounter with the animal kingdom and at every meal. Observance of the dietary rules would thus have been a meaningful part of the great liturgical act of recognition and worship which culminated in the sacrifice in the Temple. (Douglas, 1966, 57 – our italics.)

The Temple worship itself, its singular location and consequent obligation to travel to it, the ceremonies of physical prostration, the overt acts of penitence expressed in sackcloth and fasting – all these are expressions of an anthropology and of a concept of religion which involved the whole man, body and soul, and thereby implied the value and significance of the body as essential to the whole man even in his most spiritual activities. The same notion underlies the ascetic communal practices which attracted devout men among the Jews. For example, the historian Josephus, though eventually sufficiently Romanised to adopt the name Flavius, as a youth tested his vocation in the contemporary religious communities:

> For I thought that by this means I might choose the best, if I were once acquainted with them all; so I contented myself with hard fare and underwent great trials and passed through them all. Nor did I content myself with these trials only; but when I was informed that one, whose name was Banus, lived in the desert and used no other clothing than grew upon trees and had no other food than that which grew of its own accord and bathed himself in cold water frequently, both night and day, in order to preserve his chastity, I imitated him in those things, and continued with him for three years. When I had accomplished my desires, I returned

to the city . . . and began to conduct myself according to the rules of the sect of the Pharisees, which is of kin to the sect of the Stoics, as the Greeks call them.[14]

Another marked characteristic of the Jews throughout their history was their firm, almost obsessive, antipathy to idols or images of God. This was undoubtedly connected with their monotheism and is embedded in the fundamental Decalogue which was essential to their special covenant-relation to Yahweh: 'Thou shalt not make unto thee a graven image, nor the likeness of any form that is in heaven above, or that is in the earth beneath, or that is in the water under the earth. . . . Thou shalt not bow down to them, nor serve them, for I the Lord thy God am a jealous God.' (Exod. xx, 4f.) But it is also connected with their concept of this single God, with ideas of His dignity, His otherness, His essentially spiritual and transcendent nature. There is only one tolerable image of God and that is the one which He Himself made: 'And God said, Let us make man in our own image, after our likeness, and let them have dominion. . . . And God created man in His own image, in the image of God created He him; male and female created He them.' (Gen. i, 26f.) 'Image' (*selem* in Hebrew) means a representation in the form of a statue and is translated in the Septuagint by the word *eikon* and should therefore be understood in a very concrete sense.[15] The word 'likeness' (Hebrew *demut*) is more abstract, but is sometimes also used concretely, almost as 'model' (cf. II Kgs xvi, 10ff). Two further texts from Genesis are perhaps worth passing notice: 'When God created man, He made him in the likeness of God. . . . When Adam had lived a hundred and thirty years, he became the father of a son in his own likeness, after his image, and named him Seth.' (Gen. v, 1, 3). Man is made in the image and likeness of God and this characteristic is a permanent possession, which continues to exist and be transmitted even after the Fall. The moral connotations of this fact are expressed in our second quotation: 'Whoever sheds the blood of man, by man shall his blood be shed; for God made man in His own image.' (Gen. ix, 6). Murder deserves a peculiar stigma and punishment since it desecrates the image of God which is in every man. In accordance with the characteristics of Jewish thought, the idea is presented in a very concrete context: man, existing in flesh and blood, is the image of God and therefore God is concerned that no one should shed his blood.

Naturally, scholars have paid attention to this notion of representation, attempted fine distinctions between 'image' and 'likeness' and considered the senses in which man can be said to 'represent' God. Two theories might be briefly mentioned:

(1) That man 'represents' God by his upright posture which differentiates him from animals who proceed on all fours or 'on their belly' and who, consequently, in spite of their numbers and variety, cannot provide his complement – a companion suited to him (Gen. ii, 18ff). This interpretation could be a mythological rationalisation of the Jewish horror of bestiality (cf. Lev. xviii, 23) which, apparently, was not so strongly felt in other early civilizations whose myths represent a period in which man ate and mated with animals.[16] This theory has been objected to on the grounds that this part of Genesis stems from the priestly tradition which is essentially anti-anthropomorphic in its concept of God.

(2) Man represents God who has delegated to him a lordship, a stewardship over the rest of creation, particularly over its zoological life, as indicated by Genesis i, 26: 'Let us make man in our image, after our likeness; and let them have dominion over the fish of the sea, and over the fowl of the air, and over the cattle, and over all the earth, and over every creeping thing that creepeth upon the earth.' This notion seems to be a theme[17] which recurs through the Old Testament. The eighth psalm tells of God's transcendence, of the marvels of His heavenly creation and continues:

> What is man, that Thou art mindful of him?
> And the son of man, that Thou visitest him?
> For Thou hast made him but little lower than God
> > (or 'the angels')
> And crownest him with glory and honour.
> Thou madest him to have dominion over the works
> > of Thy hands;
> Thou has put all things under his feet:
> All sheep and oxen,
> Yea, and the beasts of the field;
> The fowl of the air, and the fish of the sea,
> Whatsoever passeth through the path of the seas.
> > (Ps. viii, 4–8.)

The apocryphal book, Ecclesiasticus (probably composed *c*. 200 B.C.), while accepting the brevity of human life, speaks of mankind as follows:

> He endued them with strength by themselves,
> And made them according to His image;
> And put the fear of man upon all flesh,
> And gave him dominion over beasts and fowls.
> > (Eccles. xvii, 2–3.)

The Book of Wisdom seems to develop the notion of 'image'. It contrasts the false Epicureanism of the ungodly 'reasoning with themselves, but not aright':

> Come on, therefore, let us enjoy the good things
> >   that are present:
> And let us speedily use the creatures like as in youth.
> Let us replete ourselves with costly wines and ointments:
> And let no flower of the Spring pass us by:
> Let us crown ourselves with rosebuds,
> Before they be withered:
> Let none of us go without his share of our voluptuousness:
> Let us leave tokens of our joyfulness in every place:
> For this is our portion,
> And our lot is this. (Wisd. ii, 6–9.)

with the true end of man which consists in immortality through Wisdom:

> For God created man to be immortal,
> And made him to be an *image* of His own eternity.
> Nevertheless, through envy of the devil came
> >   death into the world:
> And they that do hold of his side do find it.

It was because of their fundamental and deeply instilled hatred of false images that the orthodox Jews so bitterly opposed the attempted Hellenisation of their country by Antiochus Epiphanes who had succeeded to the Syrian portion of Alexander's empire in 175 B.C. The introduction of the Greek gymnasium, where men exercised naked, led Hellenophile Jews to wish to conceal their circumcision and Greek attitudes seem to have been associated with a spread of pederasty and male prostitution (I Macc. i, 11–16). In spite of opposition, Antiochus continued and many Jews died rather than break their faith or law, and the Maccabees led a resistance movement which brought religious and political autonomy as well as encouraging apocalyptic literature and Messianic expectations.

Greek and Jewish attitudes towards the body

Some understanding of the enormous gap between Greek and Jewish attitudes towards the body can be derived from a consideration of the Old Testament concept of nakedness and the ideas associated with this condition. In the earthly paradise of the Garden of Eden, nakedness was a natural state, but the disorder brought about by the Fall made it have evil effects on the mind (Gen. ii, 25; cf. iii, 7). In the economic reality of historical existence, nakedness is related to poverty, destitution and exposure (Gen. xliii, 9; Deut. xxviii, 48; II Chron. xxviii, 15; Isa. lviii, 7). It is the state in which man enters the world and the condition in which he leaves it (Job i, 21; xxii, 6; cf. Eccles. v, 15), as well as being a metaphor for complete vulnerability (Habb. ii, 15; Nahum iii, 5). It is related to subjective shame (Isa. xlvii, 3; Lam. i, 8; Prov. xxix, 18) and objective humiliation (Hos. ii, 3; Ezek. xvi, 37; Gen. ix, 22).

Such ideas are, of course, not peculiar to the Jews or to a particular epoch. They seem general, almost natural, and are found widely among the underprivileged nations and at least in the interrogation chambers of the privileged ones. The Jews were different in that, as a result of their religious and political experience, they had long associated nakedness with the licence, orgies and debaucheries of neighbouring religions from which they sought to separate themselves (Exod. xxxii, 25). Even in the early stages of their own religion, it was linked with religious ecstasy (I Sam. xix, 23f.) and perhaps with the related religious dance (II Sam. vi, 16). It was their desire to safeguard themselves against the overt and insidious attacks of paganism that led to the codification of the laws of purity that constitute the bulk of the Book of Leviticus and centre on the great Law of Holiness (Lev. xvii–xxvi).

In this book, the concept of nakedness seems to take on a special, almost technical, meaning and it is particularly associated with incestuous and other unlawful sexual activity in the phrase 'to uncover his/her nakedness' (ibid. xx, 11–21). A similar relationship is also evident in that other great legal work, probably marking the return from exile among the heathen, Deuteronomy (cf. xxiv, 1), and it is also found in the writings of the later prophets (eg. Ezek. xxii, 10ff.; Hab. ii, 15). In this conceptual net, 'nakedness' becomes almost synonymous with 'genitalia' (e.g. Lev. xviii, *passim* – but cf. also the earlier source: I Sam. xx, 30) and it is particularly connected with pagan religious and associated moral behaviour.

Conversely, in Hebrew thought, clothes are related to status, honour and dignity. It is both a religious and social duty to clothe the naked, and particular attention is given to the proper vesting of the priests in the ceremonial provisions of Exodus which extend from head-dresses designed 'for glory and for beauty' (xxvii, 40) to 'linen breeches to cover the flesh of their nakedness' which had to extend from the loins to the thighs (ibid. 42). There are also associations between covering and cleanliness (Deut. xxiii, 14) and between clothing and protection and love (Ezek. xvi, 8, etc.).

Other relationships take their natural place in this universe of discourse. In the Jewish mind faith, fidelity and good faith are inextricably locked together and the overriding concept includes commercial faith (though not necessarily with Gentiles), religious faith, fidelity between man and man, between man and woman (especially wife) and, above all, between Israel and her God. There is a connection, both in theory and practice, between sexual licence and idolatry, between marriage and fidelity to Yahweh, between whoredom and paganism, for all may involve giving to another that which rightly belongs only to the One. This transference of imagery, which is more than a mere metaphorical truth, is found throughout the writings of the Hebrew prophets where it becomes a passionate conviction. The total cohesion of these ideas is shown by their general association and combination. In Ezekiel xxiii, Judah and Israel are typified as two nymphomaniacs, with breasts bruised by the enthusiasm of their lovers and their bodies defiled by their multitudinous connections: nakedness, lust and religious infidelity are all associated. Alienation of body is necessarily linked with alienation of soul and brings inevitable retribution and so the Jews will themselves be betrayed by those with whom they have betrayed God: 'they shall deal with thee in hatred, and shall take away all thy labour, and shall leave thee naked and bare: and the nakedness of thy whoredoms shall be discovered, both thy lewdness and thy whoredoms. These things shall be done unto thee, for that thou has gone a-whoring after the heathen, and because thou art polluted with their idols.' (Ezek. xxiii, 29f.) These ideas are grouped together throughout the writings of this prophet (cf. Ezek. xvi, 35–38; xxiii, 10, 18) together with the antithetical associations of clothing, love and faithfulness (Ezek. xvi, 8–13), but perhaps their finest expression is found in the Book of Hosea who, through his own tragic experience of the infidelity of his beloved wife, came to a new understanding of the love of God. He penetrated the nature of spiritual adultery through the effects of his wife's physical infidelity, and his writing naturally pulls together the kindred themes of clothing and love, and nakedness and lust (Hos. ii, 5–9).

The association of nakedness, sexual licence, unnatural use of the body, and paganism might be expected to produce some imbalance or bias in Jewish attitudes towards the body and, to a minor degree, this may have happened. But abuse is no argument against right use, and reaction against perversion should not be taken as the expression of a considered attitude towards the natural. The Old Testament undoubtedly appreciated physical beauty and Wolff (1975, 69–73) concludes that 'even the form of the body and God's dialogue with man cannot be divided from one another'. Similarly, there is no damning of sexuality which is taken as a natural ingredient in lawful love:

> Let your fountain be blessed, and rejoice in the
> wife of your youth,
> The lovely hind, the graceful doe.
> Let her breasts fill you at all times with delight,
> Continue to be drunk with her love.
> Why should you be infatuated, my son, with a loose woman,
> And embrace the bosom of another? (Prov. v, 18–20.)

Indeed, there is one outstanding document which presents so powerful a picture of the physical expression of love between man and woman that, almost from its first inclusion in the Biblical canon, it has been felt that it could only be interpreted as an allegory.[18] The Song of Songs is attributed, in accordance with a familiar literary device for adding prestige and authority to a writing, to King Solomon although it was written well after his time. The poem provides a number of critical problems, particularly in regard to its form and purpose. Some regard it as a collection of originally quite separate poems, some as a collection of songs to be performed in connection with a marriage ceremony, and some see it as a kind of verse drama. Fortunately, it is unnecessary for our purposes to meet these problems and we shall assume that it is an erotic poem portraying the passion, longing and ecstasy between two young lovers who, interestingly, seem to differ in race and social position.[19] It opens directly enough, though with some ambiguity:

> Let him kiss me with the kisses of his mouth:
> For thy love is better than wine. (S. of S., i, 2.)

The affair seems to develop, not uncharacteristically, with a meal out interspersed with physical embraces:

> He brought me to the banqueting house
> And his banner over me was love . . .
> His left hand is under my head,
> And his right hand doth embrace me. (ii, 4, 6.)[20]

This is followed by an apparent interlude containing remembrance of things past, the traditional association of love and Spring, and the longing for sight or sound of the absent beloved coupled with knowledge of their mutual love (ii, 8–17). The separation becomes unbearable in bed and the sleepless girl searches the dark city for her lover until, after enquiries of the police, she meets with success:

> I found him whom my soul loveth:
> I held him and would not let him go,
> Until I had brought him into my mother's house,
> And into the chamber of her that conceived me. (iii, 4.)

The scene changes to Solomon's arrival in his palanquin, adorned with gold, silver and royal purple, accompanied by an impressive armed escort to guard him against the dangers of the night (iii, 6–10) and two poems are introduced whose elaborate praise of the bride's beauty in Eastern imagery produces an occasional cultural shock. The dove-like eyes are acceptable enough, but hair like a flock of goats (iv, 2), temples like a piece of pomegranate (iv, 3) and a neck like the fortified tower of David (iv, 4) seem somewhat exotic, as does:

> Thy two breasts are like two fawns, that are
> twins of a gazelle,
> Which feed among the lilies. (iv, 5.)

Not surprisingly, all the man's senses are enthralled by the person and adornment of his destined bride:

> Thou hast ravished my heart with one look of thine eyes,
> With one chain on thy neck . . .
> How much better is thy love than wine!
> And the smell of thy perfume than all
> manner of spices! (iv, 9f.)

His loved one's lips and tongue are honey and her garments are scented with cedar: in all, she is a garden of delights which he desires to enter and so enjoy its fruits (iv, 11–16). The next episode concerns the lover's nocturnal visit to the girl's room. Though she is asleep, her heart is on watch and she hears his voice as he knocks but, unfortunately, she delays too long and has difficulty drawing the bolts on the door because her newly perfumed hands are slippery (v, 5). When she eventually gets the door open her impatient lover has gone. Another night-search follows, less happy because she is beaten up by the police and fails to find him (v, 6f.). The chapter closes with the girl's extravagant description of her lover's physical aspect (v, 10–16). He is apparently in a garden,[21] meditating on love and the physical appearance of the woman[22] which he summarises in the words:

> How fair and pleasant art thou,
> O love, for delights! (vii, 6.)

He likens her to various trees which he will climb and handle to harvest the delectable fruit (vii, 7f.). But the woman co-operates more than trees, she responds, joyfully accepting his possession and desire and inviting him to join her in the morning fields and for an evening banquet in her home when, again:

> His left hand should be under my head,
> And his right hand should embrace me. (viii, 3.)

SUMMARY

Jewish thought sometimes distinguishes body and soul, but it does not separate them. It neither over-emphasises the body nor despises it, nor does it neglect the soul or cleave it from the body as the essential element of man. Both body and soul are essential elements in the constitution of man who is the only true image of God. Soul and spirit are also distinguished and the concepts develop, perhaps somewhat influenced by Greek ideas, but Judaism remains true to itself and places the whole man at the pinnacle of creation to which he is destined to act both as lord and steward.

Man is also at a kind of *junction* between God and creation in that he shares both in the natural life of the created order and the supernatural life of God – he is linked to both because he is both physical and spiritual in his ground and destiny. Whatever may have been the influence of Greek philosophy, Judaism's independence is exemplified in its attitude to the practical matter of nudity which is derived from the conviction that man's essential nature has been flawed. Old Testament ideas may have absorbed a little from the Greeks, but they were forged in an unremitting struggle to preserve a spiritual monotheism against an idolatrous polytheism, which not only surrounded them geographically but remained a threat throughout their history. This danger has left its mark on their attitudes towards the body which, however, is not the subject of a special theology or philosophy but an integral part of their faith and practice, of orthodoxy and orthopraxis. One might say that they see the body almost as a sacrament – its use and relations (particularly sexual ones) symbolise a relationship to God and the right order of creation.

THE ORIGINAL CHRISTIAN
TEACHING

Jesus of Nazareth, recognised by his followers as the Christ (Messiah), like many other great teachers (e.g. Socrates, the Buddha) did not write down any of his instruction but apparently relied on the spoken word and the memory of His hearers for its transmission. Consequently, there are remarkable gaps in our knowledge of Christ: His birth has been placed between 6 B.C. and A.D. 5, but we have no reliable information about His personal appearance[1] and there is some doubt about the date of His death, though the weight of evidence suggests 7 April A.D. 30.

The surviving Gospels are, in their written form, far from contemporary and the oldest was probably compiled at least a generation after Christ's death.[2] Further, they are neither biographies nor complete compendia of His teaching as the Fourth Gospel points out with some hyperbole: 'But there were also many other things which Jesus did; were every one of them to be written, I suppose that the world itself could not contain the books that would be written.' (John xxi, 25.) The original Christian message was both delivered and transmitted by word of mouth and the first documents of this new faith were the *ad hoc* letters written by the early missionaries to their converts who naturally treasured them. The largest of these epistolary collections is associated with the name of St Paul, a former Pharisee, who was born and educated at the Oriental city of Tarsus in Cilicia,[3] one of the great commercial cities of the ancient world. Dio Chrysostom, a younger contemporary of Paul, was, even as a worldly Greek, shocked at the lasciviousness of its inhabitants, both men and women. This fundamentally Hellenistic city naturally had its gymnasia, baths and theatres as well as a university which, at this time, was better attended than those of Athens or Alexandria. The philosopher Apollonius of Tyana (first century A.D.), the subject of a remarkable biography written *c.* A.D. 200, studied there until he could no longer tolerate the idle and dissolute student life. The town was also the birthplace of two philosophers, Athenodorus Cordylion (first century B.C.) and the more famous Athenodorus Cananites (*c.* 74 B.C.–*c.* A.D. 7), friend of Strabo and Cicero and tutor of the future Emperor Augustus.[4]

Pauline doctrine

Since Paul has often been accused of corrupting or 'theologising' the simple teaching of Jesus, it is worth while emphasising that he is an earlier source than the Gospels which contain this allegedly 'simple teaching' and we shall begin our examination of Christian teaching by examining the Pauline doctrine of the body.[5]

It is not surprising that this member of 'the straitest sect of the Pharisees' continues the teaching of the Jewish Scriptures. In accordance with the usage of for example Proverbs v, 11 and Daniel iv, 33, Paul uses the word to signify, quite simply, the natural body of man designed by the providence of God to the conditions of earthly life (I Cor. xv, 44). As such, it is mortal (at least since the Fall) and so, in the unredeemed, can even now be described as dead (Rom. viii, 10ff.). But even our fallen bodies are the work of the Creator: they are essential to the humanity which God has made and must not be despised as inferior to the soul or as a hindrance to the higher life of man. This denigration may result from the opinions of the Gnostics and the implication of the Platonists, but was not in accordance with Hebrew thinking. On the contrary, the body was to be reverenced as a temple of the living God (II Cor. vi, 16) and it was (or could be) a suitable and acceptable sacrifice to God and an expression of the rational worship of a Christian (Rom. xii, 1). Thus, the word 'body' (because there is no implicit dichotomy between it and 'soul')[6] could be used as equivalent to 'self', 'person', 'personality', 'the whole man', etc., since Jewish (and early Christian) thought saw the body as a perfectly valid manifestation of the soul (Thornton, 1942, 298). Indeed, this grand vision of man restored to his pristine and intended integrity by the redeeming work of Christ is one of the master-themes of the entire Pauline doctrine:

> For in Him [Christ] dwelleth all the fulness of the Godhead *bodily* and in Him, who is head of all principality and power, are you made full. In Him, you were also circumcised with a circumcision not made with hands, in the putting off of the body of flesh in the circumcision of Christ, having been buried with Him in baptism, wherein you were also raised with Him through faith in the working of God who raised Him from the dead. (Col. ii, 9–12.)

The incarnation (enfleshing) of the Son of God, membership of His body which is the new Israel, the redemption of the body and its resurrection from the dead – all these doctrines cohere and form a whole. The expression 'body of the flesh' reminds us that Paul conceived of other bodies (cf. the splendid passage in I Cor. xv, 35ff. often read at Christian burials) and that he tended to use the word 'flesh' to indicate the natural frailty of the body.[7]

Paul believes that though the body ages and loses its powers, faith in God's promises can arrest or reverse these processes (Rom. i, 24). The human body is associated with powerful passions and drives which it often executes and therefore may be described as 'sinful' (Rom. vi, 6–12). The power of sin in the body is related to the weakness of the spirit which, when restored by union with Christ, breaks the unnatural dominance of sin and restores man to unified life and freedom from irrational passion and even the most powerful *external* law or pressure (Rom. vii, 4f.). Since the unnatural disassociation between will and act is related to the split between flesh and spirit, between mind and body, and to the association of sin and death,[8] Paul can cry in spiritual anguish to be delivered from 'this body of death' (Rom. viii, 13–24; cf. viii, 13).

Nevertheless, the body is an essential part of man and even in this life can be, and has been, redeemed (Rom. viii, 23), though the process is slow and painful. It is this tremendous respect for the body and its potentiality through its re-creation by Christ's incarnation which makes Paul so insistent on certain moral issues which are unfashionable today.

Corinth occupied a special position in Paul's missionary work: it was his first base where he laboured for nearly two years and it was in this city that he made the critical decision to direct his efforts towards Gentiles rather than Jews. The Corinth of St Paul was fundamentally a Roman city, founded by Julius Caesar about a century after the destruction of its Greek predecessor. With its nearby port, it had become a thriving commercial and administrative centre and already contained many magnificent buildings. After some eighteen months' activity, Paul was accused by the Jews before the disinterested Roman governor, Gallio (a brother of Seneca, the Stoic philosopher), and shortly afterwards he handed over the Church to the care of Apollos but, though 'absent in body' (I Cor. v, 3), he remained 'present in spirit' among this loved but troublesome Christian community. They seem to have been affected by the all-pervading Gnostic ideas[9] and wanted a 'spiritual' religion which would have little effect on behaviour – a comforting possession in the religious and moral climate of a cosmopolitan seaport.

Discriminate views on the purpose of the body

After Paul's departure, these lively and still semi-pagan converts seem to have got a little out of hand and his deputy, Apollos, referred a number of problems to him for authoritative resolution. These included a tendency to form rival factions or sects, the rejection of marriage by some and unlimited sexual relations among others, an outburst of litigation between members of the community, overindulgence in ecstatic utterance, a tendency to turn the Eucharist into a drunken feast, women's 'libbers' abandoning the conventional veil during services and doctrinal problems about the nature of Christ's resurrection and the consequent resurrection of Christians. The First Epistle to the Corinthians is an answer to these problems and queries, and some of them are relevant to our purpose. Chapter vi, after reproving Christians who hale each other before a pagan judge, turns to more serious delinquencies, including fraud, idolatry, various sexual offences, drunkenness, theft, malice and extortion (I Cor. vi, 8–10), which Paul condemns and not for the first time (I Cor. v, 9f.). It was apparently Paul's teaching about the abrogation of the law in the new freedom of Christ that had occasioned the full indulgence of their (redeemed) bodies in gluttony, drunkenness and sexual excess and Paul is disturbed that they had exceeded even the bounds of customary pagan behaviour, instancing the case of 'one who hath his father's wife' (I Cor. v, 1). This kind of behaviour is a misunderstanding of Christian teaching about the body (though it perhaps is significant that it could be so misunderstood) and Paul points out that the prime purpose of the body 'is not for fornication, but for the Lord; and the Lord is for the body'. God who raised up Christ's body from death will do the same for ours (I Cor. vi, 13f.). That is why they must be treated with respect, for now they are members of Christ's body as surely as limbs and arms are members of a human body. Illicit sex, therefore, is not so much unlawful as sacrilegious: 'Shall I then take away the members of Christ and make them members of a prostitute? God forbid! Do you not know that he who joins himself with a prostitute becomes one body with her? For, as it is written [in Gen. ii, 24] "the two shall become one flesh", but he that is joined to the Lord is united in spirit with Him.' (I Cor. vi, 15–17.) Though Paul's personal preference is for celibacy,[10] he does not object to the legitimate sexual act which symbolises the mutual self-giving of marriage (I Cor. vii, 1–7). His objection to harlotry may well be related to its traditional and actual association with religious infidelity since the Corinthian whores were more likely to be devotees of Venus than of Christ. His reason for singling out sexual sin is interesting: 'Shun fornication. Every other sin which a man commits is outside the body; but the fornicator sins against his own body. Do you not know that your body is a temple of the Holy Spirit within you that you have from God? You are not your own, you were bought with a price. So glorify God in your body.' (I Cor. vi, 18–20.)

In his support of marriage against its detractors, Paul gives considerable weight to the sexual aspect although he speaks in terms of the 'rights' each partner has over the other's body (I Cor. vii, 3–4).

They are not to refuse their bodies to each other except, by mutual agreement, to concentrate on prayer and even this high purpose should be approached prudently (I Cor. vii, 5-6). It is all a matter of priorities and the ultimate one is the primacy of the spiritual over the material which yet has its own importance and dignity. Sacrifice is necessary in the pursuit of any excellence and Paul naturally illustrates his argument from the gymnastic contests which were common in Corinth: 'Do you not know that in a race all the runners compete, but only one receives the prize? You should run to win. Every athlete exercises self-control in all things. They do it to receive a perishable wreath, we for an imperishable one. Well, I do not run aimlessly, nor is my boxing shadow-boxing, but I pommel my body and subdue it, lest after telling others how to win I should be disqualified myself.' (I Cor. ix, 24-7.) But the sacrifice of the body cannot be an end in itself, the merit is not in the sacrifice or training[11] but in the motivation which, in the last resort, can only be love in the highest sense. So, in the justly famous hymn to Charity, Paul explicitly declares: 'If I give away all that I have, and if I deliver my body to be burned, but have not Love, I gain nothing.' (I Cor. xiii, 3.)

Paul's attitude to the body is real and existential and when he talks of the Christian Church as the Body of Christ,[12] this is no mere metaphor but a statement of actuality with very real implications.[13] Membership of Christ gives ineffable dignity, however humble the office or the person holding it, and, above all, this unity should produce empathy: 'If one member suffers, all suffer together; if one member is honoured, all rejoice together. Now you are the Body of Christ and individually members of it.' (I Cor. xii, 26f.; cf. Rom. xii, 4-8.)

The unity of Christians in one body, by virtue of their unity with the God who took a body, separates them from others as it joins them together in their common participation in the Eucharistic body of Christ: 'The bread which we break, is it not a participation in the body of Christ? Because there is one bread, we who are many are one body, for we all partake of the one bread.' (I Cor. x, 16f.) This 'communion' or 'oneing' in the Body of Christ separates the Christian communicants from the pagans who are united by the food they share with idols,[14] and the faithful cannot share both the food of the true God and the food of pagan gods or demons since bodies absorb and become what they consume (I Cor. x, 20f.). It was Christ Himself who declared that the Communion bread was His Body and thus anyone eating it unworthily profanes the Body of Christ and consequently may suffer physical illness or even death (I Cor. xi, 23-31). Furthermore, this union with and in the Body of Christ is not

only social, but individual, so that Paul can identify his own sufferings and triumphs with the passion and resurrection of the Head:
'always carrying in the body the death of Jesus, so that the life of Jesus
may also be manifested in our bodies' (II Cor. iv, 10; cf. Galatians vi,
17).

Our earthly body is conceived as a kind of bivouac where we must
not make ourselves too much at home for 'while we are at home in
the body we are away from the Lord' (II Cor. v, 6) and the true
Christian would prefer the situation reversed (II Cor. v, 8), but in
either case, 'we make it our aim to please Him' for, in the end,
Christ's judgement on man will depend on 'what he has done in the
body' (II Cor. v, 10). Yet, even in this life, there can be moments of
ecstasy – of standing outside the body – and then it is difficult to say
whether one is in the body or out of it (II Cor. xii, 2f.).

Other New Testament writings, apart from the Gospels, need not
detain us long. The Epistle to the Hebrews, which is about the
priestly self-oblation of Christ, emphasises that His Body was the
instrument by which humanity is sanctified (Heb. x, 5, 10, cf. 22)
and also unified: 'Remember those who are in prison, as though in
prison with them; and those who are ill-treated, since you also are in
the body.' (Heb. xiii, 3, cf. 10–16). St James, characteristically, sees
faith issuing in corporeal works of mercy: 'If a brother or sister is ill-
clad and in lack of daily food, and one of you says to them "Go in
peace, be warmed and filled", without giving them the things needed
for the body, what does it profit? . . . For as the body apart from the
spirit is dead, so faith apart from works is dead.' (Jas. ii, 16, 26.)
Perfection includes the control of the body and its members,
especially the tongue which, though small, can stain the whole body
and inflame the cycle of nature (Jas. iii, 2–6). St Peter emphasises the
central moral and religious significance of Christ's taking a human
body, 'who his own self bare our sins in his body upon the tree, that
we, having died unto sins, might live unto righteousness; by whose
injuries you were healed' (I Pet. ii, 24). Jude has an obscure reference
to an angelic struggle over the body of Moses (Jude 9) and a clearer
one to carousing at the love-feasts which were associated with the
early Eucharist (the same sort of thing happened among the
Corinthians). The last book of the Bible includes among the for-
nications of Babylon (an allusion to pagan Rome) her traffickings in
the bodies of human beings (Rev. xviii, 13).

In the Gospel according to Matthew, we have a usage of the word
'body' which represents what we have come to expect of Jewish
thought. It refers to the human person and therefore part of it may
be well sacrificed to save the whole: 'If your right eye causes you to
sin, pluck it out and throw it away; it is better that you lose one of

your members than that your whole body be thrown into Hell.'
(Matt. v, 29, cf. 30). The organs of sensation affect the total personality and the more dominant they are the more pervasive their
influence: 'The eye is the lamp of the body. So, if your eye is sound,
your whole body will be full of light; but if your eye is not sound, your
whole body will be full of darkness.' (Matt. vi, 22.) The word 'body'
seems sometimes to be more or less equivalent to the sensitive flesh:
'Do not be anxious about your life, what you shall eat or what you
shall drink; nor about your body, what you shall put on. Is not life
more than food, and the body more than clothing?' (Matt. vi, 25 – all
three of these extracts are from the so-called Sermon on the Mount.)
This matter of priorities recurs in a later saying where we notice some
kind of distinction in the unified nature of man: 'Do not fear those
who kill the body but cannot kill the soul; rather fear him who can
destroy both body and soul in Hell.' (Matt. x, 28.) Matthew also uses
the word 'body' of a corpse (xiv, 12; xxvii, 52, 58f.; cf. Acts ix, 40), of
the living Body of Christ anointed in Bethany (Matt. xxvi, 12) and of
the bread blessed after the Last Supper (Matt. xxvi, 26).

Mark uses the word of the source of sensations in the story of the
woman with the haemorrhage who 'felt in her body that she had been
healed of her disease' (Mark v, 29). Some of his other uses have been
borrowed by Matthew (e.g. Mark xiv, 8, 22; xv, 43, 45).

Because of the traditional description of Luke as 'the beloved
physician', we might expect rather more emphasis on the body in his
Gospel but almost all his references are found in Matthew (due to
their derivation from a common source).[15] His only peculiar usage is
in Christ's gnomic answer to a question about the location of His
Second Coming: 'Where the body is, there will the vultures be
gathered together.' (Luke xvii, 37.)

The Fourth Evangelist adds little to this tally: he records a saying
of Christ which was interpreted as a reference to 'the temple of His
body' (John ii, 21) and shares the use of 'body' to mean 'corpse' (John
xix, 31, 38, 40). However, some additional light on New Testament
attitudes to the body may be shed by a consideration of the use of the
word 'flesh' (*Sarx* in Greek) and generally the equivalent of the
Hebrew word *basar* considered in Chapter 2.[16]

The flesh and the spirit

A very common phrase in Pauline writings is 'according to the
flesh' which often has the meaning 'humanly speaking' (Rom. i, 3;
Phil. iii, 3f.; Rom. iv, 1; I Cor. i, 26) though in context it might be
narrowed to 'racially' or 'genetically' (Rom. ix, 3; xi, 14; ix, 5, 8). It
can mean 'from a human point of view' with the implication of
superficially rather than truly (i.e. from a divine point of view) as in

II Cor. v, 16 and similarly in I Cor. x, 18 the contrast between 'Israel after the flesh' (the Jews) and the 'spiritual Israel' (the Christian Church) almost makes the distinction between appearance and reality. A similar distinction is made in the non-Pauline Epistle to the Hebrews where Christ is spoken of as a priest 'not according to the legal requirement of a carnal commandment' (actual bodily descent from a priestly tribe as in the case of the Jews) but 'by the power of an indestructible life' (Heb. vii, 16).

'Flesh', then, seems to represent the outward as opposed to the inward, material as distinct from spiritual, appearance rather than reality, human differentiated from divine; but this connotation implies no intrinsic condemnation nor contempt, though it might point to contrast or values[17] as in the case of incorporation in God's people which is other than an external mark in the body: 'For he is not a Jew which is one outwardly, neither is that circumcision which is outward in the flesh' (Rom. ii, 28; cf. whole passage ii, 17–29 and Eph. ii, 11).

'Flesh' can mean simply 'a human being', 'the human condition', sometimes with implications of the frailty involved in that state,[18] and 'in the flesh' may refer to human society and life in the world, without necessarily implying the denigration of 'worldly life'.[19] It may be applied to the ineffectiveness of human effort, even when aiming high, because (since the Fall) man has an innate weakness but the Incarnation has restored the human condition[20] so that man, renewed in Christ, can follow his higher aspirations.[21]

Though Paul sometimes seems to imply an antithesis between 'flesh' and 'spirit',[22] his disciples do not always see the exact nature of this antithesis: it is not, for instance, the lower urges of the body opposed to the higher strivings of the soul, as is made clear in the lengthy discussion of Gal. v. Freedom from law is one of the gifts of Christianity, but this freedom is not to be 'an occasion for the flesh' but for the operation of love. The opposition is really between fallen perverted humanity and redeemed converted humanity which can fulfil itself unhindered by the weakness of the flesh. When the 'flesh' is dominant, human nature is fractured – divided by a psychological war in which the flesh lusts against the spirit and vice versa. Paul's list of the 'works of the flesh' contains expected items such as fornication, uncleanness, lasciviousness, drunkenness, revellings and suchlike, but some of them should give us pause: idolatry, sorcery, emnities, strife, jealousies, wraths, factions, envyings, divisions and heresies. This group is not only more extensive but the elements are manifestly not 'bodily' sins. Indeed, in Eph. ii, 3, Paul lumps together 'desires of the flesh and desires of the mind'.

The spirit which restores psychosomatic unity to man is a partaking of the Spirit of God, mediated through Christ who in Himself has re-established the original integrity of man which is not only psychological but social (Eph. ii, 15–18; Col. i, 22). Thus 'flesh' and 'spirit' refer to what are almost attitudes of mind or spiritual states and Paul can speak of Christians as 'having put off the body of the flesh' through their union with Christ (Col. xii, 11) and earlier he makes a similar distinction between 'body' and 'flesh' (Col. ii, 23) and even uses the expression 'fleshly mind' (Col. ii, 18).

That the flesh is not intrinsically evil is both derived from and expressed by the central Christian doctrine of the Incarnation – the 'enfleshing' of the Son of God (e.g. Eph. ii, 15; I Tim. iii, 16) and therefore, among Christians, relationships can be both 'in the flesh' and 'in the Lord' (Phil. 16). The Christian belief in 'the resurrection of the flesh', as distinct from Greek ideas of the immortality of the soul, and the central act of worship involving communion in the Body and Blood of Christ are of a piece with the essential doctrine.

Besides the noun 'flesh', Paul uses two adjectives: 'fleshly' which means made of human flesh, sensitive as opposed to stone (II Cor. iii, 3); and another, usually translated 'carnal'. The latter is opposed to 'spiritual' (Rom. vii, 14), but not necessarily in a derogatory sense since care for the human needs of the Jews can be a kind of recompense for their spiritual contribution to the world (Rom. xv, 27). In this example, 'carnal' could be translated 'material' and so also in I Cor. ix, 11 where Paul claims some material recompense for his spiritual work. Elsewhere, it seems merely equivalent to 'human' (II Cor. i, 12; x, 4) sometimes with the implication of 'weak' or 'childish' (I Cor. iii, 1, 3, 4) and with associations of jealousy and contention.

The language of other New Testament writers is similar. St Peter exhorts Christians, who are only transient dwellers in the world, to abstain from the 'passions of the flesh that war against the soul' (I Pet. ii, 11). Like St James (Jas. i, 10f.), he emphasises the impermanence of the flesh which, as Isaiah says, is 'like grass' (I Pet. i, 24), yet it is of the essence of man and for this reason Christ took it, with all its weaknesses, upon Himself so that He might restore it and give it eternal life (I Pet. iii, 18; iv, 1; ii, 24). Because man is a unity, the bath of baptism is not a mere removal of dirt from the body but 'an appeal to God for a clear conscience' through the bodily resurrection of the incarnate Christ (I Pet. iii, 21). The time before baptism should provide enough opportunity for the unregenerate flesh to indulge in 'licentiousness, passions, drunkenness, revels, carousing and lawless idolatry' but, once joined to Christ, the convert should live the rest of his earthly life ('time in the flesh') no longer driven by human passions but guided by the will of God (I Pet. iv, 2f.).

St Peter takes up the Jewish idea that 'the flesh' continued a shadowy existence in Sheol and seems to teach that, between His death and resurrection, Christ preached the Gospel to the dead in recognition of both the fallen and redeemed state of humanity (I Pet. iv, 6; cf. iii, 18f.). The Second Epistle of Peter associates human dissolution with human passion, and eternal life with divine unity (II Pet. i, 4), and it indicates problems arising in the infant Church as it realised that the Second Coming of Christ was not to be as soon as some expected. The pseudepigraphal letter reflects a time after the death of Peter when his teaching has been contaminated by Gnostic and pagan ideas and the gospel of liberty is becoming an excuse for libertinism (II Pet. ii, 10–22).

The letter to the Jewish Christians (possibly of Rome), which we know as the Epistle to the Hebrews, throws light on an earlier situation (c. A.D. 67) and naturally uses Jewish language and ideas. 'Flesh and blood' is equivalent to 'humanity' (Heb. ii, 14) and 'fathers of our flesh' to 'human parents' (Heb. xii, 9), while 'in the days of His flesh' is a Hebraism for 'while He lived on earth' (Heb. v, 7). The 'carnal ordinances' of the Jewish law are temporary regulations concerning the body and related to the old priesthood which are abrogated by the High Priesthood of Christ whose self-sacrifice in the flesh sanctifies the whole man, body and soul (Heb. ix, 10–14; cf. vii, 16). Because God and man are united in Christ's flesh, the curtain (symbolised by the veil in the Jewish Temple) which separated God from man has been destroyed and a new route has been opened from God to man through His flesh (Heb. x, 20).

The less theological James associates human selfish desires (in this case, greed for money and possessions) with both the desires of the flesh and the consequent just punishment of the flesh in the fires of God's judgment (Jas. v, 1–3ff.). John, emphasising as always the love of God and the responsive love of man in and through the 'enfleshing' of the Logos, wrote (c. A.D. 90) a letter stressing the reality of Christ's humanity against the heresy of the Docetists who argued that it was only 'an appearance'. Such teachers might claim prophetic inspiration, but there is a sure test for such claims: 'Every spirit which confesseth that Jesus Christ is come in the flesh is of God.' (I John iv, 2; cf. II John 7). The true Light has come (John i, 4, 9; iii, 19; viii, 12; xii, 46, etc.) and its arrival both spotlights true values and throws false ones into relief, especially the contrast between worldly love and divine love: 'Love not the world, neither the things that are in the world. If any man love the world, the love of the Father is not in him. For all that is in the world: the lust of the flesh, and the lust of the eyes, and the vain glory of life, is not of the Father, but is of the world. And the world passeth away and the lust thereof; but he that doeth the will of God abideth for ever.' (I John ii, 16). This critical passage lies behind the mediaeval concept of 'luxuria' and was also used mistakenly to support contempt of the body and a variety of puritanisms and ascetic theories. In fact, it calls on Christians to see 'the world' (the social construction of reality prescinding from God) for what it is and its force is perhaps more clearly expressed in a modern translation:

> Never give your hearts to this world or to any of the things in it. A man cannot love the Father and the world at the same time. For the whole world-system, based as it is on men's primitive desires, their greedy ambitions, and the glamour of all that they think splendid, is not derived from the Father at all, but from the world itself. The world and all its passionate desires will one day disappear. But the man who is following God's will is part of the Permanent and cannot die. (Phillips, 1955, 239.)

An even stronger warning against false teaching or heresy is found in the letter of Jude, possibly written by the stepbrother of Jesus c. A.D. 70. It naturally contains many traditional Jewish associations: fornication and apostasy (Jude, 7), analogies between the infamous sins of Sodom and Gomorrah and contemporary perversions where 'defilement of the flesh' is linked with contempt for authority and heavenly glory (Jude 8). Yet the Christian is called, for the love of God, to help the offenders however much he is revolted by the garments which they have befouled through their incontinence (Jude 22f.).[23]

In the Book of Revelation, 'flesh' is only used to mean 'food', i.e. 'meat'. The great beast eats the flesh of the harlot (Rev. xvii, 16) and, at the end of the world, the carrion birds feed on the flesh of men and horses (Rev. xix, 18, 21). We will conclude with a brief examination of the use of the word 'flesh' in the Gospels. St Mark is generally held to be the earliest and to represent the Petrine tradition which was reduced to writing, c. A.D. 70. Its first occurrence is a citation of Gen. ii, 24, the archetypal statement of human unity through the male–female conjunction[24] of marriage: 'and the twain shall become one flesh, so that they are no more twain but one flesh' (Mark x, 8; cf. parallel in Matt. xix, 5f.). Later in the same Gospel, 'no flesh' means 'no human being' (Mark xiii, 20; cf. parallel in Matt. xiv, 22 and similar uses in Luke iii, 6 and John xvii, 2). 'Flesh' refers to natural human weakness when the apostles fell asleep in Gethsemane (Mark xiv, 38; cf. Matt. xxvi, 41) and Matthew uses 'flesh and blood' to mean 'human resources' (xvi, 7) and in Luke 'flesh and bones' express real humanity as opposed to pure spiritual existence (xxiv, 39 – account of a Resurrection appearance).

In Johannine thought, the normally weak flesh becomes the perfect embodiment of the Divine Logos (John i, 4) and those who receive Him may also become children of God so that they are no longer mere humans, 'born of bloods'[25] or of 'the will of the flesh' or even of the will of man, but of God (John i, 13). The same idea is reiterated in the conversation with Nicodemus about 'the second birth', since 'that which is born of the flesh is flesh; and that which is born of the Spirit is spirit' (John iii, 6). These are not alternatives, but stages in the advance to full humanity. In the great discourse about the heavenly bread, which John places after the miraculous feeding of the 5,000, Christ talks of faith and eternal life: 'If any man eat of this bread, he shall live for ever; and the bread which I will give is my flesh for the life of the world.' (John vi, 51). When the language is objected to, Jesus reiterates and strengthens His words, adding 'blood' to 'flesh' as though to emphasise His point that He is talking about human totality: to eat His flesh and to drink His blood means to absorb His full and exemplary humanity. Those who do so have eternal life now and they do not assimilate an alien 'soul' because it is the Logos which has become 'flesh'. The primary reference is to faith in Christ and union with Him, although the realistic imagery points to the Eucharist which is a continuing material means of spiritual life. The fact of the divine power and initiative in the transformation of the flesh is stated in John vi, 63: 'it is the Spirit that giveth life; the flesh profiteth nothing'.[26] St John has a usage, already found in St Paul, where 'according to the flesh' means 'humanly', 'in a human manner' (John vii, 15).

The remaining New Testament examples occur in St Luke's Acts of the Apostles. They are few in number and all occur in chapter ii, summarising St Peter's sermon after Pentecost, and are applications of Old Testament texts to the new dispensation (Acts ii, 17, 26, 31). The last is interesting inasmuch as Peter equates 'thy holy one' of Ps. xvi, 8–11 with 'the flesh of Christ' in his application.

The New Testament usage is thus continuous with and often repeats that of the Old Testament. There is no denigration of the body but, on the contrary, the belief that the transcendent God has become immanent in the flesh adds a new dimension to the concept of the body which is already affecting both ecclesiology and a sacramental view of creation.

SUMMARY

The surviving Gospels were probably written at least a generation after Christ's death and were based upon his verbal teachings. They cannot be considered either as biographies or as complete summaries of his instruction.

The earliest Christian writings were carefully prepared letters from the early missionaries to their converts, and St Paul's Epistles to the Corinthians are the largest, earliest and probably best known.

Paul taught that the physical body of man was created by God and therefore not to be despised as inferior or lacking in dignity. Much of Paul's doctrine was an enlargement of Judiac thought that saw the body as a manifestation of the soul – helping man re-establish himself in his original and pure state – and formed the basis of the Pauline doctrine. He saw the unity of Christians in the Body of Christ by virtue of the communion service and so the use of the terms 'body' and 'flesh' could mean both the physical body of the individual and the corporate Body of the Church. In fact the essence of Christianity lay essentially in the 'enfleshing' of God, as expressed in the Incarnation and Eucharist, and the Coming of Jesus helped narrow the gap between God and His creation, with His resurrection further solidifying that belief.

However, this religion was too materialistic for the Gnostics and others who had contrasting views about God and matter, Body and Spirit, and much misunderstanding of the Pauline doctrine prevailed. Paul has often been accused of corrupting or theologising the simple teachings of Jesus, but then he was an earlier source of the Gospels that allegedly contain the 'simple teachings'. But even Paul's disciples sometimes did not always see his comparisons between the 'flesh' and the 'spirit'.

In later ages, when the mediaeval mind seemed more concerned with the building up of man than with the analysis of his being, much of the Gospels and other New Testament writings, which were in fact an expansion of the various aspects of the Pauline doctrine, were misunderstood and falsely used to support contempt of the body and a variety of puritanism and ascetic theories.

4

THE STRUGGLE FOR SURVIVAL IN THE ROMAN WORLD

From the death of the last eye-witness of the Incarnation to the establishment of Christianity occupied two centuries, which inevitably contained a great deal of activity and adjustment. The first century saw the abandonment of a national/racial religion in favour of a universal or Catholic one, and the second volume of Luke's history of the Church (the Acts of the Apostles, written *c.* A.D. 80) has as its main themes the shift from Jew to Gentile and the transference of the centre of interest from the Jewish capital Jerusalem (destroyed by Titus in A.D. 70) to Rome, the metropolis and navel of the world.[1]

This same century allowed the Roman government gradually to distinguish between Judaism, which was a *religio licita* (permitted cultus) whose members were often protected and even favoured, and Christianity, which, lacking this legal protection, became increasingly the object of official and popular attacks from the time of Nero (A.D. 54–68). The first Christians seem to have expected an almost immediate return of the Lord whom their evangelists had seen ascending into heaven (Acts i, 11)[2] and this conviction made planning for the future irrelevant and speculation on the philosophy of the body even more so. The anticipation of a cosmic Judgment had scarcely faded when they were forced to face the capricious judgment of a secular court and violent and unnatural death.

The menace of Gnosticism

The first persecutions began in A.D. 64 when the Christians were apparently made scapegoats for the great fire of Rome and consequently appear for the first time in secular annals:

> Nero fastened the guilt and inflicted the most exquisite tortures upon a group hated for their abominations, whom the populace called Christians. Christus, from whom the name had its origin, had been condemned to death in the reign of Tiberius by the procurator Pontius Pilate and the pernicious supersitition, thus suppressed for a moment, was breaking out again not only in Judaea, the original source of this evil, but even in Rome where all things horrible or shameful from all parts of the world collect and become popular. (Tacitus: *Annals*, xv, 45, tr. Lewis and Reinhold, 1966, II, 226.)

The detached Roman aristocrat, concerned with the villainies of the emperors, nevertheless seems to share the vulgar opinion of this new minority group who were 'hated for their abominations' which, in the popular mind, included infanticide, cannibalism and incest.[3] Under torture, those first arrested implicated others until 'an enormous number', according to Tacitus, or 979 according to the records of the Roman Church, were convicted, apparently not so much for their proven involvement in the fire as for the attributed 'hatred of the human race'. Nero, the well-known amateur performer and impresario, took the opportunity for a novel promotion: '[The Christians] were covered with the skins of wild beasts and torn to death by dogs, or they were nailed to crosses and, when daylight failed, were set on fire and burned to provide light at night. Nero had offered his own gardens for the spectacle, and was providing circus games, mingling with the populace in the dress of a charioteer or driving a chariot.' (Lewis and Reinhold 1966, II, 227). According to tradition, St Peter died in this Vatican Gardens entertainment, being crucified upside down as an entr'acte between two chariot races (cf. John xxi, 18f.) and, a year or two later, St Paul also met his death in Rome but, profiting by his privileged position as a Roman citizen, was merely beheaded on the Ostian Way.

The deaths of leading apostles, authentic witnesses of the unwritten teaching of Christ, made the Gnostic danger more pressing. This general religious movement seems to have attempted to penetrate the new faith almost from its origin. Gnosticism was characterised by its secret tradition, transmitted to initiates not to the general public, by its use of magic rites and formulae and by its prime purpose of freeing the soul from association with the body in particular and the material world in general. Its central concept was of the unbridgeable chasm between spirit which was good and matter which was bad. This naturally led to a dualism: matter was to be despised and hated as the source of all evil and, as such, it could not have been created by the good Supreme Deity, but by some lesser power, angel or demiurge.

Simon Magus is an early figure in the attempt to 'disembody' Christianity by 'spiritualising' it in accordance with Gnostic principles. He appears by name in Acts viii, 9–11 and his, or similar, teaching is combated in the Epistles and elsewhere in the New Testament. Gnosticism's characteristic contempt for the flesh and consequent denial of Christ's resurrection is opposed (e.g. I Cor. xv, 12; I Tim. iv, 3). In practice, despising the flesh led to one of two extremes: libertinism on the principle that the body is so contemptible that its behaviour does not matter, or rigid asceticism because it must be utterly crushed. Both are opposed in the canonical writings (the former in I Cor. vi, 9f.; Rev. ii, 14; II Pet. ii, 10; Jude 8; the latter in Col. ii, 16–21; I Tim. iv, 3ff.; cf. v, 23).

When these first attempts failed, the gnosticisers continued their attempt to pervert the original teaching by adducing gospels, epistles and acts of their own composition and claiming a spurious authority by the attachment of apostolic or other well-known names. These forgeries led, during the second century, to the establishment of the authentic New Testament and other tests of true apostolicity such as the 'apostolic succession' of bishops and the confession of the 'apostolic faith' in formal creeds.

In spite of heresy from within and persecution from without, the young Church quickly spread and, by the end of the first century, had established communities in cities[4] throughout the Roman Empire. The word 'christian' was first coined in Syrian Antioch; St Paul and St John were associated with Ephesus, Mark and Apollos with Alexandria; Revelation contains letters to Ephesus, Smyrna, Pergamum, Thyatira, Sardis, Philadelphia and Laodicea; Paul worked in Athens and Rome, as well as Asia Minor, and the new faith rapidly reached Cyprus, Malta and Crete. By the second century there were churches in North Africa, Gaul and Spain and during the same period Christian missionaries passed the frontiers of the Roman Empire to Persia and Edessa and possibly even to India.

The establishment and organisation of such plantations was a prime concern to the second generation of Christian writers and this is the purpose, for example, of the *Letter of St Clement*[5] written from Rome to the Corinthian Church about A.D. 95. It is concerned with faith and order, with the internal peace of the Church and, above all, with charity on the model of the Master who gave 'His blood for us, His flesh for our flesh, His soul for our souls' (Lake, 1930, I, 95). Besides the self-sacrificing example of Christ, attention is drawn to the Roman martyrs Peter and Paul and other more recent witnesses. These last may be a reference to the renewed persecution with the imperial authority of Domitian (A.D. 81–96) which had caused the death of a number of Roman citizens, including some very illustrious ones, and had extended to the provinces of Bythinia, Asia and possibly Palestine. The Book of Revelation mentions martyrs in Pergamum and Smyrna and its author was possibly exiled to Patmos in this same persecution. Clement's letter indirectly throws some light on the character of its author, who seems to have been a converted Jew with a sympathetic understanding of what is noble and good in paganism (indeed his own writing shows Stoic influence) and he specially praises the created world as the work of God; he comes over as an early example of Christian humanism: 'his Christianity is not at all that of which the pagans will make a bugbear, as the religion of a *gens lucifuga* [a species that shuns the light]; he is a man of the widest and most truly human sympathies' (Lebreton and Zeiller, 1944, II, 343).

Sporadic persecution continued under Trajan (A.D. 98–117), in spite of his more judicious policy and refusal to accept anonymous accusations,[6] and the victims included Clement, condemned to the mines; Simeon (bishop of Jerusalem), crucified; and Ignatius (bishop of Antioch) who was sentenced to be thrown to the beasts in Rome. As Ignatius was conveyed to his place of execution he wrote a number of letters to the Christian Churches on the way – hasty last messages about peace and order from a man journeying to his death. He shows great awareness of the insidious poison of Gnosticism and proclaims Catholic Christianity, with its emphasis on the real incarnation of the Son of God, as the only antidote:

> Refuse to listen to the speech of those who do not speak to you of that Jesus Christ, the descendant of David and of Mary, who was really born, ate, and drank, and really was persecuted under Pontius Pilate, was actually crucified and died before the eyes of those in heaven, on earth and under the earth, and in truth was raised from the dead. . . . But if, as some godless affirm, his suffering was only an appearance[7] (when, in fact, it is they who lack reality) then why am I in chains and why do I desire to fight with the beasts? (*Trallians*, ix, x, tr. Lake, 1930, I, 221, cf. *Smyrnaeans*, ii.)

Incarnation and the Eucharist

There is an obvious connection between the Incarnation and the Eucharist: both are manifestations of the flesh of Christ and both are the source of our bodily resurrection. It is logical for those who deny the former to despise the latter: 'They abstain from the Eucharist and from prayer because they do not admit that the Eucharist is the flesh of our Saviour Jesus Christ who suffered for our sins which the Father raised up by His goodness. They who deny the gift of God are perishing in their disputes; but it were better for them to have love that they also may attain to the Resurrection.' (*Smyrneans*, vii). The eucharistic bread, like the incarnate body, is the bond of unity and peace and therefore humanity's antidote against death (Eph. xx). Both are the signs and media of God's love and the Christian's share in this love makes him able to say that he himself is the bread of God (Rom. iv,). For this mystic, the 'oneing' in the flesh of Christ obliterates the world and the ghastliness of his coming martyrdom: 'I have no more pleasure in corruptible food, nor in the joys of this life. I desire the bread of God which is the flesh of Jesus Christ and for

drink I desire His blood which is incorruptible love.'[8] (Rom. vii.) The
emperor Trajan was succeeded by Hadrian (A.D. 117–38), a great
administrator and voluptuous philhellene[9] who loved a beautiful boy
called Antinous who died in mysterious circumstances:

> He was Hadrian's male concubine and he died in Egypt, either
> through falling into the Nile, as Hadrian declared, or because he
> was offered as a sacrifice. The latter is probably the truth because
> Hadrian was so curious that he meddled with soothsaying and
> magical arts. Either because of his love for Antinous, or because
> Antinous had died for his sake (as his purposes needed the
> voluntary self-sacrifice of a human life), Hadrian honoured the
> dead youth so much that he built a city in the place where he had
> died, naming it after him. He placed statues[10] and busts of An-
> tinous in almost every city throughout the Empire. He even wished
> to see a special star of Antinous in the heavens and was pleased
> when his companions helped him to concoct the story that An-
> tinous' soul had become a star never before seen in the entire
> heavens. (Dio Cassius: *Historia Romana*, lxix, 11.)

Hadrian was no friend of Christianity, but he was antipathetic to
disorder and mob violence and therefore required that anti-Christian
proceedings should follow the due process of law and not be the
result merely of spontaneous riots or erratic lynchings. His reign
produced a number of legally executed martyrs in Italy and many
Christians were killed in Palestine as a result of the savage reprisals
following Bar Kokbha's bloody Jewish revolt (A.D. 132–5).

About this time, a work called *The Shepherd of Hermas*[11] was
reaching its final redaction. It was so popular in the second century
that it had almost the status of a canonical book of the New
Testament yet it is a complex and difficult work, full of visions and
revelations but with autobiographical elements. Its author appears to
have been a freedman who made a fortune, but had an unfortunate
marriage and children who did him little credit. Initially, merely a
nominal Christian, his faith grew more pervasive as his worldly
position deteriorated and he became a visionary and lay evangelist
with a special concern about morality and the depth of divine
forgiveness. His message also contains implied criticism of
fashionable Christianity, warnings about the dangers of wealth and
the imminence of further persecution.

Like St Paul, Hermas was aware that the world was not the real
home of Christians: 'As the servants of God, you live in an alien
country for your true city is far from this city. If, then, you know that
city which belongs to you and in which you are going to dwell, why
do you here prepare lands and costly establishments and buildings

and vain residences?[12] Do you not understand that all these things are foreign to you and are under a foreign power?' (Shepherd, *Similitudes*, I, i). Yet the world is made by God, is intrinsically a pleasant and beautiful place and a suitable locale for God's revelation of Himself. We are reminded of Piers Plowman as Hermas, just before a vision, walks along a country road 'glorifying the creation of God for its greatness and splendour and might' and again when he sits alone on a hillside, meditating and keeping his fast. There are also intimations of a destined transfiguration of the cosmos through the re-creative work of Christ in the words read to Hermas by the Lady (a symbol of the Church): 'The same Almighty God who . . . by His great wisdom created the world and by His glorious counsel surrounded His creation with beauty. . . . Lo, He changes the heavens, and the mountains and the hills and the seas, and all things are becoming smooth for His chosen ones.' (*Vision* I, iii, 4, cf. Isa. xl, 4). The same sense of light and joy in a rejuvenated nature is conveyed in the scene around the Tower (another symbol of the Church) where the Maidens, who represent the Christian virtues, receive Hermas into their jocund company. He tells how 'they began to lead me round the Tower and to play with me. I too had, as it were, become youthful again and I began to play with them myself. Some were dancing, some gavotting, others were singing and I paced in silence with them about the Tower and was merry with them.' (*Similitudes*, IX, xi, 4f.)

Though the author of *The Shepherd* is a simple moralist and not a profound theologian, he is clear about the centrality of the Incarnation and its implications in both the personal and social spheres. The Shepherd, who is the central teacher, explains one of his parables as follows:

The Holy Spirit which pre-exists, which brought into being all creation, was made by God to dwell in the flesh which He willed. Therefore this flesh, in which the Holy Spirit dwelled, served the Spirit well, walking in holiness and purity, and did not in any way defile the Spirit. When, therefore, it had lived nobly and purely, and had laboured with the Spirit, and had worked with It in every deed, conducting itself with strength and courage, He chose it as companion with the Holy Spirit; for the conduct of this flesh pleased Him, because it was not defiled while it was bearing the Holy Spirit on earth. Therefore He took the Son and the glorious angels as counsellors that this flesh also, having served the Spirit blamelessly, should have some place of sojourn, and not seem to have lost the reward of its service. For all flesh in which the Holy Spirit has dwelt shall receive a reward if it be found undefiled and spotless. (*Similitudes*, V, vi, 5–7.)

The passage is ambiguous and seems to refer to either the con-junction of the Holy Spirit with the Humanity of Christ or to man's partaking of God's spirit or to both ideas simultaneously. Whatever reading we take, the message is that human flesh, through its association with Divinity, is to be elevated into a permanent association with God Himself. The moral implications follow: 'Guard this flesh of yours, pure and undefiled, that the Spirit which dwells in it may bear it witness and your flesh may be justified. See to it, lest the idea enter your heart that this flesh of yours is mortal and you abuse it in some defilement. For if you defile your flesh, you defile also the Holy Spirit, and if you defile the flesh you shall not live.' (Ibid. V, vii, 1–2). However, defilements, which took place in the past when the true significance of the body was unknown, can be healed by the power of God,[13] 'if, for the future, you defile neither the flesh nor the spirit; for both are in communion, and neither can be defiled without the other. Therefore, keep both pure, and you shall live to God.' (Ibid. V, vii, 4.) This admonition is clearly directed against the Gnostic tendency to separate spirit and flesh and to regard the latter as contemptible and its acts as unimportant. Against this complete dualism, Hermas teaches the Catholic tradition by asserting the present significance of the flesh and the hope of its future resurrection. He also maintains the traditional association between paganism and adultery, though in his treatment of marital infidelity he is far from the extreme rigorist position (*Mandates*, IV, i, 4–10).

The ascent of Christianity

The persecution forecast by Hermas did return to Rome, claiming two popes, a priest and a number of laymen in the reign of the next emperor, Antonius Pius (138–61), although he followed the example of his predecessor in condemning popular commotions and irregular proceedings. Further afield, the bishop of Jerusalem was martyred, and the aged Polycarp, bishop of Smyrna, together with eleven of his congregation, became victims of a popular uprising to which the proconsul of Asia had yielded.[14] We owe some of our knowledge of such events to the development of a new kind of Christian writing, that of the Apologists who were Christian intellectuals, often trained and professional philosophers, who demanded a rational consideration of their case. The first representatives of this genre, such as Quadratus and Aristides, did not make a very impressive beginning, but soon more powerful voices were to be heard. Among these was Justin Martyr, described as 'orthodox Christianity's first theologian',[15] who tried to present Christianity not only as the true religion, but as the true philosophy, the true Hellenism, and the true political loyalty.

Justin was the son of a rich man and used his economic independence to pursue truth from one philosophical school to
another. He tried, in turn, Stoicism, Aristotelianism, and
Pythagoreanism, until he found temporary satisfaction in the New
Platonism which offered him a single God who incorporated the
Good and Beautiful as well as the True. Neo-Platonism also
presented the concept of the Supreme Logos (Mind or Reason) of
which the good philosopher could catch glimpses in the inferior
world of matter if he constantly purified his own 'logos' of the body
which weighed it down to earth. Finally, in his intellectual
pilgrimage, Justin came to the Gospel which he saw as the perfection
and summation of philosophy, especially of Platonism, since it
presented the Logos incarnate in the flesh. Having found what he
believed to be the final truth, Justin became a peripatetic teacher,
staying in a number of cities until he had gathered round himself a
little school of Christian philosophy and then moving on. He interspersed his task of local teaching with the composition of defences
(*Apologies*) for Christianity, which he addressed to prominent intellectuals and to the government itself which was headed by the
philosopher emperor Marcus Aurelius from A.D. 161 to 180.

Justin's literary work offers little to our purpose but, apart from
the centrality of the incarnate Logos, he makes an indirect contribution by insisting on an objective morality, founded on truth and
not on opinion: 'And against the objection that human conventions
are diverse: one thing being considered good and another evil by
some, whole others esteem as good what is bad to the former and
what seemed to them good is reckoned as bad . . . we know that the
Right Reason (the Logos immanent and transcendent) proved that
not all opinions nor all teachings are good, but that some are evil,
while others are good.' (*Apology* II, ix). However, the humane
emperor was not impressed by a religion which seemed to him to give
little value to intellect, unnaturally welcomed suffering and did not
conform, so, though there was no stiffening of the legislation against
it, Christian martyrs multiplied (probably due to the need for
scapegoats in a time of increasing public misfortunes which included
wars, epidemics and cataclysms). An outbreak of violence in Antioch
resulted in several deaths, two bishops meeting their death in Asia
Minor and another in Athens. Felicitas and her seven sons were
executed in Rome after a formal trial, as was Justin himself after
being delated by a rival Cynic philosopher. These were followed by St
Cecilia and others in Rome and there were further martyrdoms in
Greece and Gaul.

A vivid contemporary account of events of A.D. 177 in Lyons
survives,[16] which not only witnesses to the heroic faith of Christians

and their confidence in the resurrection of the body in spite of all that could be done to destroy it, but also shows something of the hysterical hatred of the mob and their irrational suspicions. These received support when pagan domestics, under the threat of torture, attested that in their master's house they had witnessed Thyestean banquets and Oedipedean incest: anthropophagy of their own children and sexual relations between mother and sons.

In such a climate of opinion, Justin's intellectual challenge was not likely to be very effective any more than such a reasoned assertion as this from the apologist, Athenagoras (c. A.D. 177): 'For nothing that is endowed with reason and judgment has been created, or is created, for the use of another (whether greater or less than itself), but for the life and continuance of the being so created.' (*On the Resurrection of the Dead*, xii). There is a good deal of potentiality here in regard to sexual ethics and social attitudes and institutions, including slavery, but the full working out was to be long delayed. It is interesting that Athenagoras goes on to 'prove' the resurrection from this axiom about human dignity. In an age of persecution, when the body was constantly menaced by diabolically ingenious tortures and ignominious death, belief in a glorious resurrection was obviously a great consolation. The pagans maliciously tried to deprive the Christians of this hope by the type of death they inflicted and by attempting to destroy their remains completely.

Athenagoras argues that the Christian attitude to the body is immeasurably superior to that of the heathen since they hope to enjoy its highest life for ever:

> Will those who take as their motto in life, 'Let us eat and drink, for tomorrow we die' . . . be regarded as pious folk? And are we to be regarded as impious, we who know that the present life is short and of little worth, we who are animated by the single desire to know the True God and His Word; the unity of the Son with the Father, the communion of the Father with the Son, the nature of the Holy Spirit, and the unity and distinction between the Father, Son and Holy Spirit, we who know that the life we await is beyond verbal expression (provided always that we leave this world pure of every stain), we who love mankind so much that our love extends beyond our friends. . . .?' (*Apology*, xii.)

Another apologist, Tatian, was an Assyrian by birth who had travelled to Rome and became a convert and disciple of Justin. He tended to be egocentric, proud and boastful but, at first, discovered in Christianity an expression of the freedom and dignity of man: his liberation from Fate (*Discourse*, xi), and his existential continuance through the resurrection of the body as against the imperfect Greek notion of the immortality of the soul (ibid. vi). He saw the harmony within the diversity of the differing parts and functions of the human body as an analogy of the greater diversity within the unified cosmos (*Discourse*, xii) and suggested that any apparent disharmony results from the machinations of daemonic forces (ibid.). Some extracts from this chapter may communicate something of its flavour.

> Man is not, as the croaking philosphers say, merely a rational animal capable of understanding and knowledge; for, according to them, even irrational creatures appear to be possessed of understanding and knowledge.[17] The singular differentia of man is that he is 'the image and likeness of God', and by 'man' I mean not one who performs actions similar to those of animals but one who has advanced far beyond mere 'humanity' to God himself.[18]

Having thus established man's essential distinction, Tatian goes on to analyse (like many other Christian thinkers) the concept of 'God's image and likeness'. On the one hand, animals have bodies and a kind of rationality; on the other, demons do not have bodies but are spiritual structures: man is different from either. 'Nor can the likeness to God be in man's body, since the perfect God is without flesh, but man is flesh: the bond of the flesh is the soul, that which encloses the soul is the flesh.'[19] Tatian seems to consider man as essentially a psychosomatic entity and he almost takes up the Aristotelian position that the soul is the 'form' of the body. But he also seems to allow the possibility of this diad becoming a triad through the indwelling of God the Spirit: 'Such is the nature of man's constitution: and, if it be like a temple, God is prepared to dwell in it by the Spirit – His representative. But, if it be not such a habitation, man excels the wild beasts in articulate speech only. In other respects, his life-style is like theirs, as one who is not a "likeness of God".'[20] It is the pursuit of the material and untruth[21] which corrupts the unique nature and destiny of man. One form of this disharmony is to reduce his unified general excellence to some specific type of physical excellence, a process which reaches its nadir and ultimate decadence in such 'men' (virile types) as pugilists and gladiators: 'You slaughter animals so that you can eat their flesh and you purchase men to supply a cannibal banquet for the soul, nourishing it by the most impious[22] blood-letting.' Athletic activities that are less bloodthirsty than the 'games' still share, in their degree, the same misconception of truly human activity: 'I have seen men weighed down by bodily exercise, and carrying about the burden of their flesh, before whom rewards and medals were set, while the adjudicators cheer them on, not to deeds of virtue, but to rivalry in violence and discord: and he who excels in the giving of blows is the one who receives the prize.'

After the martyrdom of his master Justin, Tatian seems to have regressed and have abandoned Catholicism for Gnosticism. Irenaeus provides us with this information, together with some indication of the cause of this change:

> Elated and puffed up by his title of Teacher (Doctor), as though he were superior to the others, he founded a school of his own. In it he postulated the existence of certain invisible Aeons, similar to those of Valentinus, he copied Marcion and Saturninus in denouncing marriage as defilement and fornication, but he made an original contribution by adding to these ideas the notion that Adam was not saved. (Irenaeus: *Against the Heresies* I, xxviii, cf. III, xxxvii.)

Clement of Alexandria records that Tatian opposed not merely fornication but also marriage and procreation (*Stromata*, iii, 12) and, in a tantalizing fragment, remarks: 'And he [Tatian] taught that women were punished on account of their hair and ornaments by a[n angelic] power placed over these things, which also gave strength to Samson by his hair, and punishes those who by the ornament of their hair are urged on to fornication.'[23] That such ideas were the result of an over-spiritualising of Christianity and rested on different principles from true asceticism was clear enough to the highly disciplined Jerome who (in his commentary on the prophet Amos) tells us that Tatian totally forebade intoxicating drink and also relates Tatian's peculiar doctrines to a deficient belief in the Incarnation:

> Tatian, a man who maintained that the flesh of Christ was only an appearance, pronounced all sexual connection impure. He was also the very violent heresiarch of the Encratites and employed this sort of reasoning: 'If any man sows to the flesh, of the flesh he shall reap corruption'; but, the man who is joined to a woman sows to the flesh; therefore, he who takes a wife and sows to the flesh, of the flesh he shall reap corruption. (Jerome: *Commentary on the Epistle to the Galatians*, cf. his *Against Jovinian*, i, 3.)

This is a very significant extract: it shows the tendency to quote authorities, especially St Paul, and the kind of faulty reasoning that results from a syllogism which changes the meaning of its terms in the process of development. We have already given some consideration to the many meanings of 'flesh' in the Pauline writings, since it is this very kind of transferred meaning which has caused much muddled thinking in the development of Christian attitudes towards the body and/or flesh.

Encratism (whose adherents were mentioned in the passage from

Jerome) was a heresy which seems to have begun about A.D. 170. Its name is derived from a Greek word meaning 'self-control' and its basic teaching was that sex is essentially evil and hence always sinful and impermissible to the pure. This idea was attractive to the Montanists[24] with their millenarianist expectations, and the Gnostics Marcion and Valentinus found it very conformable to their basic dualism. In Tatian, the principle of sexual abstinence was almost the prime ingredient in his notion of the Christian life.[25]

Some Encratites preferred to baptise none but virgins, male or female, but they would, as a concession, extend admission to couples who had shown their 'repentance' by separating. Others merely gave virgins priority in the baptismal queue. The basic Encratist doctrine, which necessarily made married couples into second-rate Christians, not only represented a perversion of Christian values[26] but also produced some bizarre practices of which one of the most popular and long-lasting was the habit of a man and woman living together while preserving their virginity and regarding this asexual association as the only worthy Christian 'marriage'. Barr (1966, 18) comments:

> It is easy to see that the Encratist notion is a logical consequence of the gnostic condemnation of matter. As one of the most powerful material forces, sex becomes the most thoroughly condemned. When Encratism is a product of millenarianism or some other form of false messianism, it represents preparatory self-purification or self-punishment. Unreasonable sexual taboos are a perennial temptation of human religion. They spring from man's unconscious linking of sex and guilt, a link forged in childhood in the selfishness of immature sexuality, and sometimes strengthened later by genuinely guilty, selfish sex. But religion should not condemn sexuality as evil.[27] True religion respects sexuality and consecrates it.

The reign of the next emperor, Commodus (A.D. 180–93) almost provides a gloss on this theme. Both humanly and functionally, he was a worse emperor than Aurelius, but he was less inflexible in his application of the law against Christians. Nevertheless, perhaps as a hangover from the dutiful previous regime, martyrs were produced including, in A.D. 180, the first names from Africa. A few years later, in Asia, there was a recrudescence of persecution which was described as 'especially cruel' and, about the same time, Rome produced a martyr of senatorial rank in the person of Apollonius.

The stabilisation of this uneasy situation seems to have been due largely to the exertions of one Marcia, a slave-girl who became the favourite mistress of Commodus and eventually his wife (though without the imperial title). She was a Christian, the friend and foster-daughter of a Christian priest named Hyacinth, and she used her considerable influence to ameliorate the position of her co-religionists and to protect them from the application of the existing laws. As a result of her activities, Christians were able to appear publicly at the imperial court (one even attained the office of chamberlain) and magistrates endeavoured to dismiss cases against Christians. Marcia personally procured an imperial pardon for a group of Roman Christians (among them the future Pope Callistus) who had been given the capital sentence of penal servitude in the mines of Sardinia.

As the second century draws to its close, the situation of the Church is clearly changing. From its Palestinian origins it has approached the boundaries of the Roman Empire in all directions and, in some areas, has advanced well beyond them. It has survived both intense and sporadic persecution, driven millenarianism from a central to a peripheral and even heretical belief, developed a universal organisation round the episcopate and an established liturgy, creed and canonical scriptures. Because of these essential and necessary activities, especially the need to meet the menace of Gnosticism, Christian thinkers have been unable to give their full attention to the systematic exegesis of Christian doctrine and its implications. Yet the Christian voice is beginning to be heard and its intellectual claims for attention are being asserted by the Apologists and it may be fitting to close this section with citations from the last of these: Minucius Felix, a Latin writer from the reign of Alexander Severus (A.D. 193–211).

> Is it necessary to raise statues to God, if man is His image? Why should one build temples to Him, seeing that the universe which He framed with His hands is not able to contain Him? How can one enclose this Immensity in a small chapel? It is our souls which must serve as a dwelling-place for Him and He wants us to consecrate our hearts to Him. Of what use is it to offer victims to Him, and would it not be an ingratitude, when He has given us all that is born on earth for our use, to give back to Him the presents He has given us? Let us realise that He requires of us only a pure heart and an upright conscience. To conserve one's innocence is to pray to God: to respect justice is to honour Him. We win His favour by abstaining from all fraud, and when one saves a man from danger, one offers Him the sacrifice He prefers. These are the victims and that is the worship we offer Him. Amongst us, he is the most religious who is the most just. (*Octavius*, xxxii, 3, tr. Lebreton and Zeiller, 1944, 487.)

As Minucius Felix is writing openly to pagans and from the

traditional viewpoint of the apologist, he makes use only of general arguments and does not open up the secret foundations of Christian belief and behaviour. He is concerned only with what his contemporaries could see of the significant external actions of Christians and not with the hidden springs from which those actions issued. Thus, his only continuous argument is drawn from the spectacle of Christian virtues, especially as they are displayed in the supreme witness[28] of bodily martyrdom:

> What a fine spectacle for God is that of a Christian who fights against pain, who vindicates his liberty in the face of kings and princes, yielding only to God to whom he belongs, who surmounts, triumphant and victorious, the magistrate who condemns him. . . . This is because the soldier of God is not abandoned in pain, is not destroyed by death. A Christian may appear to be unfortunate, but he is not. . . . Do you not realise that no one would wish, without reason, to expose himself to such torments, and that he could not endure them without God? . . .
>
> Peaceful, modest, assured of the goodness of our God, we support the hope of future happiness by faith in His ever-present Majesty. Thus we rise again to a happy life and here below we already live in the contemplation of that future. (We despise the contempt of the established philosophers) whom we know to be corruptors, adulterers, tyrants, and posessed of an inexhaustible loquaciousness against what are their own vices.
>
> We, who make manifest our wisdom, not by our mantle[29] but by our soul, the greatness of which is not in words but in life, we glory because we have actually grasped what these men have striven unsuccessfully to find in spite of all their great endeavours. . . . It is our will that superstititon should be forced to retreat, that impiety be expiated, and true religion be respected.
> (*Octavius*, xxxvii–xxxviii – abbreviated.)

SUMMARY

The first two centuries of the Church's existence were a time of continuing crisis. It had no sooner adjusted itself to the fact that the Second Coming of Christ was not to be immediate than it was involved in a struggle for survival in the face of State persecution from without and insidious attempts to corrupt by 'spiritualisation' its doctrine from within. This was obviously no time for considering its attitude towards, and developing its ideas about, the human body. That body was likely to be torn to pieces at any time by the most ingenious methods of a sadistic age. Nevertheless, not only are possible growth-points preserved but some of the implications are faintly discerned: the centrality of the doctrines of the Incarnation, Resurrection and Communion in the Eucharistic Body of Christ is constantly asserted; the psychosomatic unity of man is maintained against heretical distortion and there is asseveration of the dignity of the human body. Perhaps the story of Marcia whose attractive body was a means of saving members of the Body of Christ was more significant than most historians seem to realise and, at any rate, we can assert that in spite of persecution and confusion the essential ingredients of a balanced yet religious attitude towards the body are preserved through this age of endurance.

5
THE BEGINNINGS OF SYSTEMATIC THOUGHT

In the third century of the Christian era, its intellectual world continued to be wracked by the never-ending quarrels of 'schools', professors (often former or continuing philosophers who saw Christianity as the ultimate 'wisdom') and theologians. Of these intellectuals, Heer (1966, 13) comments: 'These circles were united only in contempt for the masses whom they regarded as sunk in superstition. Generally, they tended to deny both the Trinity and the divine-human nature of Christ. They hated personal, existential *and* philosophical interpretations of sin. The incarnation, suffering, and the necessarily historical character of creation were repellent to them.'

Their homes and the centres of their teaching were in the Eastern part of the Roman Empire and many of their ideas and approaches were undoubtedly affected by the characteristic Eastern attitudes to the body which were arriving from as far afield as India.

Period of transition

The African Tertullian (*c.* 155–220), the first theologian of the West (if one exempts Irenaeus), was opposed to intellectual 'establishment' on many grounds. There was a long-standing 'African nationalism' which resented the dominance of Rome and, as a member of the oppressed classes as well as a 'provincial', Tertullian bore grudges against the cultural world which dominated the official and aristocratic attitudes. The burning heat of the African sun not only delineated things in black and white, but also seemed to produce sharp conceptual antitheses: between philosophy and religion and, especially, between flesh and spirit. There was nothing in common, declared Tertullian, between philosopher and Christian, between Rome and Jerusalem. Indeed, the philosophers were the patriarchs of the heretics (*Apology*, xlvi; *De Anima*, iii) and reason itself was of dubious value. 'I believe because it is impossible', he asserted defiantly as the summary of his conviction that the values of this world were utterly opposed to Christian values.

Yet Tertullian was far from consistent. His most firmly dated work is a lengthy polemic against the Gnostic Marcion, in which he insists on the reality of Christ's flesh and the centrality of the Incarnation (*Adv. Marcion*, II, xxvii; cf. IV, xliii), together with emphasis on the facts of Christ's real death and the veritable resurrection of His Body (ibid. V, x). 'Flesh' is synonymous with 'body' (ibid. V, xv) and though it is the servant of the soul (ibid. I, xxiv) yet both soul and body make the whole man and, unless both are saved, man is only half saved and God is less than good:

> What else is man than flesh, since doubtless it was the corporeal rather than the spiritual element from which the Author of man's nature gave him his designation? 'And the Lord God made man of the dust from the ground' not out of some spiritual essence: this came afterwards from the divine afflatus – 'and man became a living soul'. What, then, is man? Made, no doubt of it, from the dust and placed by God in Paradise, because He moulded him, not breathed him, into being – a fabric of flesh, not of spirit. (*Adv. Marcion*, I, xxiv, tr. Holmes, 1868, 47.)

The Catholic faith is integrated and, within its limits, Marcionism is self-consistent too: 'You are the only man who hates his own flesh, for you rob it of its resurrection. It will be only right that you should hate the Church also, because it is loved by Christ on the same principle. . . . For myself, I shall now endeavour to prove that the same God is the God of man and of the Christ, of women and of the Church, of the flesh and of the spirit. . . .' (Ibid. V, 18). It was as an unanswerable argument against Marcionism and other heresies that the lawyer Tertullian developed the Roman legal idea of 'prescription'. He imagined Marcion and other claimants as bringing a suit against the Catholic Church for the title to correct interpretation of the Scriptures. The Church's claim is that it includes all Christian communities from those originally founded by the Apostles and these, and indeed all episcopal churches, are unanimous and opposed to the heretics in their interpretation. This unanimity, coupled with the continuous historical possession from the Apostles and Christ Himself, demands a verdict against the false claimants in accordance with the principle of Roman law that prior and uninterrupted possession of goods establishes rightful ownership against subsequent claims.[1] This may be a good argument, but it also represents the first incursion of legal thinking into Western theology: an alien intrusion which was to have serious, if not disastrous effects in the future. It seems paradoxical that the originator of Roman Catholic legalism should shortly afterwards adopt an extreme 'spiritualist' position in virulent opposition to the orthodox church. Psychologically, he was always an extremist: seeing things in black and white. He seems to have been converted by the heroism of African martyrs,[2] soon showed signs of complete intransigence himself and was so impressed by the uncompromising spirit of the

Montanists that he became one himself.

Montanism, like all millenarian movements, promoted martyrdom: if there was not a persecution going on, it would provoke
one. For it was better to die now in an act of witness, than to perish,
undistinguished, with the rest of the world at the Last Judgment.
The city of this world could, and would, go to hell, but the Montanists, including Encratists, doctrinaire teetotallers and con-
scientious objectors, would not go with it since, 'in pure spirit', they
had separated themselves from the evil, sensual world, and from the
institutional Church which, in their eyes, had accommodated itself
to it.[3] To Tertullian, once he had adopted this position, Catholicism
was a foul compromise and he threw all his energies into the building
up of a Montanist counter-church. 'Yet, like so many extreme
ascetics, Tertullian clung with glowing sensuality to the world and its
wisdom, so that to attain the final state of perfection he had to
condemn the world as rational, sensual and materialist.' (Heer,
1966, 13.)

We should not, therefore, expect from Tertullian (especially in his
later period) any balanced statement of the Church's attitude
towards the body but, nevertheless, some of his remarks might be
found of interest. He always insisted on the reality of Christ's human
body and, when he wrote *On the Flesh of Christ* against the Gnostics,
he distinguished between 'the flesh of sin' and 'the sin of flesh'.[4]
Christ did not come to destroy the former; on the contrary, He
exalted it to the right hand of the Father in heaven and will return in
it at the Second Coming 'in all the exaltation of the Father's glory'.
What has been abolished in Christ is not *carnem peccati* (sinful
flesh), but *peccatum carnis* (sin in the flesh) – not the material thing,
but its present condition; not the substance, but its flaw. Consequently, by our union with Christ through baptism, our own bodies
have been promised eternal life,[5] and indeed Christianity teaches the
natural glory of the flesh, as God created it by His 'manipulation':

What enjoyment of nature is there, what product of the world,
what relish of the elements, which is not imparted to the soul
through the medium of the body? Is it not by means of the body
that the soul is supported by the entire apparatus of the senses:
sight, hearing, taste, smell, touch? Is it not by the body's means
that the soul has a sprinkling of the divine power, since there is
nothing that it does not effect by its faculty of speech, even when it
is only tacitly indicated? . . . The arts arise through the flesh;
effect is given to the pursuits and powers of the mind through the
flesh; in addition, all work and the business and duties of life are
accomplished through the flesh; and so, in the last resort, the

living acts of the soul are the works of the flesh, so that for the soul to cease to do living acts would be nothing less than sundering itself from the flesh. Similarly, the very act of dying is a function of the flesh, even as the process of life is. Now, if all things are subject to the soul through the flesh, their subjection is equally due to the flesh. That which is the means and agent of your enjoyment must needs also be the partaker and sharer of your enjoyment. So that the flesh, which is accounted the minister and servant of the soul, also turns out to be its associate and co-heir. And if this is so in temporal things, why not also in things eternal? (*On the Resurrection of the Flesh*, vii.)

Tertullian is prepared to do more than defend the body as an essential element of our human nature;[6] he argues that Christianity, by its provision for the flesh, has given it the highest possible honour and respect:

Let us now consider its special relation to Christianity and see how vast a privilege before God has been conferred on this poor and worthless substance. Indeed, it would suffice to say that there is not a soul that can in any way procure salvation, except it believe while it is in the flesh, so true it is that the flesh is the very condition on which salvation hinges. And though the soul, in consequence of its salvation, is chosen to the service of God, it is the flesh which actually renders it capable of such service. Indeed, the flesh is washed (in baptism) that the soul may be cleansed; the flesh is anointed that the soul may be consecrated; the flesh is signed with the cross so that the soul too may be fortified. The flesh is shadowed with the imposition of hands so that the soul may be illumined by the Spirit, the flesh feeds on the Body and Blood of Christ that the soul likewise may fatten on God. Thus, they who are united in the service [to God] cannot be separated in their recompense [from God]. (Op. cit. viii, tr. Holmes, 1870, 229f.)

There is not only a necessary connection between the Incarnation of the Son of God and our own resurrection; nor is it merely that the sacramental system of the Church, which is the Body of Christ, fits in with this economy. The coherence extends to Christian practice: whether it be 'conflicts of the soul, fastings and abstinences', the vocation to celibacy or to holy widowhood, or 'the modest restraint in secret' upon the monogamous marriage bed – all alike are 'fragrant offerings to God, paid out of the good services of the flesh'. The flesh can make even greater sacrifices as when it is 'dragged out to public view and exposed to the hatred of all men' and subsequently imprisoned, sent to concentration or work camps, or 'racked by every kind of torture that can be devised' until, finally spent, it struggles to render 'its last turn for Christ by dying for Him' (ibid.).

Theological controversies

About a generation after Tertullian had written these words, persecution broke out again when, in A.D. 250, the Emperor Decius decreed that every subject of the Empire should, personally and publicly, offer incense to the Roman gods and obtain a certificate to testify to this act of civic loyalty. Some Christians treated the requirement as social rather than religious, and complied; others obtained a certificate by bribery or other means, without performing the required ceremony; and others paid with their lives for refusing. When the crisis was over, the certificate-holders swarmed to the Church for absolution and faced the hierarchy with a difficult decision. Some authorities were for permanent excommunication for apostasy, others (including the profound and prolific writer Cyprian, bishop of Carthage[7]) were for absolution after long and heavy penances.

Novatian (fl. 249–62), who was acting as locum tenens in Rome due to the recent martyrdom of Pope Fabian, was a 'hard-liner' and when the new pope, Cornelius, supported Cyprian, he like other purists before him founded a new sect to maintain the perfect way. Thus the tension in Western Christian thought was continued and the pressures of Novatianism were aggravated by movements from the East, associated on the one hand with Origen and on the other with Arius. Origen (fl. c. 222–54) was the culmination of the Platonising movement in the early Church. His system raised God above all material creation with which he had only a functional contact, and next to the Supreme Being was an infinite world of pure spirits. These only existed to love and be loved, and when the ardour of love cooled in some of them these were imprisoned in bodies: more or less gross, according to the distance they had fallen from their primordial existence of the highest and most total love. Least fallen were the good angels, while the greatest decline produced the demons. In between were bodies whose spirits are still capable of a little love: human being who can, by Christ's grace, painfully re-ascend to their primal state of pure disembodied love by means of asceticism. These ideas exemplify the extreme ascetical notion that the human body is an evil thing which must be shed like a chrysalis if the soul is to ascend to its proper place.

As a teenager, Origen sought the release of bodily martyrdom and was saved from this fate by his mother, although his father perished. He devoted his adult life to maintaining and developing Christian

Platonism in the Catechetical School of Alexandria, a Christian institute of higher studies. The main purpose of this institution was to transform the Christian religion into a philosophy of pure spirit, whose highest good was not faith but knowledge (gnosis) and where the Christian sage would be as detached from and unmoved by the world as God was believed to be and consequently able, as the result of unremitting training and study, to rise at will beyond the limits of space and time to the realms of pure spirit. Origen's inexhaustible will and energy in study, teaching and writing earned him the nickname of 'Brass-Belly' (Chalchenteros) and his spirit of bodily sacrifice also led him to self-castration and to the prisons of Decius where he eventually died through ill-treatment. His far-ranging ideas included a cyclic view of history and an imperfect view of the nature of Christ and the completeness of His revelation. Of him, Heer (1966, 14f.) remarks:

> He had no more sympathy for Church and state than for the 'historical Christ' and the 'unspiritual' faith of the common people. With Plotinus and other Neoplatonists, Origen believed that God is pure spirit, an insubstantial monad. His task in life was to reinterpret both Old and New Testaments spiritually by means of allegory, which would, of course, be compréhensible and available only to those few civilised gnostics who could recognise in it the doctrine of the spirit. Since God is wholly transcendent, man is wholly free, i.e. he can at any time rise to self-mastery through reason and asceticism.

Arius (fl. 318–36) was another Alexandrian who sought to reconcile the Greek mind and the intelligentisia of the Hellenic East to Christianity,[8] in this case by emphasising the unity of the Godhead to such an extent as to make the Son a mere creature, albeit the first and most perfect creature. The ensuing theological conflict threatened to split, not only the Church (at last resting from persecution as a result of Constantine's Edict of Toleration in A.D. 313), but also the State on which Constantine wished to impose a unitary faith, sufficiently vague as to be universally acceptable. As the result of another Alexandrian, Athanasius, supported by Western theologians and bishops, the true and full divinity of Christ was established as the orthodox Christian faith. Apart from its theological significance, this doctrinal struggle was of fundamental cultural importance:

> This resistance of the Western bishops created the West as a self-conscious unity. The West emerged in the battle for the 'freedom of the Church', the mystery of the Trinity, and the divine and

human nature of Christ. 'By rejecting the mystery [of Christ and the Trinity], Arius necessarily denied the legitimacy of the society which had risen to be the steward of that mystery.' That society was the Roman Church. The Church attained its independence by rescuing the mystery of the Trinity and the God-man, christ, from the clutches of the Greek theologians and emperors.[9]

This independence was dramatically manifested in the person of Ambrose, an unbaptised aristocrat who was chosen bishop of Milan (374–97) by popular acclaim when, as civil governor of Liguria and Emilia, he arrived to keep order at the riotous episcopal elections. He proved a staunch opponent of Arianism, a popular leader, a highly competent statesman and administrator, and a bishop morally and socially strong enough to impose public penance on the autocratic emperor Theodosius in A.D. 390. Although he was subsequently recognised as one of the four outstanding teachers (*egregii doctores*) of the Western Church,[10] Ambrose was not a professional theologian but a practical bishop, concerned with the day-to-day life and problems of those committed to his charge. He had conscientiously read Philo, Origen and Basil, and had some acquaintance with other Greek divines, but he had no interest in speculation and distrusted philosophy against which he often warned his hearers and readers. In his eyes, religion was not élitist but for all, and it had to be based on the authority of the Scriptures and the Catholic creeds, since right thinking was the indispensable foundation for right living. Like Tertullian, he was a lawyer and tended to view Christianity from a legal point of view, but this predisposition was balanced by mysticism: his longing for God and for the love of God. His typical Roman equipoise was also shown in his regard for both personal religion and ecclesiastical doctrines and instititutions. Mysticism was no excuse for individualism: 'On the contrary, he held that the personal relation of the soul with God or Christ is dependent on a correct apprehension of Trinitarian and Christological truth, and is capable of being realised only in the Church and with the help of the Church's sacraments.' (Dudden, 1935, II, 557.)

Ambrose's views

It is no surprise to see associated together belief in the incarnate Lord, in His mystical Body, the Church, and in the sacramental body of the Eucharist, but we must pass over these interrelations to consider Ambrose's ideas about the human body. These derive from the sense of sin of a saint and mystic, and the consequent appreciation of the extent to which man has fallen short of the high nature and destiny which was his at creation. Yet in spite of his sensibility, this writer avoids the exaggerated pessimism and sharp dichotomy of some of his predecessors.

Both men and women are part of the good creation of a good God and it is necessary for them to obey the ancient Greek precept, 'Know thyself' first before they attempt the ascent to the supreme knowledge of God. Ambrose defines man as 'a living animal who is mortal and endowed with reason' (*De Noe*, 10) and declares that though he was created last of all things, yet he is God's *chef d'œuvre* (*Ep.*xliii, 19), His most precious work (*Expos.* ps. cxviii, xx, 6), the consummation and flower of all creation (*Hexaem.* VI, 75) in whose making God took special pains (*Expos. ps.* cxviii, x, 8, 9, 13) and who consequently can be described as the 'glory of God' (*Hexaem.* vi, 50). He is God's friend (*Ep.* xliii, 3) for whom the world and all things in it exist (*De excess. Sat.* ii, 87) and he has lordship and dominion over all:

> [God] granted to him, as to that creature who was nearest and dearest to Him, all the things which are in the world, that he might want for nothing which is necessary either for life or for the good life; some of which things were to be supplied by the abundance of earthly plenty to minister pleasure; while others by the knowledge of heavenly secrets were to arouse man's mind through love and the desire of that discipline which should enable us to reach the summit of the divine mysteries. Both of these possibilities are most excellent gifts: on the one hand, to have subject to him all flying and creeping things and fishes and, in his capacity as lord of the elements,[11] to have the use of the sea and, without toil or want, to abound in all things (after the model and likeness of his adorable Creator) to live in the greatest plenty; and, on the other hand, to open paths for himself and progress so as to ascend to the royal abode of heaven. (*Ep.* xliii, 11, cf. *Ep.* xlv, 16; *De Noe*, 86; *Expos.* ps. cxviii, x, 18.)

The opportunities open to this hybrid or psychosomatic entity are limitless for 'although in body, he has analogies with the beasts; yet in mind, he is numbered among the inhabitants of heaven' (*Ep.* xliii, 7). This paradoxical creature even surpasses heaven, in a sense, since 'Heaven is of the world, man above the world; for the former is a portion of the world, the latter is an inhabitant of Paradise and the possessor of Christ. Heaven is thought to be undecaying, yet it passes away; man is deemed to be corruptible, yet he puts on incorruption: the fashion of the first perishes, the latter rises again as being immortal; yet the hands of the Lord (according to the Scriptures) formed them both.' (*Ep.* xliii, 9.)

The human body is both beautiful and useful (*De Noe*, 18; *De Officiis*, I, 83, 220) and, indeed, it can be described as a superb work of divine art (*Hexaem*. VI, 47; *Expos.ps*. cxviii, xvi, 6) and it not only surpasses in comeliness and grace the bodies of all other animals (*Hexaem*. VI, 54; *De Instit. Virg*. 20; *Expos. ps*. cxviii, x, 6), but it is an image in miniature of the cosmos itself.[12] Yet, our flesh is, by its nature, mortal and, though bodily illness can be a means of grace (*Ep*. xxix), death 'is the common fate, not only of man but even of states and countries'. Transitoriness is part of the human condition, whether considered individually or socially, as Ambrose reminds Faustinus, grieving excessively over his sister's death:

> Do not the carcases of so many half-ruined cities, the states laid out on their biers before your very eyes, do not these remind you that the passing of a single woman, holy and excellent as she was, is much less to be deplored, especially as the city-states are laid prostrate and destroyed for ever while she, though removed from us for a while, continues to live a more blessed life elsewhere?
>
> It may be that you will assert that, though you are sure of her merits and faith, yet you cannot endure the feeling of regret when you no longer see her after the flesh – which is a bitter grief to you. But does not the apostolic saying influence you that 'henceforth we know no man after the flesh; yea, though we have known Christ after the flesh, yet now henceforth know we Him no more'? For our flesh cannot be perpetual and enduring, it must needs die that it may rise again, it must be dissolved that it may rest and sin come to an end. (*Ep*. xxxix, 3, 5.)[13]

These last words are a reminder of the fundamental belief that the supreme handiwork of God has been flawed as a result of the Fall and the pristine unity of its elements shattered. In particular, the flesh has ceased to be subordinated to the reason and, reversing the order, has asserted itself unreasonably, sometimes beguiling and seducing the reason itself to sin (*Ep*. xlv, 17; *Expos. ev. Luc*. iv, 63) and sometimes forcibly overpowering it and compelling its submission (*De Isaac*, iii; *De Bono Mortis*, 26). This triumphant revolt of the flesh is what is meant by sin: 'Sin is walking according to the flesh: for he who has his life-style according to the wisdom of the flesh lives for indulgence and pleasure and the allurements and desires of the flesh. But the wisdom of the flesh is emnity with God. So that they who are "in the flesh" cannot please God.' (*In ps*. xxxvii, enarr. 5.)

Since concupiscence is the most vicious and fundamental passion of the lower nature (*De Jacob*, i, 1, 5), this word can be used to describe the general decontrol of that nature so that it is possible to say 'concupiscence is sin' (ibid. i, 13, 16). Thus, the flesh, which is not the body yet is irretrievably associated with it, has become the enemy of the soul which it persistently seeks to carry away into sinful enslavement (*De Isaac*, 3; *De Bono Mortis*, 26; *De Jacob*, i, 15). For this reason, the greatest precautions must be taken to prevent the soul being dominated and taken over, even absorbed by the body (*De Bono Mortis*, 40).[14] Prevention is largely a matter of the will whose freedom Ambrose repeatedly asserts. 'Why then do we accuse the flesh of weakness? Our members [i.e. our body] can be instruments of iniquity or instruments of righteousness. The originator of sin is not the flesh but the will. The flesh is merely the servant of the will.' (*De Jacob*, i, 10; cf. i, 1; *Hexaem*. I, 31). Yet the will can only act freely when enlightened by spiritual knowledge and even the soul is divided; for although part of it (the 'spirit') is rational, there is another and irrational part (the 'anima', source of drives and emotions) which connects[15] the 'spirit' to the body and tends to take the side of the flesh (*De Abraham*, i, 4; ii, 2, 57). Therefore the good man has to detach himself not only from the flesh but also from the fleshly element in his soul (*Expos*. ps. cxviii, xx, 46), a process which Ambrose calls 'the circumcision of the heart'[16] (*De Abraham*, ii, 78). When this process has been completed, man can rise to the vision of God (*De Bono Mortis*, 49) but not before, 'since it is not possible to be at home with God and with the flesh at the same time' (*De Isaac*, 54).

This psychological experience, together with the evils of a society which, in the declining decades of the Western Empire, was obsessed by luxury, avarice and selfishness, leads Ambrose to speak disparagingly of the body, which he describes as 'abject and vile' (*De Paradiso*, 16) and as 'mud' which soils the soul (*De Bono Mortis*, 12). The body is not only an obstruction, it makes no practical con-tribution to the higher life of man: unless he disengages himself from it, he will appreciate neither virtue nor truth (ibid. 10, 11). Awareness of a world and society abounding with physical and moral evil and of a corrupted human nature makes it possible to consider life as a misfortune and death as a positive advantage (ibid. 4, 12, 28). Even unspoiled nature, though appreciated, is viewed from a practical point of view or as a source of symbols of the supernatural world (Dudden, 1935, II, 474ff.). The Christian, and implicitly every potentially 'human' being, is alienated (more fully than Marx ap-preciated): heaven is his true home, to which he must flee, renouncing (as far as he is able) the contemporary world with all its pleasures, customs and conventions (*De Abraham*, i, 4). Man, in order to be fully human, must have his priorities right,[17] both of psychology and sociology. He must remember that the body differs in substance from the soul (*De Bono Mortis*, 26), being fashioned of clay (*Ep*. lxxii, 19; *De Noe*, 86; *Expos*. ps. cxviii, x, 10, 15, 18; *De Paradiso*, 540), or rather, compounded of the four elements:[18] earth, air, fire and water (*De Fide*, ii, 12; *De Virginibus*, iii, 21; *De Isaac*, 59). The body also differs from the soul in nature and tendency: 'That which is according to the nature of the body is contrary to the nature of the soul, and what is according to the nature of the soul is contrary to the nature of the body.' (*Ep.* lxxii, 17, cf. *De Inst. Virg.* 11.)

On the other hand, the soul is our 'true substance': 'In what do we consist? In the substance of the soul and in the vigour of the mind. That is all our portion. We are not flesh, but spirit.' (*Exhort. virginitatis*, 68). That is to say, that man is not a half-and-half creature, a kind of psychosomatic Centaur, composed of equal parts of body and soul. In the last resort, the essence of man is his 'living soul', created immediately by God and infused by Him into that particular body of which it is the destined animating principle (*Expos.* ps. cxviii, x, 10; *De Cain*, ii, 36; *De Bono Mortis*, 26, 42). The body is thus an instrument or organ of the soul (ibid. 25, 27; *De interpell. Job*, ii, 36). It is the soul which is 'the man' (*Hexaem.* VI, 46; *Expos.* ps. cxviii, x, 11), while the body is only the 'envelope' or 'vesture' of the man (*De Instit. Virg.* 18; *De Cain*, ii, 36; *Hexaem.* VI, 39; *Expos. ev. Luc.* vii, 123). Ambrose makes this point frequently: 'What we are is one thing; what is ours is another. The wearer of the garment must be distinguished from the garment.' (*De Isaac*, 3; cf. *Hexaem.* VI, 42; *De Bono Mortis,* 27). 'We are souls, our members are our garments. The garments must be cared for, so that they do not get torn or fall into disrepair, but even more must the wearer care for and preserve himself.' (*De Isaac*, 79). 'Without the soul, the flesh is nothing. "What shall a man give in exchange for his soul" which is not merely a small portion of himself but the very substance of all that is distinctively human in him?' (*Hexaem.* vi, 43.) It follows that, if the soul is so immeasurably the superior element in man, it ought not to be 'mixed'[19] or 'confounded' with the inferior element which the body is (*De Bono Mortis*, 26). It is the function of the soul to govern the body and to use it for its own purposes:[20] 'The soul is the user, the body for use; hence the one is master, the other servant.' (*De Bono Mortis*, 27). 'Let not our soul become flesh; but let our flesh, being obedient to the soul's direction, become soul.' (*Expos.* ps. cxviii, iv, 7). Thus the ideal condition is obtained when the flesh, in complete submission to the higher nature, becomes simply 'an appendage to the soul' (*Expos. ev. Luc.* vii, 141).

It is consonant with this attitude that Ambrose should say that 'bodily pleasures enervate the mind' (*De Isaac*, 2) and that, when he admires beauty, he should do so grudgingly since it can be a snare for souls (*De Officiis*, I, 83; *De Bono Mortis*, 16). Women are a source of temptation (*De Officiis*, I, 87) and the clergy are advised to avoid looking at them (ibid. I, 255). However, Ambrose was never a monk (unlike most of the characters hitherto mentioned) and, though he encouraged Eastern monasticism in Milan, he is not obsessed by sex nor does he see it as the only, or even the chief, carnal sin. Sins of the flesh include the love of material possessions, for earthly goods are a positive disadvantage to the Christian life (ibid. I, 28, 29; II, 16). Ambrose also believed that property was theft[21] and that it was God's will that the land should belong to all. He also distinguished between ownership for use and ownership for profit (ibid. I, 132; De Viduis, 5; Expos. ps. cxviii, viii, 22). Private property is contrary to both the laws of God and of nature and these same laws make all men equal.[22]

Riches provoke his greatest condemnation for, in his eyes, they denuded a man of 'the likeness of God' and clothed him with 'the likeness of the devil' (De Officiis, I, 244):

> What rich man does not daily lust after what belongs to others? Which of those who have the most wealth does not endeavour to eject the poor man from his small-holding and to drive out the indigent from his ancestral fields? Who is content with what he possesses? What rich man does not burn to possess his neighbour's estate? The peasants are leaving their lands in a body. The poor man migrates with his family of little ones; behind him follows his wife, weeping bitterly as though she was escorting her husband to the grave. (De Nabuthe, 1.)

Worldly power is also castigated, for this brings no real happiness and should be despised by Christians (De Isaac, 78) and even more contemptible are the worldly gaieties and amusements of this life which are utterly empty (De Fuga, 4). Even the pleasures of the mind can be carnal, in a sense, for unless they are directed to their highest object (i.e. the knowledge of God), they are dangerous. Worldly philosophy is often no more than a tissue of futile obscurities (De Officiis, I, 122), and its pursuit is not only pointless but a mere culpable curiosity (De Interpell. Job, i, 29).

Society is so shallow and disordered that it is better to die to such a world than to live for it and, indeed, when one's duty[23] has been done, death may be legitimately sought as an end good in itself. This death may take a variety of forms: the willing acceptance of the course of nature, martyrdom or an ascetic mortification but, whatever way it is sought, the motives must be right: 'Let our flesh die so that in it all that is sinful may die; and, as though coming to life from the dead, let us rise to new works and to new life.' (De Officiis, I, 185.) 'Ascetic mortification is practicable for all and ascetic mortification is "the imitation of death".' (De Bono Mortis, 9, 10, 16; De excess. Sat. ii, 40.)

Nevertheless, we are, in fact, in the world and we have a body, however bad the former and weak the latter, and Ambrose sometimes writes of the flesh even with indulgence (*Ep*. lxiii, 91; *De Jacob*, i, 10). Certainly, the body ought to be reasonably cared for and not neglected (*Ep*. xxxvii, 42; *De Isaac*, 79), and the senses themselves are only evil when they are directed by an evil heart (*Expos*. ps. cxviii, xvi, 3, 6). We must not ignore nature (*Expos. ev. Luc*. vii, 201) but, on the contrary: 'Let us imitate Nature: conformity with Nature provides us with a formula of discipline and a standard of rectitude.' (*De Officiis*, I, 84). What is according to nature is seemly and virtuous, for God made all things very good; and conversely, that which is contrary to nature is shameful[24] (*De Officiis*, I, 222; III, 28.)

This same realism makes Ambrose avoid the millenarian attitude of unreserved condemnation of worldly duties or even of worldly interests and he explains the concept of 'renouncing the world' as meaning the 'renunciation of vices, not of the use of things' (*De Isaac*, 6) – a very important distinction. Consequently, marriage and its associated sexual activity is not to be despised, but regarded as a good and necessary institution for the propagation of the species,[25] though a rightly motivated virginity is to be regarded even more highly (*Expos. ev. Luc*. viii, 37; *Apol. David*, 56; *De Virginibus*, i, 34; *Ep*. xlii, 3). Even worldly wealth, the object of some of Ambrose's most mordant scorn and invective, can provide some good, since it offers its possessors an opportunity for the exercise of virtue (*Ep*. lxii, 92, cf. ii, 11).

> Why do you seek to accumulate riches as though they were necessary? Nothing is so necessary as to know what is not necessary. Why do you cast the blame on the flesh? It is not the lust of the belly, but the desires of the mind that make a man insatiable. Is it the flesh which obliterates the hope of the future? Is it the flesh which removes the sweetness of spiritual grace? Is it the flesh which defers in every way to the frantic domination of vain opinions? The flesh prefers that frugal temperance, which relieves it of its load, which endues it with health, for so it rids itself of sharp anxiety and obtains tranquillity for itself. But riches in themselves are not blameable . . . for he who gives to the poor redeems his soul. Therefore, even in these material riches there is scope for virtue. (*Ep*. lxiii, 91.)

Ambrose was a practical man with a sense of order and a deep awareness of the growing social and psychological disorder of his time. He wished to reapply the principles of discipline and authority which had once made Rome great to the spiritual life which, like many other Christian teachers before and since, he saw as a combat and a training ground. As both soldier and athlete have to develop the strengths and fortify the weaknesses of their body for higher purposes than immediate gratification, so all Christians are called to be spiritual athletes and must train themselves in a similar way. The following from his letters develops this idea.

What is the world but a kind of arena of spiritual strife? . . . The promoter of this contest is Almighty God . . . the prizes are the fruits of the earth and the lights of heaven – the former for use in this present life, the latter as a token of eternal life.

Man as a wrestler makes a late entry into the (cosmic) contest. He raises his eyes to heaven and sees that even the heavenly creation 'was made subject to vanity' (Rom. viii, 20) . . . He sees that 'the whole creation is groaning with birth-pangs, waiting for the redemption' (ibid.). He sees that labour awaits us all. He raises his eyes, he sees the encircling lights . . . and he chastises his body that it may not be his enemy in the combat. He anoints it with the oil of mercy, he exercises it with daily trials of virtue, he smears himself with dust, he runs for the finishing tape 'but not as uncertainly' (I Cor. ix, 26).

He aims his blows, he lunges with his arms, but not into empty space for he hits the adversary whom he cannot see . . . It is he who sets up the blow, but it is Christ who strikes; it is he who lifts up his heel, but Christ who directs it to the ground. . . . Fittingly, therefore, did man (for whom the race was prepared) enter the scene last, so that he might be preceded by the creation of heaven which was, so to speak, to be his prize.

But we wrestle not only 'against the spiritualities of wickedness in high places' but also 'against flesh and blood' (Eph. vi, 12). We wrestle with satiety, with the very fruits of the earth, with wine . . .; we wrestle with wild animals, with the fowls of the air. For our flesh, if pampered by these, cannot be brought into subjection. As St Paul says, we wrestle 'with perils of the road, with perils of the sea' (II Cor. ix, 26). . . . You see how severe our contests are. Thus the earth is man's competition-ground, heaven is his gold medal and therefore it was eminently suitable that, as a friend [of God], what was to minister to his needs should precede him [and provide] his rewards as a competitor. (*Ep.* xliii, 4–6 abbreviated.)

SUMMARY

The third century of the Christian era is a period of transition which includes both the beginning of systematic theology and also foreshadows many future developments, both positive and negative. It includes the noble contribution of Tertullian in his pre-montanist period who, in spite of his incipient Puritanism, lauds the body and its dignity and clearly sees the significance of the Incarnation and sacramental system for a proper attitude to the body. He even argues that the sufferings of the martyrs adumbrates the same principles. Unfortunately, the pressures of the last imperial persecutions brought new crises of practical discipline which were aggravated by the spiritualist (and consequently denigrating the body) tendencies of Origen who was a kind of Christian Gnostic emphasising the aristocratic and intellectual elements of Christianity at the expense of its Catholic and human ones. Theological controversies around the essential nature of the faith brought a necessity for clarification which prevented thinkers from developing the full implications of the central doctrines – a situation that was to recur many times in the history of the Church. Some of these problems were the result of a necessary attempt to express abiding Christian truth in terms of the contemporary, but essentially transitional, thought patterns and needs of a particular age – the abiding and fundamental problem of a living theology – but others were the result of the social and cultural predispositions of certain leaders. Ambrose introduces a characteristic Roman note of balance and order, but his writings also show the developing effect of the growing darkness as the Roman Empire begins to crumble under the ceaseless assaults of the bar-barians, and there is a growing note of pessimism and renunciation of the dying world.

THE ESTABLISHMENT OF THE WESTERN TRADITION

The 'conversion' of Constantine, which swiftly transformed Christianity from a *religio illicita* to the favoured religion of the emperors, naturally affected the general character of its adherents. Christianity was no longer costly: the threat of delation, banishment, torture and death was no longer associated with the name. Henceforth, the Christian profession might lead to preferment and so the really convinced sought an alternative to the popular way of nominal Christianity. They found this by 'a flight to the desert', by creating an existence where the faith, shorn of its accidental advantages, might still be sought in its essential purity. The movement started in the East, was introduced to Rome by St Athanasius *c*. A.D. 342, and consisted of solitaries, striving to be 'alone with the Alone', and various groupings of coenobites and monks.

The growth of ascetism

We have already seen[1] Ambrose suggesting ascetism, voluntary mortification, in place of the external, involuntary infliction of death, and a notable exemplar was Jerome (A.D. 345–420), an aristocrat who, from the age of eight to twenty, absorbed all that Rome could offer in lavish humanistic culture. At twenty, he received baptism from the Pope and then travelled for many years through the other great cities of the West and through the Syrian desert (the home of many ascetics) in what Heer[2] calls 'a combination of the Grand Tour and a penitential pilgrimage'. Jerome was an irritable, scholarly man who easily made friends and enemies and, shortly after he had become a priest, he was commissioned by the humanist Pope Damasus to produce a new Latin translation of the Bible.[3] Though he spent the last thirty-five years of his life as a hermit in Bethlehem, he remained a humanist[4] and his voluminous correspondence provides a mordant commentary on a world which he found both odious and attractive. Besides setting new standards of scholarship and providing new models for biography, Jerome was the first great churchman 'to cultivate noble and virtuous women and thus the founder of the Western tradition of feminine culture'.[5] But, above all, he was the propagator of asceticism, of the unending spiritual warfare, as when he, typically, calls Heliodorus from the domestic to the ascetic life:

What business have you, pampered soldier, in your father's house? Where now are the rampart, the trench and the winter under canvas? Lo, the trumpet sounds from heaven! Lo, our General comes forth amid the clouds, fully armed to subdue the world! Lo, from our King's mouth proceeds a doubly sharpened sword which cuts down everything in its path! Are you coming out, pray, from your chamber to the battlefield, from the shade into the sun's glare? A body used to the tunic cannot support a cuirass, a head that has worn a linen hood shrinks from a helmet, a hand softened by idleness is galled by the hard sword-hilt. Hear the proclamation of your King: 'He that is not with Me is against Me, and he that gathereth not with Me, scattereth.'[6]

The Roman soldier was one of the most admired products of the Roman civilisation which he did so much to create, maintain and defend. He obviously impressed Christ Himself, not to mention St Paul, by his fitness, hardihood, courage and willingness to sacrifice himself in service. He was the result and expression of an awesome discipline acquired by long training in complex physical skills and the endurance of physical discomfort. He represented a kind of athlete whose training and will were directed not towards personal excellence but the success of the body to which he belonged.

He early became a model which, *mutatis mutandis*, the Christian soldier – the member of the Church militant, was exhorted to copy in ascesis, self-sacrifice and loyalty. Here Jerome is carrying on this tradition and arguing that the monk should excel the soldier since he too has left the 'civvy-street' of lax, accepted Christianity for active service in the front line of spiritual warfare.

The same letter argues that it is a sin not to wish to be perfect and that Christ overturns the standards of a world itself made topsy-turvy by war and invasion. The Christian must flee from the worldly city to the blessed solitude: 'O wilderness, bright with Christ's spring flowers! O solitude, whence come those stones wherewith in the Apocalypse the city of the mighty king is built! O desert, rejoicing in God's familiar presence!' The values of 'civilisation' are well sacrificed: 'Does the infinite vastness of the desert seem terrible? In spirit, you may always stroll in Paradise and when you have made that mental ascent, you will no longer be in the desert. Without baths, is your skin rough and scurfy? He who has once washed in Christ does not need to wash again.'[7] But the external profession of asceticism is not enough: there are many kinds of monks and some of them are still suffering from pride, envy and malice.[8] Even when the will is right it may be assaulted by the imagination:

Oh, how often, when I was living in the desert, in that lonely waste, scorched by the burning sun, which affords hermits a savage dwelling-place, how often did I imagine myself surrounded by all the pleasures of Rome! I used to sit alone, for I was filled with bitterness. My unkempt limbs were covered in shapeless sackcloth; my skin, through long neglect, had become as rough and black as an Ethiopian's. Tears and groans were my portion every day; and, if sleep ever overcame my resistance and fell upon my eyes, I bruised my restless bones against the naked earth. I have nothing to say about food and drink. Hermits have nothing but cold water even when they are sick, and for them it is a sinful luxury to partake of cooked dishes. But although, in my fear of hell, I had condemned myself to this prison where my only companions were scorpions and wild beasts, I often found myself surrounded by troupes of dancing-girls. My face was pale with fasting and though my limbs were cold as ice, yet my mind was aflame with desire and the fires of lust kept bubbling up before me even when my flesh was as good as dead.[9]

Just as a successful athlete has to consider psychological elements in his total training (ascesis), so the Christian attitude must look beyond the hardening of his body. Physical austerities can have the effect of arousing desire and increasing the power of the imagination (as St Anthony found to his horror). Christian discipline and self-mastery should be both total and balanced, but unfortunately it was not within the competence of the psychological knowledge of St Jerome's day to appreciate that some kinds of mortification may aggravate the very ills they seek to cure.

However, this harsh discipline is never proferred as an end in itself. The purpose of abstinence is to bring back to Paradise those who lost that state of bliss through greed and we are not to think that God 'the Lord and Creator of the universe, takes any delight in the rumbling of our intestines, the emptiness of our stomachs or the inflammation of our lungs; but because this is the only way of preserving chastity'.[10] And, important as chastity is, that by itself is by no means enough: 'No man shall applaud himself on the Day of Judgment on account of his mere bodily chastity, for then men shall render account for every idle word that they have spoken, and abuse of a brother shall be counted as the sin of murder.'[11] Similarly, though Jerome believes that virginity is a higher vocation than marriage,[12] mere physical virginity is not enough. Even those who pursue this state with the right motives can lose the inner condition by mental activity: 'Those are the evil virgins, virgins in the flesh but not in the spirit: foolish virgins who, having no oil in their lamps, are shut out by the

Bridegroom.'[13] He takes seriously the Scriptural warning (Phil. iii, 19) that the end is destruction for those whose god is their belly, yet there is no intrinsic merit in fasting: 'If you have fasted for two or three days, do not think that you are better than those who have not fasted. You fast and are irascible; another eats and wears a smiling face. You work off your irritation and hunger by quarrelling with others; your neighbour feeds in moderation and gives thanks to God.'[14]

It is only because the body is good and is created by a good God that it can be worthily sacrificed or mortified.[15] If, like the Manichees, you believe that the body is evil because all matter is essentially evil, then there cannot be a cult of virginity: 'Such virgins as are alleged to exist among different heretics or with the filthy followers of Manes must be considered, not virgins, but whores. If the devil is the author of their body, how can they honour a thing fashioned by their foe?'[16] The ascetic life can only rightly exist in its proper relation to the self-sacrifice of the incarnate God and within His Body, the Church:

> For our salvation, the Son of God became the Son of Man. Ten months he awaits birth in the womb, He endures distress, He comes forth covered with blood, He is swathed in napkins, He is comforted with caresses. Though He hold the world in His closed hand, He is contained in the narrow space of a manger. I say nothing of the thirty years He lived in obscurity, content with His parents' poverty. He was scourged and says not a word. He was crucified and prays for His crucifiers. . . .[17]

It is love alone that facilitates sacrifice and endurance, and the ascetic's abnegation restores to a self-indulgent world a sense of proportion which may be lost even by Christians: 'And yet we frown if our food seems to lack savour and we fancy that we are doing God a favour if we add water to our wine. If that water is a trifle too warm, the servant must pay for it with his blood: we smash the cup, knock over the table and the whip whistles through the air.' Fallen man and a decadent society are a mighty combination that can overwhelm the real nature and destiny of man; the world and flesh in alliance make any concession to the body hazardous: 'At a banquet it is hard to preserve one's chastity. A sleek skin is a sure sign of a foul mind.'[18] And, on general grounds, the Roman baths are not a suitable preparation for the life of a nun, even if Constantine had prohibited mixed bathing:

> Speaking personally, I altogether disapprove of baths for a full-grown virgin. She ought to blush at herself and be unable to

behold her own nakedness. If she mortifies and enslaves her body by vigils and fasts, if she desires to quench the flames of lust and check the hot passions of youth by cold chastity, if she hastens to spoil her natural beauty by deliberate squalor, why should she rouse a slumbering fire by the incentive of baths?[19]

The power of sensibility

Because of its nature, the body will eventually fail, even in its good works: 'In the case of old men, almost all bodily excellences are changed and they decrease, while only wisdom increases. Fasting, sleeping on the ground, moving to and fro, hospitality to strangers, defence of the poor, perseverance in standing at prayer, visiting the sick, manual labour to earn money for alms-giving – in fact, not to be tedious, all actions that depend on the body's agency diminish as the body decays.'[20] The care of failing, or sick, bodies (particularly if they belong to the poor) is an excellent work and very suitable for religious women. In his panegyric on the patrician matron, Fabiola, Jerome makes much of this:

> In the first place, she founded an infirmary[21] and gathered into it sufferers from the streets, giving all a nurse's care to their poor bodies eroded with sickness and hunger. Need I describe here the diverse troubles from which human beings suffer: the maimed noses, the lost eyes, the scorched feet, the leprous arms, the swollen bellies, the shrunken thighs, the dropsical legs, the diseased flesh alive with hungry worms? How often did she carry on her own shoulders poor filthy wretches tortured by leprosy? How often did she wash away the purulent matter from wounds which others could not even bear to look at! She put food into their mouths with her own hand and, even when a man was but a breathing corpse, she would moisten his lips with drops of water.
>
> I know that many wealthy and devout persons, because they have queasy stomachs, perform this work of mercy through the agency of others and show their charity through the purse rather than through their hand. I do not blame them, nor do I, in any way, construe their lack of fortitude[22] as lack of faith. But, while I excuse their weakness, I extol to the skies the ardent zeal that perfect courage possesses. A great faith makes light of discomfort: it knows the retribution that fell on the rich man, clothed in purple, who in his pride refused Lazarus aid (Luke xvi, 19–31). The sufferer whom we despise and cannot bear to behold, whose very aspect turns our stomachs, is a man like ourselves, formed of the same clay, made from the same elements. Whatever he suffers, we may possibly suffer also. Let us regard his wounds as our own. (*Ep*. lxxvii, 6.)

Such passages as this indicate that a new sensibility[23] has entered the world: a sensibility which, to be maintained, requires a subordinationism in the old Greek trinity of goodness, beauty and truth, and a bodily discipline which will free and order the intelligence, imagination and will. A side-effect will be the playing down of carnal love and the spiritual interpretation of the Song of Songs which the Christians have inherited with the rest of the Jewish Scriptures. In his advice on the education of the young girl Paula, Jerome writes that it must be read only after proper preparation for, 'if she were to read it too early, she might be harmed by not perceiving that it was the song of a spiritual bridal expressed in fleshly language' (*Ep.* cvii, 12, cf. *Ep.* xxii, 1).

This change of attitude, or rather clear perception of priorities, was undoubtedly conditioned by the nature of the age.[24] Dr Johnson remarked that the thought of his imminent death concentrated a man's mind wonderfully and the concentration of St Jerome (and his contemporaries) on 'the things that abide' was naturally affected by awareness of the impending catastrophe whose signs were plain to the sensitive throughout the civilised world. Jerome's own native town in Dalmatia had been half-destroyed by the Goths in A.D. 377 and both his parents probably died when it was sacked.[25] He had experienced the transitoriness of both human life and human achievement, and even when he had abandoned the world and all it had to offer for the solitude of his hermitage in Bethlehem, its tremors still reached and affected him. The earthquake reached its climax in A.D. 410 when the Goths sacked the Eternal City and 'the head of the whole world' fell, spreading terror and consternation throughout the known world. There had been previous signs and warnings:

> For a long time now, we have felt that God is offended with us but we do not try to appease Him. It is by reason of our sins that the barbarians are strong, it is our vices that bring defeat to the armies of Rome; and if this were not enough carnage, civil wars have spilt almost more blood than the sword of the enemy. . . .
>
> For twenty years and more, the blood of Romans has been shed every day between Constantinople and the Julian Alps. . . . How many matrons, how many of God's virgins – ladies of gentle birth and high position – have been made the sport of these beasts! Bishops have been made prisoners, presbyters and other ranks of the clergy have been murdered. Churches have been destroyed, horses stabled at Christ's altar and the remains of martyrs dug up.
>
> >   Sorrow and grief on every side we see
> >   And death in many a shape.'

The Roman world is falling, and yet we hold our heads erect instead of bending our necks.[26]

Even Jerome's attempt to find a suitable spiritual retreat in Palestine for Fabiola had been frustrated by an invasion of Huns from beyond the Caucasus: 'Flying hither and thither on their fast horses . . . these invaders were filling the whole world with bloodshed and panic. . . . Everywhere their arrival was unexpected, their speed outstripped rumour, and they spared neither religion, nor rank, nor age; nay, they had no pity even for wailing infants. Children who had only just begun to live were forced to die and, in ignorance of their fate, smiled amid the brandished weapons of the foe.'[27]

But these premonitions and earlier experiences in no way lessened the traumatic shock of the fall of Rome itself:

> I was so stupefied and dismayed that, day and night, I could think of nothing but the welfare of the Roman community. It seemed to me that I was sharing the captivity of the saints and I could not utter a sound until I had some more definite news. All the while, full of anxiety, I wavered between hope and despair, torturing myself with the misfortunes of others. But when I heard that the bright light of the whole world was quenched, or rather that the Roman Empire had lost its head and that the entire world had perished in one city then, indeed, 'I became dumb and humbled myself and kept silence from good words'.[28]

The memory was still vivid when, years later, the aged Jerome, in spite of public calamity and private sorrow, was still applying himself to his labours. In A.D. 412 he recalls the time when his community

> heard that Rome was besieged, that its citizens were purchasing their safety with gold, and how after they had been thus despoiled, they were besieged again; so that they lost not only their substance, but their lives as well. The city which had taken the whole world was itself taken; nay, it fell by famine before it fell by the sword and there were but a few found to be made prisoners. Mad hunger drove people to impious food: men tore at one another's limbs, and the mother spared not the baby at her breast, reabsorbing into her body that which her body had lately brought forth.[29]

There are profound lessons and serious implications in all this: a disaster of such magnitude should bring Christians to their senses and recall them not only to true values, but to a sense of proportion:

. . . the world is falling in ruins, but our sins still grow. The glorious city that was the head of the Roman Empire has been engulfed in one terrific blaze. There is no part of the world where you may not find refugees from Rome. Venerated churches have collapsed into dust and ashes. Yet still our hearts are fixed greedily on money.

We live as though it was our last day but we build as though we were going to inhabit this world for ever. Our walls glitter with gold, gold gleams from our ceilings and upon the capitals of our pillars: yet Christ is dying on our door-steps in the persons of His poor, naked and hungry.[30]

With the collapse of the social order, with life made tenuous amidst such universal calamities, death may come as a blessing, rather than as a curse: 'He who has escaped from this world's light is not so much to be mourned as he is to be congratulated on having escaped from such great evils.'[31] The world, with all its comforts and conveniences, is approaching dissolution and destruction. Since we are bound to lose its goods anyway, it is a more moral, meritorious and manly thing to abandon them of our free will than to wait until they are taken from us: 'May our renunciation of the world be a matter of free-will and not of necessity! May we seek poverty as a glorious thing, not have it forced upon us as a punishment! However, in our present miseries, while swords rage fiercely about us, he is rich enough who does not lack bread: he has power beyond his needs who has not been reduced to slavery.'[32]

We have emphasised matters which do not directly seem to be concerned with the Church's attitude to the body, but all thinking (even theological thinking) is socially conditioned and it is our conviction that the psychological effects of the barbarian invasions, with the consequent destruction and degradation, had a very important effect on Christian thinking, almost driving it to renunciation and mortification. The body was degraded in fact by atrocity and famine and the struggle for mere survival inhibited that leisure which is the necessary basis for culture.[33] It would be a thousand years before European civilisation climbed slowly out of the abyss into which the barbarians had hurled it. But one mind of giant stature was already addressing itself to the task.

Foundations of Western theology

St Augustine (A.D. 354–430) may be known to some only as the man who besought God to grant him chastity and continence 'but not yet'[34] and to others as the man who in violent reaction against bodily pleasure strait-jacketed the Western Church into extreme puritanism. To others, he is one of the intellectual giants of European history, indeed 'a maker of history and a builder of the bridge that was to lead from the old world to the new'. (C. Dawson in D'Arcy, 1930). He has left us the literary materials to form our own judgment: *On the Trinity* which laid the foundations of an independent Western theology; *The City of God*, occasioned by the fall of Rome, which attempts a vast reassessment of the social and political structuring of mankind (Bourke, 1964, 13); and, above all, the widely read *Confessions* which, apart from other values, introduced a new genre into European literature. These are merely some of the masterpieces of a literary output equal in bulk to about fifteen volumes of a modern encyclopedia.

Augustine was the inventor of a school of theology and of a lasting form of the religious life. He was a mystic who managed to inspire Reformation theologians as well as being counted one of the *egregii doctores* of the Roman Catholic Church. His writings contain memorable apothegms and insights of the greatest profundity, so that even the most superficial reader is soon convinced that he is in the presence of a towering intellect and an original genius. The great German historian of Western theology, Adolf Harnack, remarked: 'It would seem that the miserable existence of the Roman Empire in the West was prolonged until then only to permit Augustine's influence to be exercised on universal history' (cited in *The Confessions*, tr. Sheed, 1943).

Above all, Augustine was a passionate man: a man of deep emotions, responses and desires. He was fond of food, obsessed by sex, could be carried away by music and intensely moved by the play of light; but supremely, he relentlessly pursued truth in the passionate conviction that the human soul *could* find understanding, if it used to the utmost what it had been given. In this fervent quest, he explored all available intellectual avenues: the wisdom of Cicero and the classical tradition, the new and popular teaching of the Manichees,[35] the spiritual idealism of Porphyry and Plotinus, and his own deeply felt and scrupulously analysed experience. This included teaching in a grammar school and the contemporary equivalent of a university. Following his appointment, at the age of twenty-eight, to the chair of rhetoric at Milan, he met St Ambrose and, impressed by his teaching and personality, Augustine became a catechumen.[36] In spite of this commitment, his mind was still open: he explored and finally rejected the claims of astrology and, at the age of thirty, he was still wrestling with the theoretical problem of evil and the practical one of chastity. He was much impressed by the story of St Anthony[37] and by the conversion of a number of his friends and acquaintances to the ascetic life. He became convinced that the way of perfection was the only way for him and he was finally converted and received into full membership of the Church at the age of thirty-two in A.D. 387. Four years later he became a priest and in 396 he was made bishop of Hippo, near Carthage, an office which he held until his death in 430, just before the besieging Vandals captured and sacked the town.[38]

In the midst of a civilisation which was collapsing, not only morally but also politically, amidst the fires and swords of the barbarians, Augustine singlemindedly sought eternal goodness, beauty and truth and, above all, the total peace and fulfilment which can only be found in God,[39] though it is reflected in creation and in man and his works. After his conversion, the smouldering fire of his passionate love for God burst into flame and everything other than God was purged from his value-system.

Looking clearly and dispassionately[40] at the world around him and closely examining the depths of his own soul, Augustine became convinced that nature was not evil (since the only God had made it), but that it was totally flawed in what should have been its highest point – man himself, and that this disaster was the result of the first man's turning away from God:

> That the whole human race has been condemned in its first origins, this life itself – if we may call it life – bears witness by the host of cruel ills with which it is filled . . . by the profound and dreadful ignorance that produces all the errors that enfold the children of Adam . . . by the love of so many vain and hurtful things . . . the crimes of wicked men which nevertheless spring from that root of *error and misplaced love* which is born with every son of Adam.[41]

The main result of this Original Sin is a psychological disorder in man: the schism between intelligence and will, between soul and body, and the consequent loss of 'right order' which produces false priorities and inordinate affections. All this is the just retribution for, and the inevitable result of, the Fall of Adam: 'Man, who by keeping the commandments should have been spiritual even in his flesh, became fleshly even in his spirit; and, as in his pride he had sought to be his own satisfaction, so God in his justice abandoned him to himself.' (*CG*, XIV, 15). Mind and flesh no longer serve the will, the body falls prey to infirmity and pain, and even natural pleasure is corrupted: 'Pleasure is preceded by a certain appetite which is felt in the flesh like a craving, as hunger, thirst and that generative appetite which is most commonly identified with the word "lust" – though this is the generic word for all desires.' (*CG*, ibid.)

Lust or concupiscence is inordinate desire, desire that has lost its priorities, that has escaped the mind's control, and this is always true, whether the lust be for revenge (anger), or for conquest (which Augustine interestingly calls 'opinionativeness'), or for applause (boasting), or money (avarice). He points out that although some lusts have specific names, others do not, 'for who could readily give a name to the lust for ruling?' (*CG*, XIV, 15). Physical desire, then, is not the only disordered emotion; anger has much the same characteristics 'because, even when exercised towards objects which wisdom does not prohibit, [these passions] are moved in an un-governed and inordinate manner, and consequently need the regulation of mind and reason'. Nevertheless, there seems to be more disorder in the former than the latter, since

> he who in his anger rails at, or even strikes, someone, could not do so unless his tongue and hand moved at the authority of his will, as they are similarly moved when there is no anger. But the organs of generation are so subjected to the imperative of lust, that they have no motion except that which lust itself communicates. It is this that we are ashamed of; it is this which blushingly hides from the eyes of onlookers. Rather will a man endure a crowd of wit-nesses when he is unjustly venting his anger on someone, than the eye of a single man when he is innocently copulating with his wife. (*CG*, XIV, 19.)

It is this complete independence of the sexual organs from the control of the rational mind and will which wish to use them that convinces Augustine of their fundamental disorder, more extensive and complete than any other disintegration consequent upon the Fall. This is why the word 'lust' has become attached to the ar-chetypal example of *physical* desire,

> the lustful excitement of the organs of generation, and this lust not only takes possession of the whole body and its outward members but also makes itself felt inwardly so that it moves the whole man with a passion in which mental emotion is mingled with bodily appetite, so that the resulting pleasure is the greatest of all bodily pleasures. Indeed, so possessing is this pleasure that, at the moment of time in which it reaches its consummation, all mental activity is suspended. (*CG*, XIV, 16.)

It is this suspension of man's higher faculties as the result of a physical activity which is the crux of the matter. Mental activity is held to be man's highest attribute, the very thing which distinguishes him from the brute creation, and so, when it ceases, it would appear that he ceases to be man. Hence the grave suspicion of such an all-consuming experience. [42]

Augustine also refers frequently to the other characteristic of sexual desire: its lack of subordination in due submission to mind, reason and will and its exemplification of disintegration and disorder in the total man:

> Sometimes this lust importunes men in spite of themselves and sometimes it fails them when they desire to feel it, so that though lust rages in the mind it does not stir in the body. Thus, strangely enough, this emotion not only fails to obey the legitimate desire to beget offspring, but it also refuses to obey lascivious lust; and, though it often opposes its whole combined energy to the soul that resists it, sometimes it is also divided against itself and, while it moves the soul, it leaves the body unmoved. (*CG*, IIV, 16.)

However, things were not always so, nor will they be always so. Against those who, because of their contempt for the body, argued that there could not have been procreation in the earthly Paradise, Augustine argues that there certainly would have been procreation, by willing and co-operative bodies, yet without lust (*CG*, XIV, 21, cf. 23). Similarly, in answer to those who argued that in the Resurrection all would rise with a male body, because man was – according to Genesis – the primal creature, Augustine supports the opinion that there will still be sexual differences in the resurrection-body:

> For (then) there shall be no lust which now is the cause of confusion . . . in these bodies vice will be withdrawn but nature will be preserved. And the sex of a woman is not vice but nature. [Her body] then shall indeed be superior to carnal intercourse and child-bearing; nevertheless, the female members shall remain, adapted not to the old uses but to a new beauty which, so far from provoking lust, shall excite praise to . . . God. (*CG*, XXII, 17.)

Against the extreme spiritualisers or dualists, Augustine maintains that there is nothing wrong with the body in itself and, though he is fond of quoting 'the body weighs down the soul' (Wisd. v, 15), he more than once points out, in reference to this very text, that 'it is not the body, but the corruptibility of the body which is a burden to the soul' (*CG*, XIII, 16, cf. XIX, 18) and that corruptibility is, of course, no part of God's design in the creation of man but solely a consequence of the Fall:

> Our parents were so created that, had they not sinned, they would not have been dismissed from their bodies by any death but would have been endowed with immortality as the reward of their obedience and thus lived for ever with their bodies. Further, the

saints will, in the resurrection, inhabit those very bodies in which they toiled. But no corruption or unwieldiness shall attach to their flesh, nor shall any grief or trouble cloud their felicity. (*CG*, XIII, 19.)

In the resurrection, flesh is not transformed into spirit but is restored to is proper subordination 'with a perfect and marvellous readiness of obedience, so that it responds in all respects to the will that has entered on immortality – all corruption, all reluctance, all slowness being abolished. For that body will not only be better than it ever was here, even in its best state of fitness, but it will surpass the bodies of our first parents before they sinned.' (*CG*, XIII, 20, cf. 22.)

The contemporary idealism which wished to reject the body or to see spiritual progress as a process of bodily divestation is constantly opposed by Augustine who saw such notions as contrary to fundamental Christian beliefs: the Incarnation, sacramentalism and the resurrection of the flesh. He continually rejects the anti-materialism which was so prominent in the religion and philosophy of his time: 'It is not necessary for the blessedness of the soul that it be detached from a body of any kind whatsoever, but that it receive an incorruptible body.' (*CG*, XXII, 26). It is not the thing in itself but its corruption following its perversion which is the source of trouble: 'To obtain blessedness, we need not quit every kind of body, but only the corruptible, cumbersome, painful, dying bodies – not such bodies as the goodness of God contrived for the first man, but only such bodies as man's sin entailed.' (*CG*, XIII, 17). However, apart from its corruption, the human body is naturally fragile and extremely vulnerable. In a fallen world, the happenings which can hurt it are legion:

What numberless casualties threaten our bodies from outside – extremes of heat and cold, storms, floods, inundations, lightning, thunder, hail, earthquakes, houses falling; or from the stumbling, shying or vices of horses; from countless poisons in fruits, water, air, animals; from the painful or even fatal bites of wild animals; from the insanity which a mad dog communicates, so that even that animal which is most gentle and friendly to its own master becomes the object of intenser fear than even a lion or dragon, and the man, whom by chance it has affected with this pestential contagion, becomes so rabid that his parents, wife and children dread him more than any wild beast!

What disasters are suffered by those who travel by land or sea! What man can leave his own house without being exposed on every side to unforseen accidents! If he returns home sound in limb, he may slip on his own door-step, break a leg and never

recover. What can seem safer than a man sitting in his own chair?
Yet Eli the priest fell from his and broke his neck. (I Sam. iv, 18.)

How many accidents do farmers, or indeed all men, fear that
the crops may suffer from the weather, or the soil, or the ravages
of destructive animals? Usually, they feel that the danger is past
when the crops are gathered and stored. Yet, to my certain
knowledge, sudden floods have driven the labourers away and
swept the barns clear of the finest harvest. (*CG*, XXII, 22.)

The reader may think that Augustine was a profound pessimist,
always looking on the dark side and in his gloomy imagination seeing
disaster lurk everywhere. But in reality, he was a realist, regarding
the world as it is, unbemused either by romantic or scientific optimism. His world was, in fact, disintegrating before his eyes: apart
from the natural disasters and accidents due to an undeveloped
technology, barbarism and disorder, war and all its attendant evils
were penetrating even to the centre of the Pax Romana and finally
overthrowing the stability of nearly 1,000 years. But Augustine could
also see the less obvious elements in the picture: the goodness of God
contrasted with human evil, the persisting glories of creation in spite
of its corruption by sin. Even the human body, the very seat of
concupiscence, whose disordered wants prevented the ascent of the
mind to God, the spoilt carapace that was doomed to die – even this
still bore the marks of glory with which the Creator had originally
endowed it:

What goodness of God, what providence of the great Creator, is
apparent in the human body though it dies like that of the beasts
and is, in some ways, weaker than theirs! Are not the organs of
sense and the rest of its members so placed, and is not the appearance, form and stature of the body as a whole so fashioned, as to
indicate that it was made for the service of a rational soul? Its
posture, the flexibility of the hands and of the speech-organs
support this impression and, even apart from its aptness to the
tasks required of it, there is such a symmetry in its various parts
and the maintenance of such beautiful proportions that one is at a
loss to decide whether, in the creation of the body, the greater regard was paid to utility or to aesthetics. What is certain, is that no
part of the body has been created for use which does not also
contribute something to its beauty. (*CG*, XXII, 24.)[43]

This wondering apprehension of the marvels of our mortal bodies:
their superb design, their symmetry and proportion, the whole so
nicely fashioned that it becomes a problem to decide whether their
Creator's aim was primarily functional or aesthetic, the assured

conclusion that even those parts which were designed for use also contribute to the total beauty – these are not the morbid musings of a misanthropic ascetic, but the conclusions of an ordered mind that contemplates all that God has made with awe, respect and delight. Augustine goes on to say that if we knew more about the body, its structures and organisation, we should be even more appreciative of what he calls the *coaptio*[44] or harmony of the body both in its internal and external structures and operations. If we could apprehend the human body in its totality 'even those inward parts which seem to have no beauty would so delight us with their exquisite design as to afford a profounder satisfaction to the mind (of which the eyes are but the ministers) than the obvious beauty of the body which so gratifies the eye' (*CG*, XXII, 24). Even in the visible structures of the body, beauty (according to Augustine) is never sacrificed to utility and, indeed, some parts of it seem to have no other reason for their existence than adornment. He therefore concludes that God, in creating man, paid more regard to comeliness than necessity since, 'in fact, necessity is a transitory thing; and the time is coming when we shall enjoy one another's beauty without any lust – a situation which will especially redound to the praise of the Creator' (*CG*, ibid.).

Since the body, both totally and in each of its individual parts, is good and beautiful, how are we to explain that shame which, at all times and among all cultures, seems to have been attached to the sexual organs and their activities? Augustine recognises that this is an unnatural or learned response and was not felt by man at his first creation. He explains it by its relation to the peculiarly irrational and inordinate nature of sexual concupiscence:

> Shame is very specially connected with this lust, and rightly so. The sexual members themselves, being moved and restrained not at our will but by a certain independent autocracy, so to speak, are also rightly called 'shameful'. Their condition was different before sin for, as it is written, 'They were naked and not ashamed' (Gen. ii, 25). It was not that they were unaware of their nakedness, but that nakedness was not yet sinful because lust did not yet move their sexual organs without the consent of their will; the flesh, by its disobedience, did not yet testify to the disobedience of man . . . they had no consciousness of their members warring against their will. But, stripped of grace, that their disobedience might be punished by an apt retribution, a shameless novelty was initiated in the movement of their bodily members which made nakedness indecent. At the same time, it made them observant [of these involuntary movements] and also made them feel shame. (*CG*, XIV, 17.)[45]

The uncontrollability of the sexual organs provides fundamental evidence of the disorder in fallen man's nature, the breakup of the psychosomatic unity, the destruction of an integrity which was related to the order between God and man and the unity between God and man. Therefore Adam and Eve were compelled to conceal the mark of their shame, the visible signs of a disordered human personality in which the body was no longer the willing servant of the mind. So they had to wear *caches-sex* or 'cinctures for their privy parts' and Augustine explains that the Hebrew word in Gen. iii, 11 (translated as 'apron' in the Authorised Version), is usually rendered in Latin by *campestria*, the word for the training-shorts which served 'a similar purpose for the young men stripped for exercise on the *campus*' (*CG*, XIV, 17.)

Since, according to Augustine's beliefs, all mankind was descended from these common parents, Augustine concluded that all human beings have inherited this disorder and its accompanying shame:

> Shame modestly concealed those parts that lust disobediently moved in opposition to the will which was thus punished for its own disobedience. Consequently, all nations – being propagated from that single stock – have so strong an instinct to cover the shameful parts that some barbarians do not even uncover them in the bath but bathe with their drawers on. Also, in the dark solitudes of India, though some philosphers go naked and are therefore called 'gymnosophists',[46] yet they make an exception in the case of these members and cover them up. (*CG*, XIV, 17.)

Further evidence of the extreme disorder of human sexuality is derived from the shame which seems inextricably attached to copulation, even when there is no logical reason for it in such situations as when it is socially acceptable and legally permissible. Even within the intimate relations of the family, when people usually behave most naturally and uninhibitedly, the disorder is still manifest.

> Lust requires for its consummation darkness and secrecy. This is not only the case when unlawful intercourse is desired, but even in respect of such fornication as the earthly city has legalised. Even where there is no fear of punishment, these tolerated pleasures still shrink from the public eye. When facilities are provided for this lust, secrecy is also provided: though lust found it easy to abolish legal prohibition, shamelessness found it impossible to do without the veil of retirement. Even shameless men call this activity shameful and, though they love the pleasure, dare not display it publicly.

What! Does not even conjugal intercourse, sanctioned as it is by law for the propagation of children,[47] legitimate and honourable though it be, does not even it seek retirement from every eye? . . . The greatest master of Roman eloquence [Cicero] says that all right actions wish to be set in the light, i.e. desire to be known. But this right action has such a desire to be known that it even blushes to be seen! Everybody knows what happens between husband and wife in order that children may be born. Is it not for this very purpose that wives are married with such ceremony? Yet, when this well-understood act is performed for the procreation of children, not even the children already born from the union are allowed to witness it. This right action seeks the light, inasmuch as it seeks to be known, yet it dreads being seen. Why should this be so, if not because that which is, by nature, fitting and decent, is accompanied by the shame-begetting penalty of sin whenever it is performed? (*CG*, XIV, 18.)[48]

It is difficult to emphasise sufficiently the centrality of the notion of order in Augustine's thought. It affects his thinking on almost every topic and is closely associated with such other key concepts as Love, Harmony, Tranquillity, Obedience and Peace.[49] The antonym of 'order' is perversion; peace is 'the tranquillity of order' (*CG*, XIX, 13), and virtue is 'the order of love' (*CG*, XV, 22). Things are only evil through lack of proportion, inordinateness: getting the proper order wrong. Right order underlies every good:

The peace of the body, then, consists in the duly-proportioned arrangement of its parts. The peace of the irrational soul is the harmonious repose of the appetites and the peace of the rational soul is the harmony of knowledge and action. The peace of body and soul is the well-ordered, harmonious life and health of the living creature. Peace between man and God is the well-ordered obedience of faith to eternal law. Peace between man and man is well-ordered concord, Domestic peace is the well-ordered concord between those of the family who rule and those who obey.[50] Civil peace is a similar concord among citizens. The peace of the celestial city is the perfectly ordered and harmonious enjoyment of God and of one another in God. The peace of all things is the tranquillity of order. Order is the distribution which allots things, equal and unequal, each to its proper place. (*CG*, XIX, 13.)

Creation itself is a manifestation of order in the material world[51] and the source of any disorder in any part of it is the result of disobedience to or non-co-operation with its inbuilt order. Man is the chief manifestation of this and it is important to see what he was and what he is still destined to be by God, as well as to see him as he is. Hence, Augustine has much to say about the condition of Paradisal man and about the condition of redeemed man in his resurrection body. Man's Paradisal condition was essentially marked by order or harmony and integrity or wholeness. In that original state there was no want, neither hunger nor thirst, no senility, disease or accident: 'Soundest health blessed his body, absolute tranquillity his soul.' Both macrocosm and microcosm were in order: there was neither excessive heat nor excessive cold in the environment and man felt neither fear nor desire within himself. Sadness and buffoonery were alike lacking, but true gladness flowed ceaselessly from the presence of God. From the beginning the human species was sexually differentiated, yet there was unity in this duality: 'the honest love of husband and wife a sure harmony between them'. A similar unity in duality marked the joint operations of body and soul in the individual. The physical state produced neither distressing effort nor wearisome langour and, congruently, with this total order, harmony and unity, Augustine postulates that there was no sick concupiscence. In Paradise, the sexual organs were as much under voluntary control as other members and sexual relations could take place with 'a tranquillity of both soul and body', without the stimulus of fiery enticement and without any breach of psychosomatic unity. Sexual congress would result from the spontaneous ability of both partners in the act and no pain would accompany the resultant birth. He remarks, rather enigmatically, that both conception and foetal development would be independent of lust but affected by will and nature. Sexual intercourse would be a placid obedience to the will and not a violent act of concupiscence (*CG*, XIV, 26).

For the same reasons, Augustine speculates on the nature of the resurrection-body (*CG*, XXII) and, in passing, disposes of the puerile objections to this essential article of the Christian faith (ibid. 12, 20). He is inclined to think that abortions will share in this grace (ibid. 13) and is certain that infants will (ibid. 14), though their bodies will be developed to their full potential so that all the resurrected will have the bodies of maturity and not those either of infancy or of old age (ibid. 15). All physical blemishes which marred our beauty in this life will be removed so that, though the natural substance of the body will remain, it will be entirely beautiful and perfect – especially in regard to proportion (ibid. 19). He did, however, consider that there might be a partial exception to this principle in the case of the martyrs whose bodies might still bear glorious traces of their wounds, since these would be marks of honour, giving added lustre to their appearance (ibid.).

However refined the substance of the resurrection-body may be, nonetheless it will be a real body in accordance with man's essentially composite nature. The reason why, in some Biblical texts, it is called a 'spiritual' body is not because it is itself spiritual but because there will be no conflict between it and the spirit (ibid. 21). It will possess new powers which might be called supernatural, though, in fact, we have intimations of these even in our present condition and

> it may very well be that, in the future world, we shall see the material forms of the new heavens and the new earth in such a way that we shall most distinctly recognise God present everywhere and governing all things, material as well as spiritual. It could be that we shall see Him, not as we now understand the invisible things of God – by the things which are made, seeing him vaguely and partially reflected in them and more by faith than by physical sight – but by means of the bodies with which we shall be clothed and which will give us that direct vision wherever we shall turn our eyes. (Ibid. 29.)

Such was God's creation of man in the beginning and such, by His grace, will be His re-creation at the end of the world but, in the meantime, we are in this flesh which is corruptible and vulnerable.

This condition provides special difficulties for those who are seeking the Ultimate in the right order of things, for the disordered flesh produces problems for the spirit.

> Irrespective of the miseries which in this life are common to the good and the bad, the righteous undergo labours peculiar to themselves, insofar as they make war upon their vices and are involved in the temptations and perils of such a contest. For, though at some times it is more violent and at other times slacker, yet without intermission does the flesh lust against the spirit and the spirit against the flesh. Consequently, we cannot do what we want and extirpate all lust; we can only refuse consent to it as God gives us ability and so keep it under. We have constantly to be on the watch lest the semblance of truth deceive us, lest a subtle discourse blind us, lest error involve us in darkness, lest we should take good for evil or evil for good, lest fear should hinder us from doing what we ought or desire should precipitate us into doing what we ought not, lest the sun go down upon our wrath, lest hatred should provoke us to render evil for evil, lest unseemly or immoderate grief consume us, lest an ungrateful disposition make us slow to recognise benefits received, lest calumnies fret our conscience, lest our rash suspicion deceive us over a friend, or others' false suspicions of us give rise to too much uneasiness, lest sin reign in our mortal bodies to obey its desires, lest our members

be used as instruments of unrighteousness, lest the eye follow lust, lest thirst for revenge carry us away, lest sight or thought dwell too long on some evil thing that gives us pleasure, lest wicked or indecent language be willingly listened to, lest we do what is pleasant but unlawful and lest in this warfare, filled so abundantly with toil and peril, we either hope to secure victory by our own strength or attribute it, when secured, to our own strength and not to His grace of whom the Apostle says: 'Thanks be to God who giveth us the victory through our Lord Jesus Christ.' . . . But yet we are to know this, that however valorously we resist our vices and however successful we are in overcoming them, yet as long as we are in this body we have always reason to say to God, 'Forgive us our debts'. But in that kingdom where we shall dwell for ever, clothed in immortal bodies, we shall no longer have either conflicts or debts, as indeed we should not have had in any time or in any condition had our nature continued upright as it was created. (Ibid. 23.)

It is worth quoting this long passage on the human condition according to St Augustine, since it reminds us once more that the traditional concept of the 'flesh' or 'body' does not connote simple bodily impulses which are forbidden because they are pleasurable. Augustine is operating on a much more profound level: the leitmotiv of this passage is truth; truth in thought, truth in act, truth about people, true order, true attribution, and the moral principle is that such truth is difficult enough for men to attain but impossible if we allow the disorder in our human condition to get out of hand, and this is the justification for a total asceticism – the discipline of mind and body which can only succeed through the grace of God. Besides these inward and, so to speak, spiritual conflicts with the flesh, life in the body can produce additional harassment, particularly when under pressure.

Has not the madness of thirst driven men to drink human urine and even their own? Has not hunger driven men to eat human flesh and not even the flesh of bodies found dead but that of bodies slain for the purpose? Have not the fierce pangs of famine driven mothers to eat their own children, incredibly savage as this may seem? In conclusion, to speak of sleep which is justly called repose: how little repose there is in it sometimes when it is disturbed by dreams and visions, and with what terror is the wretched mind overwhelmed through the appearance of things presented to it in this way and which, as it were, so stand out before the senses that we cannot distinguish them from realities. How wretchedly do false appearances distract men in certain illnesses! With what an astonishing variety of apparitions are even healthy men sometimes deceived through the evil spirits who produce these delusions for the sake of perplexing the senses of their victims, if they cannot succeed in seducing them to their side! (Ibid. 22.)

We can understand the nightmares produced in its citizens by the multifarious horrors which accompanied the collapse of the Roman Empire before the assaults of the barbarians: such dreams merely reflected the reality of the day. We can also sympathise with Augustine's concern that the rational soul could be overwhelmed by the side-effects of a fevered body. The understanding of the delusions referred to in the last sentence requires familiarity with the accounts left by the ascetics, particularly the Desert Fathers,[52] of their demonic visitations. The temptations of St Anthony are perhaps the best known of these and they were to produce a subject for painters for many centuries to come.

In spite of these concomitants, there is still so much good in our earthly condition that Augustine can give very serious attention to the view of some philosophers that man's chief good is to be found in this life and especially in his body. Yet, Augustine argues, these manifest goods suffer from the limitations of their nature:

> Is the body of the philosopher excempt from every pain that may dispel pleasure, from every disquietude that may banish repose? The amputation or decay of any of its members puts an end to the body's integrity, deformity can blight its beauty, lassitude its vigour, sleepiness or sluggishness its activity – and which of these may not assail the flesh of even the wise man? Comely and fitting postures and movements of the body are numbered among the prime natural blessings, but what if some sickness makes them tremulous? What if a man suffers from such an acute curvature of the spine that his hands reach the ground and moves like a quadruped on all fours? Do not these things destroy all grace and beauty in the body, whether it is at rest or in motion? What shall I say of the fundamental blessings of the soul: sense and intellect; of which one is provided for the perception, and the other for the comprehension, of truth? But what kind of sensation remains when a man becomes deaf and blind and where are reason and intellect when disease makes a man delirious? (*CG*, XIX, 4.)

He reiterates that it is not the body itself, but its proneness to decay that 'weighs down the soul' repeating one of his favourite texts (Wisd. ix, 15). But, just as a man can expect too much from his body, so he can also despise it to such an extent that he cannot conceive of its resurrection as the culmination and reward of the spiritual life. One of his arguments against such imbalance takes the following form:

> What is to prevent the earthly body being elevated to a heavenly body, since a spirit (which is more refined than any kind of body) is now tied to an earthly body? If so small a piece of earth is capable of maintaining union with something better than a heavenly body so that it can receive sensation and life, will heaven disdain to receive or even retain this sentient and living fragment which derives its life and sensation from a substance more refined than any heavenly body?[53]

In general, Augustine generally maintains the Pauline distinction between 'flesh' and 'body'[54] and repeats and expands the apostle's exposition of 'living after the flesh' and 'living after the spirit'. For example, he points out that the Pauline distinction is not the same as the difference between the Epicureans 'who place man's good in bodily pleasure' or the non-philosophers 'who are so prone to lust that they cannot delight in any pleasure save such as they receive from bodily sensations' and the more 'spiritual' philosophers, such as the Stoics, 'who place the supreme good of man in the soul'.[55] From the Christian point of view, both these opposed groups alike 'live after the flesh' since they both trust in human self-sufficiency (cf. *CG*, XIV, 2). The germinal Pauline passage (Gal. v, 19–21) itself clarifies what is really meant by 'living after the flesh': 'For, among the works of the flesh which he said were manifest and which he cited for condemnation, we find not only those which concern the pleasures of the flesh . . . but also those which, though they be remote from fleshly pleasure, reveal the vices of the soul.' (*CG*, XIV, 3). Indeed, to abstain from fleshly pleasures for the wrong reason can be described as 'living after the flesh' and both 'carnalities' and 'animosities' are equally 'works of the flesh' (ibid.). This point is best summarised by a typical and revealing Augustinian aphorism: 'As the life of the flesh is the soul, so the blessed life of man is God.' (*CG*, XIX, 26.)

Body and soul are alike created by God and therefore neither of them can be evil or hated by God, for He hates nothing but sin. Sin, for man, is a disorder and perversion of which the fundamental mark is a turning away from the Creator in favour of the things which He has created.[56] Not only the body, but even that more ambivalent concept 'the flesh', 'is to be healed, because it belongs to ourselves: it is not to be abandoned to destruction as though it were alien to our nature' (*CG*, XV, 7). The flesh, the world, and earthly things are all essentially good and all, even now, are capable of good if they are kept in their place, i.e. their proper order in the universe of reality.

The balanced Christian view is determined by the fundamental doctrine of the Incarnation, the belief that the Word of God has become flesh: 'For, even if His Incarnation showed us nothing else, these two wholesome facts would be enough: that true divinity cannot be polluted by flesh, and that evil spirits are not to be considered better than ourselves because they do not have flesh.' (*CG*, IX, 17, cf. *De Trinitate*, XIII, 22.)

To the thoughtful Christian, 'body' is a pregnant concept, constantly giving birth to new ideas and insights and bringing to light connections and interrelations. It is not an accident that, in theology, the word is used equally of the natural body of man, of the incarnate Body of Christ, of the unity in one flesh of man and woman, of the mystical Body which is the Church, and of the gift which is received in the sacrament of the altar. Augustine, perhaps more than other Christian authors, was aware of the root meaning behind these various usages.[57] One example must suffice:

> He, then, who is in the unity of Christ's body [i.e. of the Christian membership] – of which body the faithful are accustomed to receive the sacrament at the altar – that man is truly said to eat the body and drink the blood of Christ. Consequently, heretics and schismatics, being separate from the unity of this body, are able to receive the same sacrament, but not with profit to themselves – rather to their hurt – for they are not in the bond of peace which is symbolised by that sacrament.' (*CG*, XXI, 25, where the old notion of spiritual adultery also recurs.)

The City of God, that social body whose head is Christ, forms the New Adam, the sum of redeemed and recreated humanity and makes up a cosmic 'perfect man' (*CG*, XXII, 18).[58]

This speculation opens up matters which are beyond our present terms of reference and we will descend from the heights of theology to Augustine's realistic appraisal of the beauty of the human body: 'Beauty is, indeed, a good gift of God; but, so that the good may not think that it is a great good, God dispenses it even to the wicked.' (*CG*, XV, 22.)

SUMMARY

By the beginning of the fifth century the Catholic Church was beginning to make its mark on the world in the care of those neglected by the State, the institution of general hospitals, the care of widows and orphans on a large scale, the opening up of new careers for women, etc. The cessation of external persecution had led some to the conviction that Christian life could never be easy, even in a neutral or even friendly State, and that the sharpness of its challenge must never be allowed to become blunt. The same minds saw the easy corruption of a Church which was part of the Establishment and set it a new challenge in the renunciation and austerity of the religious life. There is the exemplification of a sacrificial love of God and the brethren and a realised vision of the Incarnate Christ in the person of his 'little ones', and we have glimpses of a charity which overcomes mental prejudice and involuntary physical repugnance. In short, we are aware of the entry into the old and dying world of a new and vital sensibility.

Yet there are signs of over-reaction against the corruption of the world and the laxity of nominal Christians, a tendency to deny the good in order to praise the better. Above all we are aware of the influence of political events. The slow disintegration and decline of Roman civilisation reached its climax in the cataclysmic fall of Rome itself – the undoubted end of a world and what must have seemed like the end of the world. We have tried to show at some length the effect of this event on a sensitive observer who fully appreciated the gifts of Rome – though he had preferred those of the Church – as an example of what, to a greater or lesser degree, must have been the impact on millions. It was generally and genuinely believed that Rome was in fact the Eternal City and that her fall would presage the end of the world. Apart from the psychological effects one must assess the effects of the almost total breakdown of law and order, of education and trade, of banking and communication. The nearest analogy would be the state of the world after a total atomic war: shock, disintegration, a struggle to survive, the salvaging of indiscriminate remains, at the worst a mental breakdown and at the best a complete reassessment of all previous assumptions and values.

The fall of Rome was the dreadful fulfilment of the worst fantasies of an apocalyptic vision, the shaking of the foundations of the world, the triumph of barbarism, force and disorder, the disappearance of their opposites in smoke and flame. The Church survived as, in some sense, the heir to Rome both for good and ill. What remained of classical culture and learning survived with her as accidental luggage of the Benedictine monks who, in seeking first the Kingdom of God, had almost all things of earlier culture added unto them. The single individual who bestrides the classical world and the mediaeval one is the genius Augustine, whose passion and intellect have affected all subsequent Christian thought, attitudes and practice.

THE DARK AGES

The Fall of Rome was the sunset that heralded the arrival of the Dark Ages and in that dusk appears Boethius whom Gibbon called 'the last of the Romans whom Cato or Tully [Cicero] could have acknowledged for their countryman'.[1] He was one of the most accomplished men of his time: orator, poet, musician, mathematician, philosopher and, among his other bequests, he transmitted the works of Aristotle to the Middle Ages through his Latin version. When Theodoric the Goth made himself master of Italy (493–526), Boethius became the head of his civil service and a senator and Boethius' sons were created joint consuls in A.D. 510.

Boethius's interpretation of life

Scarcely a year after this signal achievement, Boethius lay in solitary confinement, stripped of his honours and awaiting death at the hands of his barbarous master.[2] In this situation he wrote *The Consolation of Philosophy* which, in succeeding centuries, was republished more frequently than any other book except the Bible and *The Imitation of Christ* (Heer, 1966, 28). It owed its phenomenal popularity to its belief in an ordered and rational world in spite of all the evidence to the contrary in the Dark Ages. It asserted that God was good and that He created and governs the world through goodness, and that it is man's task and salvation to grasp the fullness of this truth beyond the superficial emptiness:

> Have you no good of your own implanted in you, and that you must seek your good in things external and separate? Is the nature of things so turned upside-down that a creature, divine by right of reason, can in no way be splendid in his own eyes save by the possession of lifeless chattels? You place yourself below the lowest of things when you judge these low things to be your good . . . man is so constituted that he only excels other things when he knows himself, but he is brought lower than the beasts if he loses this self-knowledge. (*Consolation*, II, v.)

Even more abstract goods, like the pursuit of fame and glory which ranked so high in the value-system of antiquity, are intrinsically empty:

> For, if man is entirely mortal (which our thinking forbids us to

believe), there is no such thing as glory at all since he to whom glory is attributed is wholly non-existent. But if the mind, conscious of its own rectitude,[3] is released from its earthly prison and seeks heaven in free flight, does it not despise all earthly things when it rejoices in its deliverance from earthly bonds and enters upon the joys of heaven? (Ibid. vii.)

Here speaks no monk but a man of affairs who remembers his pride when 'in the Circus, seated between the two consuls [his own sons], he did glut the thronging concourse with the largesse for which they looked' and who has come to equate fortune with Providence through recognising that ill fortune is more likely than good fortune to reveal truth (ibid. viii). Above all, he recognises that it is Love that bestows and maintains true order: literally, it is Love that makes the world go round:

> Yet should He His care remit,
> All that now so close is knit
> In sweet love and holy peace,
> Would no more from conflict cease
> But with strife's rude shock and jar
> All the world's fair fabric mar. (ibid. Song, viii.)

All creatures naturally seek happiness, but the disordered minds of men are blinded to its true source (ibid. III, ii) and the final illusory source of human happiness is the body:

Are you fain to lead a life of pleasure? Yet who does not scorn and despise one who is the slave of that weakest and lowest of things – the body? On how slight and perishable a possession do they rely who set before themselves bodily excellence?[4] Can you ever surpass the elephant in bulk or the bull in strength? Can you excel the tiger in speed? Behold the infinitude, the solidity, the swift motion of the heavens and, for once, stop admiring things that are mean and worthless. Yet the heavens are not so much to be admired for these qualities as for the Reason that guides them.

Furthermore, how transient is the lustre of beauty! How soon it is gone! It is more fleeting than the fading bloom of spring flowers. Moreover, if (as Aristotle says) men could see with the eyes of Lyncaeus[5] and see through obstructions, would not even the body of Alcibiades,[6] so gloriously fair in its outward appearance, seem utterly loathsome when all its inner parts were open to view? From this it follows that it is not your state that makes you appear beautiful but the weakness of the eyes that see you. You may give whatever undue value you like to the excellencies of the body so long as you know that this thing which you admire, whatever its worth, can be dissolved away by the feeble flame of a three-day fever. (Ibid. viii)

The prime source of human error in pursuing these phantoms of the Good is the disintegration and separation of what is, in its nature, one and indivisible. If all man's goods are to be attained, they are to be obtained totally and together (ibid. ix). The *summum bonum* is, in fact, attainable for man because of the very nature of the universe. Its source is God and the truly happy man partakes of the divine nature. All other ends are relative to this absolute, simple Good (ibid. 10) since unity or integrity is, like happiness, an aspect of goodness (ibid. 11) and 'there is nothing which, so long as it follows nature, endeavours to resist good' (ibid. xii).

Amid the contemporary chaos Boethius wrote a work intended to help others to 'believe in a universe firmly constructed according to a clear, luminous system of law and yet open to the wisdom both of the pagan and the Christian writers of old' (Heer, 1966, 28). He also left other insights which would be considered and developed during the following centuries, including the first satisfactory definition of person[7] and a popular definition of eternity.

The contribution of the Benedictines

Apart from the breakdown of political and economic order, perhaps the chief characteristic of the centuries after the fall of Rome was the rapid growth of the ascetic movement and its organisation into communities. Lecky (1905, II, 101) identifies its central notions as 'the meritoriousness of complete abstinence from all sexual intercourse and of complete renunciation of the world', and numbers among its causes enthusiasm, reaction against the luxury and licence of the great cities, and social changes 'especially the barbarian invasions which produced every variety of panic and wretchedness'. By the fourth century we hear of ascetic communities numbered in thousands,[8] and in Egypt, the original home of this movement, it has been estimated that the monastic population was approaching that of the cities at the end of the century.

Such a phenomenon is obviously open to widely differing valuation. Lecky (1905, II, 107ff.) writes:

There is, perhaps, no phase in the moral history of mankind of a deeper or more painful interest than this ascetic epidemic. A hid-eous, sordid and emaciated maniac, without knowledge, without patriotism, without natural affection, passing his life in a long routine of useless and atrocious self-torture, and quailing before the ghastly phantoms of his delirious brain, had become the ideal of the nations which had known the writings of Plato and Cicero and the lives of Socrates and Cato. For about two centuries, the hideous maceration of the body was regarded as the highest proof of excellence.[9]

But this same unsympathetic rationalist recognises the excellency of asceticism as the great school of self-sacrifice (ibid. 154f.), the moral beauty of some of the associated legends (ibid. 156–60) and writes extensively on their tendencey to produce a kindliness towards animals (ibid. 161–73).[10] We have already mentioned the beginnings of its penetration into the West, but this received new impetus and some change of character through the influence of the Italian Benedict whose *Rule* was to establish the norm of Western monasticism and which 'for all its apparent simplicity, is one of the few great constructive works of the sixth century' (Gardner, 1911, xxii). In many ways, the 'Rule' is significantly Western if not characteristically Roman.[11] It channels the enthusiastic individualism of an extreme Eastern movement into a system with fixed laws and an emphasis on the social or community aspect of the religious life. It is essentially balanced and moderate and has even been described as possessing 'incomparable sanity' (Clarke, 1931, vi).

The Benedictine monk voluntarily binds himself, after a probationary period both for himself and the community which he desires to enter, by the threefold vow of poverty, chastity and obedience and thus witnesses to other-wordly values, then as now, for in an age when 'economic considerations dwarf all else, some at least are renouncing possessions and making many rich; that when self-indulgence and self-expression are preached as the duty of man, some are practising restraint without detriment to the fullness of their humanity; and when self-determination is the watchword of both nations and individuals, obedience is being preferred by vigorous wills.' (Clarke, 1931, viif). These virtues, in one form or another, have always been important for serious Christians, particularly for those called to the stonier paths of self-renunciation and mortification, but the characteristic Benedictine vow is none of these three but the fourth one which commits him to 'stability', to remain for ever (unless otherwise ordered by due authority) in the monastery which he first entered.[12]

St Benedict was well aware of the contrast between the transitoriness of this life and the abiding nature of God's precepts, and therefore the monks' 'hearts and bodies must be prepared like those of soldiers'[13] so that they may serve God in holy obedience. It is his intention 'to establish a school of the Lord's service, in the institution of which we hope that we are going to establish nothing harsh, nothing burdensome' (Clarke, 1931, 5). The monastery is a family of

which the abbot is the model father, its laws are the love of God and
neighbour which are exemplified in the order and discipline of the
common life. The monk is exhorted, among other things, 'to chastise
the body . . . not to embrace delights . . . to love fasting . . . not to
be given to much wine . . . or much sleep, nor to be gluttonous or to
fulfill the desires of the flesh' (Clarke, 1931, 15–19). Discipline,
particularly of the younger members of the community, includes
corporal punishment, but gentle consideration in all things is to be
paid to the very old and the very young. Food and drink is to be given
according to need, always adequate but never excessive, and the
regulations about drink exemplify the Benedictine spirit: 'We believe
that half a pint of wine per head per day suffices . . . but if the
necessities of the place, or the work, or the heat of the summer
should call for more, let it stand within the discretion of the superior
to grant more, he taking all care that neither surfeiting nor drunkenness creep in.' (Clarke, 1931, 61f.)

The Mass is assumed as the central act of worship, as for any kind
of Christian community, but the special duty or 'office' of the
monastic community is the *Opus Dei* (God's Work) which consequently receives detailed attention. It consists of seven solemnly
sung services during the day and one during the night (called 'the
Hours) which consecrate all time to the eternal God. This custom
was imitated subsequently by all religious orders, imposed on all
priests and taken up by pious laity. Hence the proliferation in the
Middle Ages of 'Books of Hours'. This supreme work was reflected in
manual and intellectual work[14] and the Benedictine motto became
Laborare est orare, i.e. work in the right spirit and prayer of a
similar nature are substantially the same thing. Benedictine culture
originated from chapter xlviii of the *Rule*: 'Since idleness is inimical
to the soul, the brethren ought to be occupied at fixed sessions with
manual work and again at fixed sessions with spiritual
reading . . . they are truly monks when they live by the work of their
hands. . . . Let everything be done in moderation, however, on
account of the faint hearted.' (Clarke, 1931, 70f). The notions of
balance and moderation here expressed are central to Benedictinism: they affect discipline, self-denial, comfort and all aspects of
the life. Clothes are to be plain and simple, made from easily ob-
tainable material, and varied according to climatic demands.
Hospitality flows from the charity which is central and exercised
continuously in the community in the patient tolerance of others'
infirmities 'whether physical or of character; let them compete in
yielding obedience; let none follow what he judges convenient to
himself but rather what he judges convenient to another; in chaste
love let them exercise fraternal charity; let them fear God; let them

love their abbot with sincere and humble affection; on no account let them exalt anything above Christ; and may He bring us all alike to eternal life' (Clarke, 1931, 105). In spite, or perhaps because, of its extreme brevity and explicit 'open-endedness', the *Rule* and the communities it regulated were so influential that the next 500 years have been called 'the Benedictine centuries'.

Among its illustrious adherents was Pope Gregory the Great (*c.* 540–604) who profoundly influenced the development of the Western Church and the structure of mediaeval society, as well as initiating Augustine's mission to the Anglo-Saxons. This invalid, suffering from incessant pain, administered the Catholic Church for fourteen years in a whirl of unceasing and vigorous activity, which extended to mundane things in spite of his conviction that the end of the world was at hand.[15] In an address of about A.D. 600 he warned:

> Behold, my brethren, we already see with our eyes what we are used to hearing in prophecy. Day by day the world is assaulted by fresh and thickening blows. Out of the once innumerable Roman people what a remnant are you today! Yet incessant scourges are still in action; sudden adversities thwart you; new and unforseen slaughters wear you away. For, as in youth the body is in vigour, the chest is strong, the neck muscular, and the arms plump, but in old age the stature is bent, the neck is withered and stooping, the chest pants, the energies are feeble, the breath is wanting for the words; so the world too once was vigorous, robust for the increase of its kind, green in its health and opulent in its resources, but now on the contrary it is laden with the weight of years, and is fast sinking into the grave by its ever-multiplying maladies. Beware then of giving your heart to that which, as even your senses tell you, cannot last for ever. (Cited in Newman, 1908, 95.)

The *Dialogues* of St Gregory, among the most popular books of the Middle Ages, were translated into Anglo-Saxon *c.* A.D. 890 as part of Alfred the Great's policy of restoring English civilisation. The book is a collection of anecdotes about saints with many miracles and visions and gives a vivid picture of the interests and concerns of those who had turned away from 'the changes and chances of this fleeting world'. It opens with the Pope's complaint that the demands of his office has distracted him from monastic contemplation:

> My unhappy soul, wounded with worldly business, now remembers my inner state when I lived in my abbey and how at that time it was above all earthly concerns, above all transitory and corruptible pelf, and how it was accustomed to dwell on nothing but heavenly matters. Then, though it was enclosed in a

mortal body, by contemplation it passed far beyond earthly
bounds and penetrated to the height of heaven itself. (Gardner,
1911, 4.)

Urged on by his interlocutor, a young monk called Peter, Gregory
tells stories of Italian saints personally or by repute known to him.
They include the abbot Equitius who as a young man endured 'many
and sore carnal temptations' which he resisted, continuing to pray
for a remedy until in a vision 'he saw an angel come unto him who
made him an eunuch and so delivered him from all those carnal
motions in such sort that never after felt he any more as though
he had not been any man at all'. Trusting in this 'great grace' he
added the oversight of nunneries to that of the monasteries he already
supervised, though he warned others not to presume to do this unless
they had received a similar gift (Gardner, 1911, 15). The same man
averted possible scandal in a women's community where one of the
nuns 'who in respect of her corruptible carcase seemed beautiful' fell
into feverish fits and declared that she would die unless treated by a
specific monk (who was in fact a witch hiding under the protection of
the Benedictine habit) (Gardner, 1911, 16).

The second part of the *Dialogues* consists of an account of the life
and miracles of St Benedict who also was much tempted in the early
stages of his ascetic life until a crisis was reached:

> There was a certain woman whom he had seen at one time whose
> memory the Wicked Spirit put into his mind and by her
> representation he so mightly inflamed the soul of God's servant
> with increasing concupiscence that, almost overcome with pleasure,
> he was of a mind to forsake the wilderness. But, suddenly assisted
> with God's grace, he came to himself and seeing many thick briars
> and nettles growing nearby he cast off his apparel, threw himself
> into their midst and wallowed there so long that when he rose up
> all his flesh was pitifully torn. So by the wounds of his body he
> cured the wounds of his soul in that he turned pleasure into pain
> and by the outward burning of extreme smart quenched the fire
> which inwardly flared in his soul fed with the fuel of carnal
> cogitations. He overcame the sin by changing the nature of the
> fire. From this time on, as he personally told his followers, he
> found all temptation of [carnal] pleasure so subdued that he never
> more felt any such thing. (Gardner, 1911, 55.)

The phrase 'came to himself' in the above passage is interesting and
Gregory himself expatiates on it a few pages later (Gardner, 1911,
58f.), pointing out that we can fall beneath ourselves by 'sinful
cogitation' or rise above ourselves by 'the grace of contemplation'.

The implication is that a lewd kind of life' is beneath man and that the 'heights of contemplation' raise man above his 'usual judgment and understanding'.

The positive and lasting contribution of Benedictinism[16] to Western civilisation is exemplified in two English monks: Bede and Alcuin.[17] Bede (673–735) was placed as a child in the newly founded monastery at Jarrow where he remained until his death, having just completed his translation of St John's Gospel – a shining example of 'stability' and sanctified work. During his lifetime, Europe was saved from Mohammedanism by two of the decisive battles of the world while he, unknowing, made his own contribution to the preserved European civilisation. His extensive works, particularly his masterpiece *The Ecclesiastical History of the English Nation*, present us with lively cameos of the age, including the memorable figures of Northern ascetics and solitary contemplatives, but always he implicitly emphasises the contribution made to material civilisation by the monk whose primary aim

> was to devote oneself to righteous works, and especially to keep oneself 'unspotted from the world', restraining mind, hand, tongue and all the other members of the body from every kind of sinful pollution; and then to help one's neighbour to the best of one's ability, by giving food to the hungry, drink to the thirsty and clothing to the cold, by receiving the destitute and wanderers into one's home, by visiting the sick and burying the dead, by snatching the helpless out of the power of the stronger, and the destitute and poor from those who laid hold on them, by showing the truth to those who erred and by submitting oneself to the demands of brotherly love, and especially for striving for righteousness even unto death.[18] (Blair, 1970, 203f.)

Such teaching and example eventually redirected the energies of some barbarians towards the rebuilding of civilisation under Christian inspiration. Perhaps the most notable of these was the Frankish Charles who provided the conditions for the first of Europe's many Renaissances.[19] The exaltation of this man, under the style of Charlemagne, into one of 'the nine worthies' of the Middle Ages marks a new attitude to the body in what was to become a kind of 'functionalist' society. Men were expected to use their talents and position in society in an ordered way so as to make their peculiar contribution to the whole and on behalf of all. Just as there was a clerical order which 'prayed for all', whose members devoted themselves body and soul to the perfect performance of this work, so there would be a warrior caste which, by a different kind of training or ascesis and another form of self-sacrifice, 'fought for all' and thus protected the ordered life in which prayer and work and good government could take place.[20] The significance of Charlemagne is marked by two near-contemporary 'lives' which present this Christian warrior king for our admiration: one, modelled on Suetonius' *Lives of the Caesars*, by Einhard, a product of the Benedictine Abbey of Fulda; the other by Notker, a monk who seems to have spent the whole of his adult life in the Abbey of St Gall.[21]

Charles is pictured as a much metamorphosed barbarian warlord whose virtues, besides heroic prowess in battle, include care for the spiritual and material welfare of his people. He could terrify men with a glance and bend a sword with his bare hands, and Notker gives a vivid description of this 'man of iron':

> topped with his iron helm, his fists in iron gloves, his iron chest and his Platonic shoulders clad in an iron cuirass. An iron spear raised high against the sky he gripped in his left hand, while in his right he held his still unconquered sword. For greater ease of riding other men kept their thighs bare of armour; Charlemagne's were bound in plates of iron. As for his greaves, like those of all his army, they too were made of iron. His shield was all of iron. His horse gleamed iron-coloured and its very mettle was as if of iron. (Thorpe, 1969, 163.)

The heroic context is also illustrated by the vignette of the giant warrior Eishere from the Thurgau who now regards those outside Charlemagne's empire as the barbarians. Notker tells how he

> mowed down the Bohemians and Wiltzes and Avars as a man mows a meadow. He spitted them on his spear as though they were tiny birds. When he came back victorious, the stay-at-homes asked him how he liked it in the land of the Winides. Contemptuous of some and angry with others, he used to answer: 'What are these tadpoles to me? I used to spit seven or eight or sometimes nine of them on my spear and carry them about all over the place, squealing their incomprehensible lingo.' (Thorpe, 1969, 157.)

We are also introduced to the bishops who were Charles' co-workers, all larger than life whether in their virtues or in their vices. They amass vast fortunes in their avarice, provide enormous banquets through their love of display and gluttony; they give themselves utterly in the service of God and the emperor, and they struggle heroically with temptations and the weaknesses of the flesh (cf. Thorpe, 1969, 117f., 121f.). One good bishop, to make amends for a minute (and justifiable) breach of the Lenten fast, not only intensified his abstinence and maintained perpetual vigils but also ministered with his own hands to the poor and pilgrims, washing their feet, giving them clothes and money to the full extent of his means, and even wishing to go beyond his means. On the holy day of Easter Saturday, [22] he collected large wine-jars from the entire city and ordered that hot baths be prepared for all the poor from dawn to dusk. With his own hands he shaved the throats of all who wished it, and with his nails he removed purulent scabs and hairy growths from their hirsute bodies. He then anointed them with unguents and dressed them in white garments, as a sign of their regeneration. (Thorpe, 1969, 116.)

It is satisfactory to be informed that, after all these exertions and when there was none left who had not submitted to these ministrations, the bishop himself took a bath and reclothed himself in spotless raiment. In view of the tendency of some to associate enthusiastic Christianity with carelessness in matters of hygiene, it is perhaps worth pointing out that some attitudes towards the body were more the result of local culture than of Christian belief. Notker himself gives plenty of examples of the Frankish contempt for foppishness or the over-consideration of the body which they discerned in more civilised peoples such as the Italians and the Byzantines who were, of course, at least as good Christians as the Franks. One illustration is perhaps particularly significant: 'There was a certain deacon who followed the habits of the Italians in that he was *perpetually trying to resist nature*. He used to take baths, he had his head very closely shaved, he polished his skin, he cleaned his nails, he had his hair cut short as if it had been turned on a lathe, and he wore linen underclothes and a snow-white shirt.' (Thorpe, 1969, 130.) Notker seems to find satisfaction in the fact that this un-naturally proud cleric, having presumed to sing the Gospel at High Mass (as it was his office to do), was, in the course of this function, attacked by a spider and died of its bite.

To return to greater matters, Charlemagne who preferred an élitism open to the talents through education to an élitism dependent on birth (Notker, I, iii in Thorpe, 95) persuaded the Benedictine Alcuin [23] to leave his native York to become a sort of minister of cultural affairs in the Frankish Empire (Boussard, 1968, 134). For a time he also seems to have been director of the palace school or imperial college of Charlemagne which, characteristically, was as open to the sons of millers as to the sons of nobles. Alcuin performed his task so effectively before his retirement to the famous and ancient Abbey of St Martin of Tours that his name not only symbolises the learning and literature of the age of Charlemagne (Ker, 1958, 101) but also its art and theology.

If one is tempted, through lack of imagination or sense of proportion, to think that the Church's attitude to the body (considered as a simple and separate thing) was, in the Dark Ages, not all that we would have it, we might ask oursleves what place the subject would take in literature produced in the aftermath of an atomic war. Dark Age Europe had much more on its mind than hygiene, physical education or recreation or a balanced approach to the human body and its nature. Fundamentally, Europe was engaged in survival and any superfluous time and energy was directed to rescuing the remains of a great civilisation and, with the help of these fragments, in building (or at least laying the foundations for) a new civilisation. This enormous task extended from acquiring the mechanics of writing and book production to the provision or support of a social order that would make life itself less nasty, brutish and short. The stupendous achievement is reflected in the reflorescence of schools and centres of higher education, the production of major works of art in painting, glass and ivory, the return of great architecture, and the continuation and development of literature in both prose and verse. To this total task and achievement the contribution of the Church in general (Boussard, 1968, 92, 106) and of monasticism in particular (ibid., 98, 100, 118–20) was both critical and indispensable.

Revival of traditional thought

The main work of the Dark Ages lay in establishing the bonds of society, ordering the Christian life and re-establishing a tradition of thought.[24] By succeeding in these almost superhuman efforts, the men and women of the Dark Ages not only made possible the flowering of the Middle Ages but they also created a new and unique cultural entity which was independent of race or of obvious geographical or linguistic boundaries. They called this creation Christendom, we call it Europe.[25] Its failures were many (Charlemagne's achievements were largely dissolved in fratricidal strife) and even some of its successes could be described as accidental. We must recognise that in a time of disorder thinking is disordered, in the struggle for existence 'male virtues' would be overvalued since might, if not right itself, seemed the only way to make right either possible or impossible. We should not be surprised at the appearance of male chauvinism' or at a depreciation of the body resulting from the exhausting struggle of idealists to escape from its insistent demands. In this period there are glaring contradictions and failures to work out the implications and consequences of accepted truths. Sexuality was ignored or rigorously suppressed. The same age that offered new influence, careers and status to women through the religious life also saw a provincial council of the Church enact that women should not receive the Eucharist into their naked hands on account of the impurity of their sex. [26]

Early monks had an attitude to the flesh that could show itself in an almost paranoic hatred of the human body, yet it was one of them, Telemachus, who in A.D. 403 interrupted the gladiatorial combats in the Colosseum and besought the spectators to renounce this inhuman passion. The frustrated audience stoned him to death for interfering with their pleasures, but his protest eventually brought about the formal abolition of the shows by Honorius as being contrary to the spirit and principles of Christianity. It was a century later before the wild-beast shows were also (temporarily) abolished.

The epitaph which Alcuin composed against his death in A.D. 804 reads:

The world's delight I followed with a heart
Unsatisfied: ashes am I and dust.
Wherefore bethink thee rather of thy soul
Than of thy flesh – this dieth, that abides.
Dost thou make wide thy fields? In this small house
Peace holds me now: no greater house for thee.
Wouldst have thy body clothed in royal red?
The worm is hungry for that body's meat.
Even as the flowers die in a cruel wind,
Even so, flesh, shall perish all thy pride. (tr. Waddell, 1929, 95)

The same century saw the production of a rollicking drinking-song about the abbot of Angers[27] which tells how the townsfolk will never see the like again of this prelate who drank so much that the wine pickled his body against corruption. As the time 'to stand and stare' marginally increases, there is growing expression of a joy in nature, in the seasons and in the flora and fauna. [28] From the next century a popular and widely distributed song has arrived whose author clearly feels the rising of the Spring sap:

Now the snow's melting,
Out the leaves start,
The nightingale's singing
Love's in the heart.

Dearest, delay not,
Ours love to learn,
I live not without thee,
Love's hour is come.

What boots delay, love,
Since love must be?
Make no more stay, love,
I wait for thee. (tr. Waddell, 1929, 144f.)

Earlier than this, as order was increasingly restored, some respite was being gained generally from the business of mere survival. The Church had seen the practical implications of some of her doctrines about the nature of man and had not only instituted holy days but, through Charlemagne, had incorporated into the social structure a legal decree that disallowed servile work on Sundays and saints' days. This prohibition was repeated by Charlemagne's son in A.D. 827 in an enactment that bade people congregate for Mass in their local church on such days.[29] People seem to have obeyed such instructions which became general, but when they had celebrated in church they did not return quietly to their hovels but spent the rest of the free day in social intercourse, in dancing, singing and buffoonery. 'They were very merry and not at all refined, and the place they always chose for their dances was the churchyard; and unluckily the songs they sang as they danced in a ring were the old pagan songs of their forefathers, left over from May-Day festivities which they could not forget, or ribald love-songs which the Church disliked.' (Power, 1939, 25.)

It had certainly been the Church's policy, as represented by the instructions that Pope Gregory had given to Augustine for his mission to England, that as much of the old customs, ceremonies, seasons and sites should be retained as were not inconsistent with the fulfilling character of the new religion.[30] The results of this wise advice, however, were not always pleasing to subsequent ecclesiastical authority, for frequently we find councils complaining that peasants (and sometimes priests of the same social class) were singing 'wicked songs with a chorus of dancing women' or that they were taking part in 'ballads and dancings and evil and wanton songs and such-like lures of the devil' (cf. Chambers, 1913, i, 161–3).

A few centuries later, stories were being told which related the dire judgments which could fall on such unrepentant and indefatigable dancers. Sometimes they explained the existence of the individual monoliths in prehistoric stone-circles as the remains of such dancers who had been petrified where they stood. There was the legend of the dancers of Kölbigk, which existed in several forms, who were punished for dancing on Christmas Eve in spite of their priest's admonitions. Nearer home there was a tale about a Worcestershire parish priest who was kept awake by churchyard dancers singing an interminable song with the refrain, 'Sweetheart, have pity'. These words so fixed themselves in the priest's mind that at Mass next

morning instead of 'Dominus vobiscum' he greeted his congregation
with the words 'Sweetheart, have pity.' This event created such a
scandal that it found its way into the gossipy chronicle of Giraldus
Cambrensis (Power, 1939, 26).

SUMMARY

The Dark Ages acquired their name from the paucity of literary
remains which means, *a fortiori*, that evidence for attitudes towards
the body is very scant indeed. However, we have seen Boethius, at the
beginning of this period, hanging on to order and reason and indicating the survival of some elements of the ancient world (if only
circuses and senators). In his work we seen the continuation of an
evaluation forced by the collapse of the old value-system. On the one
hand the body is seen to be an illusory source of happiness and, on
the other, there is emphasis on the wholeness of man and a clear
vision of his highest potential. We have noticed the rapid growth of
solitaries and monks which can be variously assessed, but there can
be little doubt of the positive effects of Benedictinism with its notion
of a rational and balanced discipline of body, mind and spirit within
a stable community. Indeed the foundations of Christendom, and
therefore of European culture, were laid in the Benedictine centuries. Both the scholarship of Bede and Alcuin and the political and
cultural achievements of Charlemagne are seen as by-products of this
characteristically Western monasticism. Physical strength is
redirected towards defence and reconstruction and the barbarians
become rebuilders of civilisation. Glimpses are seen of both old and
new attitudes towards the body and the possibility of a synthesis.
Some of the negative consequences, as well as the nearly superhuman
achievements, have been pointed to as we have tried to indicate that
the results may have been as much an existential decision as a forced
reconsideration.

MEDIAEVAL SYNTHESIS AND PROMISE

After awaiting with bated breath for the arrival of the millenarian year A.D. 1000 and finding that the world had not ended with its advent, Christian civilisation took a deep breath to march into the second millennium, celebrating the fact with a frenzied outburst of new architecture and artistic creation of every kind. These events, activities and productions are usually bundled together under the concept of the eleventh-century Renaissance whose largest and most lasting monuments are ecclesiastical buildings.

> Thereafter, after the above-mentioned year of the millennium which is now about three years past, there occurred throughout the world, especially in Italy and Gaul, a rebuilding of church basilicas. Notwithstanding that the greater number were already established and not in the least need [of repair], nevertheless each Christian congregation competed with the others in the erection of new ones. It was if the whole world, having cast of the old by shaking itself, were clothing itself everywhere with the white robe of the Church. (Cited Holt, 1957, I, 18.)

Thus Rudolf the Bald, a Cluniac monk who died *c*. 1046, mixing metaphors from a snake sloughing its skin and the imagery of Easter baptism, described the white rash of new building in the Romanesque style that was soon to be seen in every town and nearly every village of Europe.

Pursuit of purity

This is not the place to describe the riotous imagination that covered manuscripts with exuberant decoration, that made pillars into forests peopled with monsters, that converted drain-pipes into gargoyles and functional stone into genre scenes. Some of this decoration could be described as edifying, some as world-accepting wonder at the variety of life and its myriad forms, while others seem either to reflect the love of the grotesque which is almost a characteristic of the Middle Ages or to be a therapeutic exercise to exorcise the demons which were never too far away, even in church. In this riotous creation there is an abundance of bodies, naked and clothed: animal, vegetable, mineral and hybrid: and they are frequently engaged in very natural and even unnatural activities.[1]

The austere St Bernard of Clairvaux, reformer of the reformed Cluniac Order, founder of the Cistercians, found such artistic extravaganzas both unbecoming and distracting – especially when they appeared in monasteries:

> To what purpose are those unclean apes, those fierce lions, those monstrous centaurs, those half-men, those striped tigers, those fighting knights, those hunters winding their horns? Many bodies are there seen under one head or, again, many heads to a single body. Here is a four-footed beast with a serpent's tail; there a fish with a beast's head. Here again, the forepart of a horse trails half a goat behind it or a horned beast bears the hinder quarters of a horse. In short, so many and so marvellous are the varieties of divers shapes on every hand, that we are more tempted to read in the marble than in our books, and to spend the whole day in wondering at these things than in meditating on the law of God. For God's sake, if men are not ashamed of these follies, why at least do they not shrink from the expence? (*Apologia to William of St Thierry*, tr. Coulton, 1938, IV, 72f.).

So conspicuous expenditure and unedifying frivolity were banished from Cistercian houses, the precious metals of the altar plate used by other orders was replaced by wood and base metal and Cistercian architects, in their pursuit of purity, produced their own building style which still, even in ruin,[2] impresses by its sheer unadorned beauty.

St Bernard was the most influential individual of his age and it has been said that 'an adequate account of his career would embrace the entire history of the first half of the twelfth century' (Taylor, 1938, I, 408). The figure of this gentle ascetic, harder with himself than with anyone else, one of those rare characters who, like Augustine, was obsessively in love with God, is projected clearly across the dividing ages:

> As a helpmeet for his holy spirit, God made his body to conform. In his flesh was visible a certain grace, but spiritual rather than of the flesh. A brightness not of earth shone in his look; there was an angelic purity in his eyes and a dove-like simplicity. The beauty of the inner man was so great that it would burst forth in visible tokens and the outer man would seem bathed from the store of inward purity and copious grace. His frame was of the slightest and most spare of flesh; a blush often tinged the delicate skin of his cheeks. . . . His hair was bright yellow, his beard reddish [with some white hairs towards the end of his life]. Actually of medium stature, he looked taller. (*Contemporary Biography*, tr. Taylor, 1938, I, 408f.)

We have described Bernard as obsessed with love and it is no surprise that one of his most famous commentaries is on the 'Song of Songs'. Like Augustine before him, he moved from the sanctified word *caritas* to the more secular *amor* and even *cupiditas* to indicate the element of desire in even that highest love which is the sublimation of earthly affection:

> Because we are of the flesh and are begotten through the con-cupiscence of the flesh, our yearning love must begin from the flesh; yet, if rightly directed, advancing under the leadership of grace, it will be consummated in spirit.[3] For that which is first is not spiritual, but that which is natural (animale); then that which is spiritual.[4] First, man loves himself for his own sake; for he is flesh and is able to understand nothing beyond himself. When he sees that he cannot exist by himself alone, he begins (as it were from necessity) to seek and love God. Thus, in this second stage he loves God, but only for his own sake. Yet, as his necessities lead him to cultivate and dwell with God in thinking, reading, praying and obeying; little by little God becomes known and becomes sweet. Having thus 'tasted how sweet the Lord is', he passes to the third stage, where he loves God for God's sake. I do not know if any man has perfectly attained the fourth stage in this life, the stage where he loves himself for God's sake. Let those say who have knowledge; for myself, I confess it seems impossible. Doubtless, it will be so when the good and faithful servant shall have entered into the joy of his Lord and shall be drunk with the flowing richness of God's house. Then, oblivious of himself, he will pass to God and become one spirit with Him. (Taylor, 1938, I, 422.)

Profound and intense friendships between great individuals seem to be characteristic of this age.[5] So it was between Bernard and Guigo to whom the above letter was addressed and between Francis and Clare and Dominic and Scholastica and doubtless the relationship between Abailard and Héloïse had some of the same elements. Abailard was Bernard's contemporary and bitterly op-posed by the latter in spite of the fact that 'he stood for the same things intellectually which Bernard represented emotionally'. (Heer, 1966, 107).

The concept of personality had been forged amidst the disasters of the Dark Ages[6] and with the growing order of the Middle Ages it produces a new kind of total love which has significance for attitudes to the body, even if its implications have still not been fully worked out. For this reason some attention will be given to the story of Héloïse and her love for the man with the acutest mind of the time. It began in triumph, hymned by the admiring students of the nascent

University of Paris, it continued into a secret marriage and the ferocious revenge of Héloïse's clerical uncle and guardian and apparently died after their separation into the life of the cloister apart from a few personal letters.[7]

The tale is even more thoroughly mediaeval than the stories of Parsifal.[8] Love of God and love of one of the opposite sex are almost inextricably intertwined. Héloïse was only possible in the Middle Ages, but to subsequent ages she has been an exemplar of the supreme capacity for human love: 'For loving out to the full conclusions of love's convictions, and for feeling in their full range and power whatever moods and emotions could arise from an unhappy situation and a passion as deeply felt as it was deeply thought upon.' (Taylor, 1938, II, 29). Abailard, as often with the man involved, proved the less mature. The brilliant academic whose lectures were always thronged, with no sexual experience since, unlike most students, he had always had 'an aversion for those light women whom 'tis a reproach to pursue' ('H.M.' 1901, 6), fell, with all the passion and confusion of an adolescent, into love with his highly educated, intelligent and beautiful private pupil. 'I thought of nothing but Héloïse; everything brought her image into my mind. I was pensive and restless, and my passion was so violent as to admit of no restraint. . . . I would not have exchanged my happy position for that of the greatest monarch upon earth.' ('H.M.', 1901, 8.)

He declared his love nervously but Héloïse was not offended, only wishing that he had either 'not made this declaration or that [she] were at liberty not to suspect [his] sincerity' (H.M., 1901, 9). Eventually, he convinced her of the reality of his total love and an emotional union followed their intellectual one, though the latter was gradually eroded by the sheer pleasure of being in each other's presence. 'The same house, the same love, united our persons and our desires. How many soft moments did we pass together! We took all opportunities to express to each other our mutual affection and we were ingenious in contriving incidents which might give us a plausible occasion for meeting.' (H.M., 1901, 9). The admired philosopher ruefully admits the feebleness of reason when faced with overpowering emotion as Love, 'this tyrant of the mind triumphed over all my wisdom; his darts were of greater force than all my reasonings, and with a sweet constraint he led me wherever he pleased' ('H.M.', 1901, 9). His passionate assiduity was eventually rewarded and when Canon Fulbert and the rest of his household were asleep they 'improved the time proper with the sweets of love'. But physical consummation brought no relief and in his obsession he neglected both his other pupils and his own studies, giving up Aristotle for the composition of love-songs which made their relationship a general topic throughout the cathedral and university city.

Fulbert reluctantly believed the gossip and expelled Abailard from his lodging in the canonry, but the lovers maintained contact and when Héloïse discovered her pregnancy[9] she escaped with him to his sister in Brittany where he offered to marry her and sacrifice his clerical career.

> She strongly disapproved and urged two reasons against the marriage: the danger and the disgrace in which it would involve me. . . . She asked how she was to have any glory in me when she should have made me inglorious and humiliated both herself and me. What penalties the world would exact from her if she deprived it of such a luminary; what curses, what damage to the Church, what lamentations of philosophers would follow this marriage. How indecent, how lamentable it would be for a man whom nature had made for all, to declare that he belonged to one woman and subject himself to such shame. (Cited Taylor, 1938, II, 32.)

Her refusal was buttressed by quotations from St Paul, Roman and Greek philosophers, the examples of Jewish and Gentile worthies, and the sheer practical problems involved in Abailard's 'solution'. 'What sweet accord there would be between the students and the domestics, between copyists and cradles, between books and distaffs, between pen and spindle. Who, engaged in religious or philosophical meditations, could endure a baby's crying and the nurse's nursery rhymes to quieten it and all the noise of the servants? Could you put up with the dirty ways of children?' (Taylor, 1938, II, 33). Such combined occupations might be possible in the spaciousness of a wealthy household but 'the state of the rich is not that of philosophers'. There is no need to institutionalise a lapse and let 'yourself be smothered in filth inextricably. If you do not value the privilege of a clerk, at least defend the dignity of a philosopher.' Abailard remembered that Héloïse concluded her argument by declaring that it was both more fitting for him and sweeter for her that she should be his mistress rather than his wife, 'so that affection alone might keep me hers and not the binding power of any matrimonial chain; and if we should be separated for a time, our joys at meeting would be dearer for their rarity' (Taylor, 1938, II, 34).

The argument was burned into Héloïse's memory, too, for she recalls

> the extreme unwillingness I showed to marry you, though I knew that the name of wife was honourable in the world and holy in

religion; yet the name of your mistress had greater charms because it was more free. The bonds of matrimony, however honourable, still bear with them a necessary engagement and I was very unwilling to be necessitated to love always a man who perhaps always would not love me. I despised the name of wife that I might live happy with that of mistress. . . . If there is anything that may properly be called happiness here below, I am persuaded that it is the union of two persons who love each other with a perfect liberty, who are united by a secret inclination and satisfied with each other's merits. Their hearts are full and leave no room for any other passion; they enjoy perpetual tranquillity because they enjoy content. (H.M., 1901, 30f.)

Héloïse had not studied Augustine for nothing, not only are there reminiscenses in her letters but she knows that self-sacrifice is the ultimate testimony to love. There is a unity in all real love and so she asks him for whose sake she has buried herself alive in a nunnery to give the spiritual guidance that will make her life bearable. Now that their physical connection has been brutally severed cannot he who taught her physical love aid her to the heights of spiritual love? She would not be in the cloister now had there not been from the beginning a spiritual element in their love: 'Nothing but virtue, joined to a love perfectly disengaged from the senses, could have produced such effects. Vice never inspires anything like this, it is too much enslaved to the body.' (H. M., 1901, 29). It was always the whole person and not merely the male that she loved with her total being.

Abailard, inspired by Héloïse, also retired to the cloister: a renunciation doubtless facilitated by the fact that he had been emasculated by bravos hired by the vengeful, and perhaps jealous Fulbert. He put all his remaining energies into teaching, writing and the reform of his recalcitrant community. Origen had castrated himself for love that he might more perfectly follow divine philosophy; Abailard returned to her service when he had been emasculated by the hate of others; Héloïse gives us a glimpse of a supernatural union of earthly and heavenly love, the love of the flesh and the love of the spirit inextricably mingled in one person.

Outcome of the repression of carnality

The students who sang Abailard's songs would include those wandering scholars,[10] clerks in minor orders who were the first undergraduates, usually poverty-stricken yet world-affirmers. In spite of their arduous studies, they seem to have found time for wining and wenching, for gaming and rioting and for writing poetry.

They lampooned the clerical order to which they belonged and in which they hoped for preferment, they wrote exquisite verse in which we can almost sense the mediaeval spring and they sometimes over-reacted against the asceticism which some churchmen taught without burdening theory with practice. The monument of this movement is the *Carmina Burana*,[11] Golias its patron saint and the Arch-poet their major prophet. These are churchmen and they have attitudes to the body, both implicit and explicit, but unfortunately space can only be spared for a few examples. One might compare the almost innocent sensuality of:

> Under the kind branching trees
> Where Philomel complains and sings,
> Most sweet to lie at ease.
> Sweeter to take delight
> Of beauty and the night
> On the fresh springing grass,
> With scent of mint and thyme,
> And for love's bed, the rose.[12]
> Sleep's dew doth ever bless,
> But most, distilled on lovers' weariness. (Waddell, 1927, 149.)

with the near-cynicism of the Arch-poet's unrepentant confession:

> Down the broad way do I go,
> Young and unregretting,
> Wrap me in my vices up,
> Virtue all forgetting,
> Greedier for all delight
> Than heaven to enter in:
> Since the soul in me is dead,
> Better save the skin. (Waddell, 1927, 173f.)

This sensitive genius, knowing both the truth and his own weakness, prayed publicly that he might die in a tavern with a tankard in his hand and that the angels looking down might sing for the souls of all drunkards that God would look kindly upon this and all other such weaklings.

The tavern is a favourite subject for the goliards, since drinking is common to all sorts and conditions of men and 'when we are in the tavern we are not concerned with death'.[13] Love-songs are also popular, but the most frequent subject seems to be delight in Spring and nature. Other poems vary from lyrical to boozy, from bawdy to sharp satire and whatever their mood, they are always full-blooded. Their passion may be earthy but it is never pornographic, and however vicious their invective it is directed at those who preach but do not practise Christianity.[14] The goliards are the songsters of a cultural Spring which will be blighted by the Black Death[15] which hushed their songs and replaced them with the *danse macabre*. But before that final extinction their flaunting of clerical privilege and utter irresponsibility, their near and sometimes actual blasphemy, their irrepressible contempt for office and benefice until they were offered one, slowly eroded the licensed freedom in which they had lived, flourished and found a tolerable sustenance.[16]

As a result of the reforms of Pope Gregory VII (1073–85), clerks had to take a vow of celibacy before they could enter into the major orders of the diaconate, priesthood and episcopate. Much goliardic activity might have been in the nature of 'a final fling', but this regulation, demanding unnatural or heroic continence, from a large minority of the population of Western Europe was extremely popular among the laity at its inception, whatever abuses and scandals developed later. The general reforming work of this austere and dedicated prelate has been described as 'the most momentous of all the actions and movements of modern European history' (Heer, 1966, 70) and the same writer gives his reasons for what, to most contemporary readers, would seem a somewhat eccentric valuation.

> The consequences of Gregorian celibacy for Europe's spiritual history were far-reaching. A special realm of the spirit was detached from the world. An entirely new field of tension was created in which pioneers of the mind and of the heart were to set about constructing a new set of relationships between God and the world and between man and woman. A new kind of purely intellectual labour was made possible, out of which the pure research and pure science of a later age was to grow. At the same time a remarkable culture of the heart evolved. Not only were priests and nuns new men and new women in a literal sense, but all men and women were related in a new, spiritual way. Whereas the archaic world had regarded marriage and sex in terms of legal status, the post-Gregorian church spoke of spiritual and sacramental union. Love was possible outside of marriage, and there were marriages of the spirit like those of Abelard and Héloïse, or Francis de Sales and Françoise de Chantal. The single man who lived a life of celibacy resisted nature and the world and the tension generated by this resistance was inherently creative. (Heer, 1966, 77f.)

Inherently creative it may have been, but it is an old tag that the worst is the corruption of the best, and before the end of the Middle Ages clerical corruption was to become a leitmotiv expressed in almost every kind of art as well as in sermons, exhortations and strenuous efforts of bishops and archdeacons to heal it. Repression was not always creative and resulted in sadism and hysteria, particularly in some convents where not all the inmates had entered from the highest motives. Demonology was enriched by succubi and incubi: the former took the form of nubile women who invaded the beds of males struggling with celibacy, while the latter were masculine equivalents who were particularly troublesome in nuns' dormitories. Many of the tales of saints which were taken by contempories as edifying often strike the modern reader as thinly disguised sexual fantasies or as containing symptoms of mental illness. On the other hand, the *Life of St Alexis* (written by an eleventh-century canon of Rouen) tells of a young man who gave up his love for a maid in favour of a higher spiritual love, renouncing the goods of human affection for the more abiding rewards of claustral life and the story has an ending which is happy for both kinds of human love. In Saintsbury's translation, it concludes as follows:

> Without doubt is St Alexis in heaven.
> He has God with him and the angels for company.
> With him the maiden to whom he made himself strange;
> Now he has her close to him – together are their souls:
> I know not how to tell you how great their joy is. (Cited Waddell, 1927, 77)

Intellectual progress and promise

From such simplicity to the sophisticated intellectualism of St Thomas Aquinas (1225–74) may seem a great step, but perhaps it is not really far. Aquinas built an intellectual cathedral which enshrined the wisdom of the Greeks and the Christian revelation, and when he discussed the faculties which differentiate man from the beasts he has this to say:

> The contemplative life is theirs whose resolve is set upon the contemplation of truth. Resolve is an act of the will because resolve is with respect to the end, which is the object of will. Thus the contemplative life, according to the essence of its action, is of the intelligence; but so far as it pertains to what moves us to engage in such action, it is of the will, which moves all the other faculties, including the intelligence, to act. Appetitive energy moves towards contemplating something, either sensibly or intellectually: sometimes from love of the thing seen, and sometimes from the love of the knowledge itself, which arises from contemplation. And because of this, Gregory sets the contemplative

life in the love of God. . . . inasmuch as someone, from a willing love of God, burns to behold His beauty. And because anyone is rejoiced when he attains what he loves, the contemplative life is directed towards enjoyment which lies in affect; by which Love also is intended. (tr. Taylor, 1938, II, 512.)[17]

Man's ultimate beatitude embraces will and love as well as intellect, and his fulfilment is in the Beatific Vision of God. Though Aquinas' emphases have earned him the title of 'angelic doctor', he never lost sight of the true nature of man which was, so to speak, suspended between the inanimate and brute creation and the celestial hierarchy of glorious spirits. In his consideration of the original creation of man, he makes the following remarks which are relevant to our theme:

Animals lack reason. But what makes man like the animals in copulation is the inability of reason to temper the pleasure of copulation and the heat of desire. But in the state of innocence, there would have been nothing of this sort that was not tempered by reason. Not that the pleasurable sensation would have been any the less intense, as some say,[18] for the pleasure of sense would have been all the greater, given the greater purity of man's nature and sensibility of his body. But the pleasure-urge would not have squandered itself in so disorderly a fashion on this sort of pleasure when it was ruled by reason. It is not demanded by this empire of reason that the pleasurable sensation should be any the less, but that the pleasure-urge should not clutch at the pleasure in an immoderate fashion; and by 'immoderate' I mean going beyond the measure of reason. Thus a sober man has no less pleasure in food taken moderately than a greedy man; but his pleasure-urge does not wallow so much in this sort of pleasure. And this is the bearing of Augustine's words,[19] which do not exclude intensity of pleasure from the state of innocence, but impetuous lust and disturbance of mind. (Gilby, 1964, XIII, 157.)

Not only are copulation and its attendant pleasure part of our nature but it is part of our unfallen nature, and the pleasures of the flesh would be even greater than they are if it had not been for the Fall. There is nothing wrong with the pleasure, it is the abdication or overthrow of the reason through the pleasures of the body wherein the disorder lies. Even that very reason which is the crown of man's faculties is essentially dependent on the body.

It is clear. . . . that the use of reason depends in some way on the use of the powers of sense; so that when the senses are locked and the inner sense-capacities are blocked, a man does not have the untrammelled use of reason – as you can see with sleepers and maniacs. Now the senses are, in fact, the capacities of the bodily organs; so that when their organs are obstructed their activities must be obstructed too and so, in consequence, must be the use of reason. (Gilby, 1964, XIII, 181.)

There are implications here for the training of the senses and for the care of their related bodily organs. St Thomas is aware that the fitness of the body is a prerequisite for the use of reason[20] and that the full functioning of reason is not only affected by the limitations of the body but also by its corruptibility, the effects of disease and age: 'The decadence of the body imposes a burden in blocking the use of reason with reference even to things that concern a man at any stage of his life.' (Gilby, 1964, XIII, 181.)

It is not only senility which places man at a disadvantage or affects his capacity, there are problems at the other end of the life-span: not merely the problems of growth up to maturity but also the fact that the new-born human is at a disadvantage compared with other animals in respect to the mental and physical capacities of the neonate. Though 'there are other animals which do not have so finished a use of their natural bents to begin with as they do later on. . . . yet in man at the beginning of his life there is a special obstruction' (Gilby, 1964, XIII, 1811) to the rapid development of those innate faculties. This St Thomas explains is due to the peculiar physiological character of the human brain (Gilby, 1964, XIII, 181). He also seems to think that this handicap is another of the consequences of the Fall.

Attitudes to the body are not only expressed by theologians but also in the popular ideas about and attitudes towards hygiene and body care. Some popular and ignorant writers have described the Middle Ages as the 'unwashed centuries', but this is neither accurate nor fair. On the one hand, the Church and especially the monasteries were pioneers in sanitation and water supply, so that literally cleanliness was often next to godliness. On the other hand, the theory and practice of Roman civil engineering, including hydraulics, had been obliterated by the barbarian invasions and there were severe technical difficulties in the way of a hot bath. The monasteries made a communal beginning by making provision for washing before every meal by building a *lavatorium* with running water and towels at the entrance to their refectories. Complex conduit systems brought water here and elsewhere and the 'garderobes' as antiquarians call the 'neccies' were probably the first, since the Romans, to be flushed by running water.[21] We must remember, too, that bathing does not require a bath in the sense of an iron or marble receptacle large enough for the occupant(s) to assume a prone position. There is little, if any, archeological evidence of 'built-in' baths, though there are the remains of a mysterious 'cistern' at Kirkstall which could be a bath,[22] and both literature and art testify to the existence of utensils designed for an operation somewhat akin to a modern bed-bath.

Because of the difficulties involved in heating and transporting the thirty gallons or so of water involved, tubbing became a corporate affair, often involving the whole family, guests and even participants beyond this circle. Mediaeval life was much more congested than most people imagine, and domestic conditions, even in high society, were straitened so that there was little privacy of any sort. Outside the bath, nakedness was more likely to be a sign of poverty than of lubricity, and that may explain why the unclothed figure tends to appear in mediaeval art usually as a mark of humility or innocence.[23] If clothes did not make the man, they certainly indicated his status and function.[24] The Middle Ages may have been concerned with the virtue of modesty, but they do not seem to have confused it with the 'emotion' of shyness.[25] Apart from sculpture in so generally public a place as a cathedral or church, manuscripts have illustrations of knights interrupting their quest to assist ladies taking an open-air bath, and literature has a number of stories of amorous affairs which began with an almost ritualistic act of bathing together.[26]

Besides the ceremonious bathing in wealthier households (sometimes accompanied by music, food and wine) and the poor countryman's bathing in his local river or stream, there were also public baths in the towns.[27] By the fourteenth century these were a prolific and flourishing institution. In Southwark alone there were eighteen of these establishments and, besides bathing facilities, they offered barbering, bleeding and minor operations. They also provided another service which gave their name of 'stews', 'bagnio' or 'bordello' another connotation which eventually ousted the prime meaning of these various words for 'bath'. Consequently, the reforming King Henry VIII, who had no need for these public services, closed them by royal ordinance and the public bath died out until the eighteenth century when bathing was regarded as a medical and professional process rather than a cleansing and social one.

There are many other sources of evidence for the mediaeval attitude to the body, for example their sports and recreations, but these latter are probably adequately covered elsewhere.[28] However, as an example of the expressive use of the body we may give the example from the University of Paris in the late fifteenth century. This pre-eminent seat of learning had stood on its corporate privileges when Louis XI wished to enrol the students for his wars and they firmly refused, but they were sufficiently loyal to celebrate his victory by dancing seven days and nights without intermission.

It is easy to assume in the Middle Ages (and most others) that the intellectual and ascetic publications of the clergy, especially when they are the dominant literary group, are representative of the thought of the Church which essentially consists of the laity ('the people of God'). We may catch a qualifying glimpse of popular attitudes in 'The ages of faith' in popular pastimes and, by reflection, in mediaeval sermons. Because of their nature, most of these latter have not survived, but something of their content can be picked up fairly easily.[29] A glance at the index to Owst (1966) will show that there are no entries under 'flesh', 'body', 'carnal', 'corporeal', or even under 'fornication' or 'concupiscence' so it would seem, at least, that there was no obsessive hatred of the body. There is, however, a good deal of preaching against the sins of the flesh: sloth, avarice, pride, drunkenness (frequently described as 'mother of vices') and lechery (largely directed against the clergy).

Perhaps more significantly, the preachers seem to display a good deal of pessimism about matrimony of which the following short extract must serve as an example: 'Daily experience suffices to show that those who wed for beauty, for sensual pleasure or for riches swiftly lose peace of heart and rest of body and are changed into states of the greatest hatreds, discords, blows and adulteries.' (Owst, 1966, 379.) It is possible that this pessimism should not be taken entirely seriously since there is undoubtedly a strong satiric element in popular preaching of this date and much of the satire is directed against women.[30] Some have seen this as an indication of the unbalanced or even envious view of a celibate clergy, but it is more likely that it is an exaggeration of a real contemporary situation. Then people were thrown together more, there were few places where they could be alone, life was short, widow-hood or death in childbirth likely and there were powerful commercial and material interests in marriage, not only in the politico-dynastic unions of the upper class but also a good deal lower down the social scale.

Probably as a reaction against contemporary marriage and to some extent parasitic upon it arose the aristocratic and privileged notion of courtly love[31] which seems to have originated in Provence with its associations of troubadours, knights and ladies and romantic love. This movement was a kind of lay spirituality, partly Christian and partly anti-Christian. Its virtues were bodily strength, manly virtues, fealty and 'courtesy', though the latter only applies to peers in the same (upper) social class. Its reference figures are not the saints but model knights like Parzifal, Tristan and Lancelot, and its equivalent to the sacraments were the powers of woman, nature and magic. Though its means were different from the orthodox Christian ones its ends were similar, for it saw this life as a pilgrimage or quest, a progress from immaturity to understanding, in which faults are purged through suffering and man is finally redeemed by love. [32]

In spite of its origins in the aristocratic courts (Eleanor of Aquitaine was one of its proponents and exponents), this cult was basically anarchic and socially solvent, an attempt to set up a new scale of values [33] from those which had brought Europe through a long gestation to a painful birth. It is not without affinities with Catharism or Albigensianism, though this religious movement had adherents at all levels of society (except perhaps the very lowest). Catharism apparently originated in Bulgaria in the tenth century and reached northern Italy and southern France (hence the alternative name from Albi) two centuries later. It settled into an anti-Christian set of beliefs which saw no values in earthly life though its members claimed to be representing the purest and most spiritual form of Christianity. Its élite abstained from flesh in all its forms: meat, eggs, milk, marriage, sex. They described the institutional Church with their most opprobious epithet '*ecclesia carnalis*', and one reason why they considered animal life sacred was because they believed a beast's body might contain a transmigrated human soul. They replaced the Christian sacrament of Christ's Body and Blood by their own once-and-for-all *consolamentum*. This was a solemn ceremony by means of which the tested candidate was believed to receive back his own holy spirit which had been left behind in Paradise when the angels fell. Once his spirit had been strengthened and detached from the material worls, there was no further purpose in life for the 'perfect' and consequently suicide was logical, preferably by refraining from food and drink. If marriage took place among this sect it was not to be consummated, for procreation would be a sin prolonging and increasing the unnatural union of spirit and body in man. But since they were free from desire (*Ćathar* means 'pure'), men and women could sleep together without danger of procreating. Their obsession with non-procreation aroused the hostile accusation that they were accustomed to intercourse *per anum* and this practice was so identified with them that their popular name of 'Bulgars' (from their originating country) became, slightly modified, the Western European name for the practitioners of this type of coitus.

Other bodily aberrations of the Middle Ages would include the sporadic outbursts of dancing mania and public flagellation which seem to have had a markedly hysterical character. Dancing came under ecclesiastical disapproval because of its pagan associations [34] and also when, as a result of its insistent rhythms, it produced frenzy [35] or sexual orgies. Flagellation as a form of self-punishment or reparation[36] had support from church leaders at its beginning, but the growing excesses and the effects of its public performance led to their condemning it in the middle of the fourteenth century.

SUMMARY

Having provided some kind of panorama or a series of vignettes of the long and varied period we call the Middle Ages, it is perhaps time to draw these impressions together. There were those who thought all well lost for the love of God and in their supernatural pursuit found the desires and needs of the body something of a hindrance. Some have left no memorial, but we have a little knowledge of the possible heroic pursuits and achievements from the notable school of English mystics in the fourteenth century.[37] Besides the rare saints there were less balanced souls who, for various reasons, had committed themselves to the priestly or religious life and had either given up the struggle to maintain their celibacy or else compensated for it by other bodily excess or tried to distract themselves with gambling, worldly affairs or sport (especially hunting). There were also the un-balanced souls who shought release from their intolerable tensions in frenzy and self-delusion in their alleged service of either God or demonic forces.

Much of the medieval imbalance or tension was due to the contrast between their ideals and the spotted actuality and to the actual conditions of the time which produced a sharp dichotomy between the serene life of the spirit and everyday events: savage physical punishment and torture, mutilations due to men or to disease, the inconsistency of the clergy and the tyranny and caprice of the powerful. Nevertheless, as we approach the end of the thirteenth century it is possible to see the potentiality of a balanced, humane world-view.[38] Intellectual order had largely been established[39] – its monument is the sanctified common sense and sharp intellectual-ism of St Thomas Aquinas – and social order was developing in a Europe that was becoming selfconscious, though at different speeds in different countries and not without relapses. There was a breaking down of the division of sacred and secular expressed, for instance, in the use of very secular tunes for sacred services and the production of very worldly words to accompany sanctified tunes. The riotous flowering of art produced some of the masterpieces of human culture in which nature and men were portrayed with a joy enfolded by a wonder and thankfulness for God's whole creation. Perhaps the most obvious symbol of this unified culture was the Gothic cathedral which even in decay, stripped of colour, furnishings and much of its rich ornament, is still a source of wonder. Within cathedral art there was a tolerant acceptance of the human condition and of the weakness of human flesh,[40] surprising to many observant moderns, which united reality and aspiration in a building dedicated to God's service, but frequently used for mundane offices.

The same attitude has other manifestations: the cult of the fool – the licensed jester who spoke many a truth, and the institution of Carneval – the licensed farewell to the flesh which allowed a merciful safety-valve before the rigours of Lenten abstinence. It was a time of feast and festival, an attempt to sanctify time not only by Michaelmass, Christmass, Candlesmass, etc. which bear witness to the prime celebration, but also to bodily celebration[42] through dance, feasting and communal jollity. Holy days were holidays, 'feast' is still the technical word for an important liturgical celebration and the tourist and town clerk's pursuit of fiestas and festivals, with whatever motives, may indicate something of our loss.[41]

Whatever potentialities or actualities might have been slowly growing, they were scythed down by the virulent outbreaks of bubonic plague, known as the Black Death,[43] which reached Europe in the last days of 1347. Death had always been a concern of realistic mediaeval man, now it became an obsession. The *danse macabre* was born and its fleshless fingers grasp art and literature and the flagellants returned with magnified numbers and more compelling hysteria. The consequences of this lethal disease were visible in every aspect of life and thought: in agriculture and architecture, in college and cloister, in social and economic conditions, in religious beliefs and practice,[44] as well as in general attitudes and assumptions. If this disaster did not kill the Middle Ages, it rendered it too weak to survive the further crises that were to arrive in the following centuries.[45]

The eleventh century sees a second Renaissance and even descriptions of the reforming ascetic Bernard of Clairvaux emphasise the beauty of his body as harmonising with his glorious soul. He taught a love which had its foundations in the flesh and ascends to the spirit, while the story of Abailard and Héloïse represents a tragic dénouement of a love in which carnal and spiritual elements were inextricably mingled. We have told their story in some detail as its contemplation yields profound insights into mediaeval assumptions and attitudes towards the body and the nature and destiny of man, compounded of body, mind and spirit, who lives intensely in this world yet aims beyond its confines.

An attempt has been made to assess the effects of clericalism, particularly in the requirement of celibacy, in both terms of idealism

and in terms of reality. St Thomas Aquinas has been briefly considered as the epitome of the mediaeval intellectual synthesis, with
particular reference to his evaluation of the body. Finally, we have
drawn attention to some of the .possible non-literary sources from
which some idea of mediaeval attitudes in this area may be gained,
and concluded that there seems to have been signs of a most acceptable and fruitful synthesis before the onset of the Black Death
and its shattering consequences.

THE BLIGHTED FLOWER OF THE RENAISSANCE

With the Renaissance, the simplicities and unifications, real or imagined, partial or virtual, of the Middle Ages are fragmented. This is not the place to examine the concept of the Renaissance: whether it existed, what it was, or whether there was a Renaissance or several.[1] We shall assume that there was an identifiable movement in the fifteenth century which first manifested itself powerfully in Italy and that this movement, initially at least, was closely related to the revived study of the classics. It can be seen as a special case of the fascination with the ancient world and its culture which was a recurring and extremely fruitful element in mediaeval culture. However, this final fruition seems somewhat overripe, if not corrupt, and the thin withholding skin finally burst and the fruit disintegrated. Much of the unprotected seed died and some produced very strange growths indeed.

The advent of conceptualism

Disintegration was not immediate: there were noble and energetic attempts to wed the 'New Learning' with Christian tradition, and even when they failed fragments of the attempted synthesis persisted for centuries. But, from the beginning, there were obvious new movements or inordinate presentations of earlier ones. The State becomes reified and the monstrous notion becomes generally accepted that any atrocity is justified in the name of politics.[2] The attention of poet, painter and philosopher becomes more interested in man as 'the measure of things' than in God as the beginning and end of Creation. Yet much Renaissance thinking is derivative, not only in its slavish imitation of the classics but also in its unacknowledged and often misunderstood transmission of mediaeval ideas. Santillana (1956, 19) writes: 'The Renaissance hits its creative stride only when it finds really new ground in the plastic arts. But a gap always remains between the originality in the arts and the derivative aspect of the purely intellectual and verbal achievements. The accent placed on personality is not always sufficient to fill that gap.'[3]

The characteristic anthropocentrism can be seen as a demonic expression of that pride which was to the mediaevals the chief of all sins, the ultimate source of disorder in man, society and the universe at large. From another point of view, this same characteristic can be seen as Promethean, for example in these words of Tommaso Campanella, poet and philosopher, passionate Catholic and Dominican friar:

> Man was once child, was embryo, seed and blood,
> Bread, grass and sundry things, in which it pleased
> Him to be what he was, nor did he crave
> To be what now he is;
> And what is now to him so frightening
> To become fire, and earth, and mouse, and snake,
> Will be his pleasure then, and he'll be glad
> To be what he shall be, for in all things
> God's thought is shining through
> And all the past forgotten.[4]

Less orthodox thinkers displaced reason as the traditional teleological force of the universe by an almost vitalist function of matter as, for example Bernardino Telesio, who ascribed sentiency to matter, made mentality a property of matter and demanded material existence for the soul itself.[5] However, the majority opinion was a refurbishing and simplification of the mediaeval view which was accepted in common by poets, physicians, philosophers, laity and clergy.

Man was a rational animal (as Aristotle had taught) and essentially composite in his being: partly akin to the angels, who are rational and not animal, and partly akin to the beasts who are animal and not rational – he was differentiated by being corporeal *and* possessed of a rational soul. 'Soul' was more or less equivalent to 'the principle of life' and, consequently, there were not only 'rational' souls but also 'sensitive and 'vegetative' ones. The latter were held to be concerned with nutrition, growth and propagation and thus possessed by all forms of organic life. Animals possessed this, but they were also endowed with the powers of sentience. This sensitive soul subsumed the vegetative one, while the rational soul subsumed both with the addition of reason. Because of their dominant attributes the rational soul is sometimes simply called Reason and the sensitive soul, Sensuality.

This is all thoroughly mediaeval and exemplified in the tale of the saintly but somewhat boring parson[6] who expounds the accepted principles that order in both the physical and moral universe is of God but 'in mannes sinne is every manere of ordre or ordinance turned up-so-doun' and concludes: 'For it is sooth [true] that God, and reson, and sensualitee, and the body of man been so ordeyned, that everich of thise foure thinges sholde have lordshipe over that other; as thus: God sholde have lordshipe over reson, and reson over sensualitee, and sensualitee over the body of man.' This mediaeval hierarchy and ladder from the body to the life of sense, from the life of sense to the life of reason and from the life of reason to the life of God persisted not only through the Renaissance and into the Reformation era but even for centuries beyond.[7]

Against Telesio's idiosyncratic view, the general opinion was that all three kinds of soul were essentially immaterial, but they differed in that each rational soul was thought to be directly and individually created by God to be the 'form' of a specific body, whereas the other kinds of soul were mediately produced by what we would call natural developments and transmutations within the total activity of creation. Some Renaissance speculative thinkers did toy with the antique idea of metempsychosis or transmigration of souls with the implied denigration of the body,[8] but most more or less followed Aquinas'[9] orthodox assimilation of ancient ideas in believing that death was no part of the original created order and that it was not the soul's nature to leave the body, but rather unnatural of the body (denatured by the Fall) to desert the soul.

Renaissance writers, having abandoned some of the nice distinctions of their mediaeval predecessors, sometimes used 'reason' for the rational soul in its entirety and sometimes for the lower of the two faculties possessed by the rational soul (previously distinguished as 'intellectus' and 'ratio'). Traditionally, 'intellectus' was concerned with the direct apprehension of truth: 'seeing' something as self-evident – a rare human accomplishment but a normal angelic activity. 'Ratio' related to the gradual process by which one proves or acquires a truth which is not immediately apparent. These two kinds of comprehension seemed to be necessitated by both logic and experience, since nothing could be proved if nothing were self-evident as there would be no starting-point. As Lewis (1967a, 157) says: 'Man's mental life is spent in laboriously connecting those frequent but momentary flashes of "intelligentia" which constitute "intellectus".'

The sensitive soul was thought to possess ten senses or 'wits': the outward ones corresponding to the popular 'five senses' together with the 'inward wits' of memory, estimation, imagination, fantasy and 'common wit'.[10] The second of these roughly corresponds to our 'instinct', while 'imagination' is the operation of bringing to mind concepts or ideas on which 'fantasy' can work. 'Common wit' acts as a sort of co-ordinator or referee of the others: in Lewis's words (1967a, 165) it 'turns mere sensations into coherent consciousness of myself as subject in a world of objects'. Finally, as far as the activities of the soul are concerned, the vegetative soul was thought to be responsible for all unconscious, involuntary processes in our organism: nutrition, secretion, growth, reproduction, etc. including what we would call glandular activity and the operations of the autonomous nervous system.

Since they generally accepted all souls to be immaterial, Renaissance thinkers were faced with the problem of the relation of the immaterial soul to a material and mortal body. They postulated an intermediate 'spirit' or 'spirits'[11] whose failure in liaison could account for such a phenomenon as insanity without the logical contradiction of predicating insanity to the rational soul.

The soul of human beings was attached to a body which was not only a halfway point in creation (linking angelic and bestial), but was also a miniature reflection of that creation – a microcosm to the macrocosm. Thus the human body was both a link and a focal point in the great chain of being[12] which manifested the unending plenitude of divine creation, its unfaltering order (apart from sin), and its ultimate unity. This awareness is often considered to be essentially Renaissance in character,[13] but as Tillyard (1966, 11) has pointed out it is really in the purest mediaeval tradition.

In this cosmology of balance, order and correspondence, man was a sort of linchpin of the universe and, of all the correspondences (of which the mediaeval and Renaissance minds were equally fond), the most popular and exciting were the correspondences between man and the cosmos,[14] though there were other interesting ones such as those between the celestial powers and other creations, between the macrocosm and the body politic and between the body politic and the microcosm.

The human body was a microcosm in a number of senses for it, like the whole of material creation, was built out of the 'four contraries'. In the macrocosm these combine to form the four basic elements: earth, air, fire and water, but in the human body they combine to form the 'humours': hot and moist producing blood; hot and dry, choler; cold and moist, phlegm; cold and dry, melancholy. The proportion of the elements in each blending produce *temperamentum* or *complexio* from which the later uses of 'complexion', 'temperament' and 'temper' derive. These proportions vary in individuals, but the dominant element produces a definite character-type with a related somatotype.[15] Renaissance thinkers followed the mediaevals in identifying four basic elemental mixtures which placed each man in his predominant humour. The 'sanguine complexion' seems to have been most highly thought of: its possessor would be plump, cheerful and hopeful, peppery in 'temper' but not vindictive. The 'choleric' man would be tall, violent and 'highly strung', liable to anger and vindictive with it. The 'melancholic' (at the beginning of the Renaissance at least) would be fretful, a poor sleeper and what we would call 'neurotic'. The 'phlegmatic' man was the worst: pale in countenance, sluggish in body and dull in mind.

It was also believed that this basic humour was modified by a daily rhythm[16] in which each of the four humours had a successive and temporary ascendency in the individual, aggravating his state when the upsurge was that of his predominant humour – a condition that was bound to occur for a period in each twenty-four hours. The progression of dominance was held to be as follows: blood from midnight to six a.m., choler from then until noon, melancholy from noon to six p.m., and phlegm thence to midnight. If we remember that in those days human activity was more geared to natural daylight and people both rose and took to their beds earlier, we might recognise, in our own experience, some kind of support for this theory.

Ideas of the relationship between body and soul were subsequently to develop in a variety of ways, of which perhaps the most vulgar was phrenology which, in the nineteenth century, sought to associate cranial bumps with spiritual powers, but even during the Renaissance there was the germ of this idea in the association of skull size with mental powers. Erasmus (1466–1536) was aware of this presumed correlation and was consequently much ashamed of his exceptionally small head which he amplified by wearing an outsize biretta whenever he appeared in public.[17]

Dissemination of attitudes and the assertion of art

Physical care of the body, which had developed in the Middle Ages, continued into the Renaissance, at least in Italy, Burgundy and France[18] and, if he is to be taken as representing the Church's attitude to the body, it might be worth mentioning that Pope Clement VII (1523–34) built a *stufetta* or 'little stew' to embellish his apartments in Castello S. Angelo. It survives[19] in an alcove whose back wall supports a structure oddly reminiscent of the antique 'Memoria' of St Peter. The walls are warmed with hot air in the classical Roman manner, the floor is marble and, according to Wright (1960, 68), the bathroom contains frescoes by Girolamo Romanino, a pupil of Giorgione.[20] A decade earlier Raphael had designed the famous 'secret' erotic frescoes of Venus and Cupid, Cupid and Psyche, Vulcan and Pallas for the bathroom of Cardinal Bibiena in the Vatican.[21]

Problems now multiply in any attempt to trace attitudes to the body in Christian thought. With the spread of lay education, the expansion of material and the growing independence of artists, it becomes increasingly difficult to decide on the locus of 'Christian thought' though the orthodox answer would presumably place it with the laity who *are* the Church. Similarly, it is necessary not only to distinguish between theory and practice, but perhaps also between 'religious' theory and Christian lay practice. Theories designed for the professed religious, i.e. those called to the conventual or eremitical life or even those called to a celibate priesthood, are not necessarily the theories of those who attempt the Christian life 'in the world'. The breakup of the mediaeval synthesis is relevant and the confusion is more confounded by the Renaissance artists' penchant (even when they were convinced and practising Christians) for subjects from pagan mythology.[22] The Church is still, by far, the greatest patron of the arts, but when its agent is a Renaissance cardinal or bishop it is difficult to know when he is playing the role of Christian propagandist or princely patron. Furthermore, the cult of the individual (characteristic of the Renaissance) is associated with increasing artistic independence which is already producing attitudes which will develop into romantic and bohemian concepts of rebellion and unconventionality.

The notion of the artist as a mediator of truth, symbolising the immaterial through the material,[23] was an inheritance from the Middle Ages. In the fifth century, Augustine had suggested that the function of art was to imitate or parallel the plenitude and diversity of God's world and that this creativity would be truly an imitation of God and therefore a religious exercise, *par excellence*. But this remained only a suggestion, since the saint's hierarchy of values and sense of impending catastrophe did not allow its development and he reverts to his other-worldly position: 'Not that those who fashion such works [of art] are to be highly esteemed, nor those who take delight in them; for when the soul is thus intent upon the lesser things – things corporeal which it makes by corporeal means – it is the less fixed upon that supreme Wisdom from those very powers.'[24] One can sympathise with the rejection of aestheticism as a substitute religion and the preference for the contemplative life as against that of the aesthete, but there may be a third possibility. Mediaeval thinkers had seen the life and work of the artist as a special case of the operation of the Gifts of the Holy Spirit.[25] Abbot Suger had used light symbolically and created Gothic architecture for the service of God,[26] Abbot Desiderius had performed the apparently impossible task of rebuilding Monte Cassino through his faith in God's assistance,[27] Villard de Honnecourt, designer and builder of cathedrals, was proud to have had the opportunity of drawing a lion from life,[28] while Durandus had worked out a rationale making cathedral art able to exemplify every aspect of human life and to celebrate the wonder and fecundity of all creation.[29] At the very beginning of the fifteenth century, Cennino Cennini, a direct artistic descendant of Giotto, produced a craftsman's handbook which began by telling how God created humans in His own image and continued by discussing art training. He advocated that the artist's life should be modelled on that of the theologian or philosopher (a far cry from the decadence of *la vie bohème*!) because it was a contemplative oc-cupation, concerned with *theoria*, and therefore required discipline and priorities:

> Your life should always be arranged just as if you were studying theology or philosophy or other 'theories', that is to say, eating and drinking moderately, at least twice a day, electing digestible and wholesome dishes and light wines; saving and sparing your hand, preserving it from such strains as heaving stones, crowbar and many other things which are bad for your hand, from giving them a chance to weary it. There is another cause which, if you indulge it, can make your hand so unsteady that it will waver more, and flutter far more, than leaves do in the wind and this is indulging too much in the company of women. [30]

As we have seen, the nude (considered so characteristic of the Renaissance) was not unknown to Gothic art [31] nor were the fun-damental activities of the human body unrepresented. [32] What might be called the Gothic nude as distinct from a Gothic naked figure comes from the direct tradition and occurs as an illustration of Paradise in the brothers Limbourg's *Tres Riches Heures* (c. A.D. 1411) and it continues through paintings, woodcuts, drawings and engravings well into the sixteenth century. Its later forms seem to assume an anti-feminine bias in the Reformed North and there is a noticeable tendency to portray women as aggressive and dominant, but some have seen its earlier forms as erotic and realistic. [33]

Be that as it may, it seems certain that the naked figures of the early Renaissance are not intended to glorify the human body primarily, if at all, but are rather forms of symbolic communication. The Renaissance flower has its roots well in the soil of the Middle Ages and the symbolisation is largely continuous. For centuries Venus had been used as a symbol and all her attributes carried significant meaning. Most of us are still vaguely aware that Venus has something to do with lechery but in the Middle Ages she had a double aspect or there were two Venuses: 'We read that there are two Venuses, a legitimate Venus and a goddess of lechery. We say that the legitimate Venus is world-music . . . or the equal proportion of earthly things . . . or which others call natural justice. She is in the sidereal heavens,' [34] in times and in animate things. But the shameless Venus, the goddess of lechery, we call concupiscence of the flesh

because she is the mother of all fornication.'[35] In the early
Renaissance, Boccaccio is maintaining a similar distinction: 'Venus
is double. The first one should be understood as the one through
whom every honest and legitimate desire. . . . The second is that one
through whom every lascivious thing is desired.'[36] The Renaissance
was much concerned with high allegory and symbolism and used the
human body to express ideal images. The Venus with whom the
Florentines, whether poets, printers or philosophers, were concerned
was the first Venus – the symbol of harmony in heaven and earth.
Their spokesman is Marsilio Ficino,[37] an urbane but other-worldly
philosopher whose ambition was to unite the earthly wisdom of Plato
with the divine revelation of Christ.[38] He advised his princely pupil,
Pier'-Francesco de' Medici to fix his eyes on Venus, 'i.e. on
Humanitas. For Humanitas is a nymph of excellent comeliness, born
of heaven and more than others beloved of God on high. Her soul
and mind are Love and Charity, her eyes Dignity and Magnanimity,
her hands Liberality and Magnificence, her feet Comeliness and
Modesty. The whole, then, is Temperance and Honesty, Charm and
Splendour. Oh, what·exquisite beauty!'[39] One of Ficino's constant
themes was the mediaeval one of man's intermediate position between brute and God, and he modified the idea of the human soul to
express this, teaching that its lower part links us with the world of the
body and its senses, its higher part by contemplation can be in tune
with the Infinite, while in between stands reason. As his virtues are
not entirely traditional Christian ones, so his psychology reveals
modifications of the mediaeval view, yet there is more continuity
than discontinuity, for example he continues the old idea of the
'psychomachia' – the internal warfare of man's soul between his
animal instincts and the promptings of Divine Reason, a conflict that
can only be stilled by heavenly grace.

The Renaissance has something in common with Gnosticism in
that it can be seen as an aristocratic attempt to rescue truth from the
vulgar Christian mob and preserve it for gentlemen who will appreciate its subtleties. The pagan myths are metamorphised[40] by
Platonic and Christian ideas into arcane symbols through which an
intellectual and aesthetic élite can converse with each other while
hiding the supreme mysteries from the common gaze.[41] In the
Renaissance there is no cult of the body for the body's sake, that
would be unimaginatively vulgar. Rather its *representation* is used as
a vehicle to express the most profound truths, particularly in the
most Christian artists such as Michelangelo and Raphael. If there is a
new element in attitudes to the body it is possibly the abolition of the
frigidity which Stoic philosophy had identified with virtue, and this
change might be regarded as a step nearer Christianity rather than

otherwise. Theology is returning to poetic expression rather than Nominalist prose and a celebrated preacher, perhaps significantly a member of the Augustinian Order, Egidio da Viterbo, extolled the pagan mysteries as models of elegance in religion and reminded his hearers, 'As Dionysius[42] says, "the divine ray cannot reach us unless it is covered in poetic veils".'[43]

The human body, particularly as portrayed in art, becomes a symbol or quasi-sacrament of divine truths and, consonant with this traditional respect for an essential element of human nature, we find more emphasis being given in education on its care and importance. In Mantua, under the distinguished Vittorino da Feltre, arose the favoured school of the aristocratic world and to it, alongside the scions of the nobility, came the gifted poor whose instruction Vittorino proclaimed was his highest earthly aim and he gave them free tuition, board and lodging 'for the love of God'. In this establishment gymnastics and all noble bodily exercises were included as a necessary part of Christian education, and this combination of physical education with liberal studies in a single curriculum was probably the first in the world. The school was very much a religious institution and Burckhardt (1944, 127) describes its regime as 'stricter indeed than many monasteries'.

The Middle Ages had been thoroughly familiar with a metaphysical interpretation of the structure of the human body. Cosmological speculation centred round the divinely ordained correspondences between the universe and man played a large part in mediaeval discussion. The Augustinian notion of universal harmony and proportion had sunk deep and human and animal representations were built on the same geometrical principles as those which underlay the soaring cathedrals.[44] Similarly,[45] in the Renaissance a practical theory of proportions and metaphysical meaning coalesced.

> The theory of human proportions was seen both as a pre-requisite of artistic production and an expression of the pre-established harmony between microcosm and macrocosm; and it was seen, moreover, as the rational basis of beauty. The Renaissance fused, we may say, the cosmological interpretation of the theory of proportions, current in Hellenistic times and in the Middle Ages, with the classical notion of 'symmetry' as the fundamental principle of aesthetic perfection.[46]

Another important link between the Middle Ages and the Renaissance may be found in the speculations of Cardinal Nicholas of Cusa who was much concerned with the reconciliation of opposites in God.[47] This concern not only affected subsequent attitudes towards the body but also produced art and literary themes concerning the body. There were attempts to reconcile Virtue with Pleasure,[48] Sacred with Profane Love[49] and scholarly paganism with aristocratic Christianity: 'The pagan courtier who thought of himself as inspired by a Venus-Diana or a Venus-Mars was quite accustomed to translate his ideal of action into a pair of Christian virtues: Carita [Charity] united with Fortezza [Fortitude]. (Wind 1967, 95). But the balance was delicate and the affinities sometimes extremely tenuous. The transition from 'Strife overcome by Love' through 'Make Love not War' to 'Swive away and All will be Well' is very easy to make. Similarly, the transition from conceiving the body as an expression of Virtue to bringing it forth as an object of vice is equally facile and the signs of this easy descent are becoming apparent as the Renaissance exhausts itself and the tensions become more acute.[50]

Ideology of the human body

It is wishful thinking to describe the Renaissance as presenting the nude as 'an idealising form embodying a sane, sensual and celebratory eroticism' in rebellion against the Gothic nude which could only be 'justified as an embodiment of man's sexual and corporeal shame' (Melville 1973, 15), but there is a tendency in this period for the body to develop into a central concept, for it to become, in a sense, an independent entity providing the source of its own being. Order is being lost and the effects of disorder will eventually become cataclysmically evident, although some elements of the mediaeval synthesis survive until their final destruction by the mechanism of the eighteenth century. For a time all seemed well: in 1435 Donatello produced the first free-standing bronze, since classical times, in his *David* which is a celebration of the beauty of a male adolescent body and after this date the Venetians will create warm and sensual nudes by artists who are always professed and sometimes ardent members of the Church. But there can be little doubt that there is a tendency to illustrate 'Christian' or 'ecclesiastical' subjects as much for the opportunities they provided for painting nudes as for any edification purpose. Such subjects as Lot and his daughters, the drunkenness of Noah, Susanna and the elders, Joseph and Potiphar's wife become very popular after the Renaissance.

However, the High Renaissance did realise both the expressive power and the sheer beauty of the human body by 'idealising' it (probably under the combined influence of Neo-Platonism and Christianity), i.e. by seeing it as an image of something beyond itself and also as a battleground set midway between the realms of sheer matter and Pure Idea or Form. The Neo-Platonists conceived of the soul as 'imprisoned' in the body which was the sole source of all the

evils it suffered once it was deprived of the joy of its previous incorporeal existence, and became stricken by sorrow, immersed in a
swamp of grief and tears, and the prey of such tormenting passions as
mad wrath or fury.[51] Man's terrestrial state was bad enough, a sort of
Limbo or Hades where 'the deep gorge of the senses is always shaken
by the floods of Acheron, Styx, Cocytus and Phlegethon'[52] according
to Ficino, but man's sensual passions could debase the soul even
lower than this level of normal bodily life. Conversely, the soul could
be rapt from the body by Divine Love and given a taste of the
fulfilment awaiting in the supernatural realm.

The contemporary ferment of ideas left its mark on the artists who
tried to communicate it and perhaps above all on Michelangelo
whose

> powerful inhibited figures reflect the disparity between Christian
> emotion and the antique ideal, free human will and the will of
> God: the rational forms of classic sculpture were not made for the
> ecstasy of a Christian mystic, they writhe in the possession of an
> unfamiliar spirit and betray by brutal distortion, incongruous
> proportions and discordant composition the force of the collision
> of mediaeval Christianity with the Renaissance. (Morey 1935, 62.)

Space does not allow consideration of the contribution and aims of
this towering genius, perhaps the greatest artist of all time, a real
uomo universale whom the Florentines justly called 'Il divino'. Like
Dante, whom he loved so much, Michelangelo strove to construct a
synthesis in which the general was firmly rooted in the particular: 'He
speaks in things and you but speak in words.'[53] He saw the function of
the artist as depicting God's creation, and the highest painting will
consist in depicting, vying with the art of God, the most perfect of
these creatures, the highest and most complex, the one He created in
His own image and likeness: man.[54] His aim was

> to render in human bodies, in their infinite individuations, the
> history and tragedy of man and his relations with God – i.e. God
> himself and the divine world to the extent that it too enters into
> the human drama – since man participates therein to the extent to
> which the divine enters into history. The members, generally nude
> members, and the numberless faces, tell of dramas that are darker
> and darker, more and more sorrowful.

From the myths and civic ideals of the *David* to the tragic mass
of the *Rondanini Pietà*, the entire struggle of men against men
and against things is gone through, from the first emergence of
the creation from nothing to the vertiginous damnation and
redemption through the merit of the Son of Man, who, too, went

through death, finding the wrath of the judge. . . .[55]

Keen to detect the slightest movement of the soul in the vibration of a muscle, in that endless throng of bodies, almost always nude, solemn, isolated or in immense whirlwinds, he writes in the concrete individual flesh the entire story, divine and human, in a light that is more and more tragically apocalyptic as the composed and fragile initial calm gives place to a deeper and deeper awareness of sin and expiation.[56] (E. Garin in Tolnay, 1966, II, 529.)

Leonardo da Vinci, who seems only to have returned to the Church on his death-bed, apparently did not feel the same conflict: 'Identifying the beautiful with the natural, he sought to ascertain, not so much the aesthetic excellence as the organic uniformity of the human form: and for him, whose scientific thinking was largely dominated by analogy, the criterion for this organic uniformity consisted in the "correspondences" between as many as possible, though often disparate, parts of the human body.' (Panofsky, 1955, 127). But there were tensions in Leonardo: between his notion of 'correspondences' and the traditional ones, between the Renaissance concept of man[57] which he exemplified and propagated and the more moderate mediaeval concept, between his implicit if not explicit hierarchy of values and the traditional ones, between his interest in proportion and his own disproportionate ego, between his love of surfaces and his detached clinical attitude to the mechanism of the body.[58] In opposition to Michelangelo's anthropology of a soul held in bondage by the body, he believed that the body, or rather the 'quintessence' of its material elements was held in bondage by the soul. 'To Leonardo death does not mean the deliverance and repatriation of the soul which, according to the neo-Platonic belief, may return whence it came when the body has ceased to imprison it; it means, on the contrary, the deliverance and repatriation of the elements which are set free when the soul has ceased to bind them together.' (Panofsky, 1962, 182.) Yet there is much in Leonardo's attitude towards the body which can be paralleled in traditional and contemporary thought. This might be best indicated by a catena of quotations from his *Notebooks* (MacCurdy, 1952, 2 vols).

The soul desires to dwell with the body because without the members of the body it can neither act nor feel. (I, 69.)

Intellectual passion drives out sensuality. (I, 64.)

The chief good is wisdom: the chief evil is the suffering of the body. Seeing therefore that we are made up of two things, namely of soul and body, of which the first is the better and the inferior is the body, wisdom belongs to the better part and the chief evil belongs to the worst part and is the worst. The best thing in the soul is wisdom, and even so the worst thing in the body is pain. As therefore the chief evil is bodily pain, so wisdom is the chief good of the soul, that is of the wise man, and nothing else can be compared to it. (I, 64 – Leonardo wrote these words in the margin of his copy of Celsus' book on medicine.)

The senses are of the earth, the reason stands apart from them in contemplation. (I, 65.)

Sickness is the discord of the elements infused in the living body. (II, 205.)

The soul can never be infected by the corruption of the body, but acts in the body like the wind which causes the sound of the organ, wherein if one of the pipes becomes spoiled no good effect can be produced because of its emptiness. (I, 66.)

Whoever would see in what state the soul dwells within the body, let him mark how this body uses its daily habitation, for if this be confused and without order, the body will be kept in disorder and confusion by the soul. (I, 61.)

If you kept your body in accordance with virtue, your desires would not be of this world. (I, 66.)

Lo, some of them can call themselves nothing more than a passage for food, producers of dung, fillers-up of privies, for from them nothing else appears in the world, nor is there any virtue in their work, for nothing of them remains but full privies. (I, 78.)

Leonardo obviously regarded himself as more than 'a filler of privies', yet personally he was politically insensitive, always tried to assure himself a place on the side of the big battalions or powerful individuals, and though he had a profound contempt for the wisdom of the past, he was himself saturated in myths, fantasies and apocalyptic dreams.[59] Heer (1966, 216) castigates him as 'the first of a series of European intellectuals to contaminate himself by his own works and monomania'. He represents at once the highest achievement of humanism and its disordered and destructive nature. He not only tried to sell himself to the King of France as an inventor of machines of destruction but was obsessed by the notion of an all-destructive deluge which he constantly portrayed in his drawings. Some of the dikes, whose breach was to unleash that deluge, were attacked two years before Leonardo's death when an obscure theological professor in an obscure German university followed mediaeval precedent by nailing the theses which he wished to debate publicly to the door of his parish church.

SUMMARY

In this chapter we have given some attention to the Renaissance concept of the soul because of its implications with regard to the body. It is observable that the Platonising tendencies tend once more to separate body and soul and, among other effects, raise questions about their mutual relationship. Some aspects of the Renaissance seem to represent a flowering of the Christian tradition which had grown through the Middle Ages, while others seem to indicate a regression to pre-Christian notions. We have seen a pope taking the lead in changing the fashion from communal bathing to that of the private bathroom (for those who could afford such luxuries), but we may remember the hints of small and private baths in the mediaeval period. There is also some evidence in Renaissance Rome of a return to the pre-Christian association between baths and lechery.

The evidence of Renaissance public art as an indicator and propagator of attitudes towards the body has been touched on as well as its continuing iconographic and symbolic function[60] as the mediator of divine truths beyond the reach of words. Michelangelo and Leonardo have been used as giant exemplars of rapidly diverging attitudes which nevertheless have common roots and thus indicate the imminent disintegration of what was so nearly achieved.

THE ONSET OF DISINTEGRATION

After the Reformation there is no Western Church – only congeries of sects, at ferocious intellectual and even physical warfare with each other. Even the Roman Catholic Church which had led, bullied and cajoled Europe into self-consciousness degenerated into little more than a sect itself as, in the face of the growing disintegration, it retreated within a monolithic fortress and set its mind to endure a siege which was to last into the twentieth century. If there is no Church, there cannot be an attitude of Christendom to the human body, but before concluding our investigation we might attempt a general survey of the situation which led to our own day.

Undermining of spiritual potentiality

A glimpse of possibilities, so long as the centre held, is offered by the writings of Thomas More (1477/8–1535), martyr and humanist, so much 'a man for all seasons' that Marxists have seen him as a forerunner of Communism and the Roman Church has retrospectively canonised him. His masterpiece, *Utopia* (1516) gives a central place to the pleasure-principle which the Utopians distinguish into false and true, subdividing the latter:

> Some (pleasures) they attribute to the soul and others to the body. . . . They separate the pleasures of the body into two classes, the first of which floods the senses with its transparent sweetness. Sometimes this happens in the restoration [of the body] by food and drink . . . othertimes this occurs when the body rejects a surplus, as in the case of bowel movements, sexual orgasm or common scratching. Other pleasures they identify . . . with a certain delectable inner movement. They place music in this category.
>
> The other kind of physical pleasure occurs when the body is in a state of quiescence or equilibrium; that is, when its health is not affected by disease. If nothing painful exerts itself, health takes delight in itself, even though no external pleasure is applied. In spite of the fact that it calls less attention to itself and offers less to the senses than do eating and drinking, many still take health for the greatest pleasure. Almost all Utopians admit it as the foundation for all the rest, so that even in and of itself it can make our life placid and tranquil. (Greene and Dolan, 1967, 72.)[1]

But the intelligent use of pleasure, which presupposed the control of reason and will, was increasingly under a double attack; from the disordered antropocentrism of the Renaissance and the unbalanced theology of the Reformers. Both, in their different ways, overstressed human personality on the one hand and human frailty on the other. Erasmus[2] seems to have been alone in seeing that the real danger of Lutheranism was not in the desire for reform with which he, along with many other Catholics, heartily concurred, but in its attack on the central notion of human free will for, 'unless the will of man is free, man's dignity is a myth, his optimism an illusion' (Baker, 1961, 291).

It is an easy and often unnoticed step from the naturalistic to the mechanistic view of man, and this step took place within the Renaissance.[3] If man's spiritual uniqueness is lost sight of, then attention naturally focuses on the mechanical characteristics which he shares with the whole of material creation. Man's spiritual potentiality was undermined not only by secularism and materialism but by unbalanced theologians who thought that God's glory was exalted by denigrating His highest creation. 'It was inevitable that Calvin, being what he was, had fixed on this very point in order to destroy the last vestige of man's confidence in himself; by declaring man's free will eternally in bondage "under the yoke of sin" (*Institutes*, I, 82) he had, in effect, invalidated his claim to rational self-government and thus reduced him to the condition of innate depravity which has for centuries been the solace of all good Calvinists.' (Baker, 1961, 291f). It may be unfair to saddle Calvin with the excesses of his followers, but it was not long before the Puritans seemed to identify sin with anything that gave pleasure and even earlier Luther[4] had dethroned reason by describing it, inimitably, as 'the Devil's chiefest whore': By nature and manner of being she [Reason] is a noxious whore; she is a prostitute, the devil's appointed whore; whore eaten by scab and leprosy who ought to be trodden under foot and destroyed, she and her wisdom. . . . Throw dung in her face to make her ugly. She is and she ought to be drowned in baptism . . . she would deserve, the wretch, to be banished to the filthiest place in the house, to the closets.' (Cited Maritain, 1941, 33).[5] This characteristically scatological and lubricious language sets a new tone in the religious controversy and the vituperative and denigratory use of bodily functions marks a psychological shift in attitudes to the body on the part of the Reformers.[6] Modern psychoanalysts would probably identify Luther as a characteristic anal type: he himself records that he received his great moment of enlightenment while at stool, that apparitions of the Devil were accompanied by maladorous breakings of wind and his *Table Talk* described how a female

Lutheran put the Devil to flight by venting her effluvia on him.

There is a peasant vulgarity about Luther which, despite his self-contradictions and desire to overthrow every authority but his own, makes him somewhat sympathetic. But it is otherwise with the cerebral Calvin who was above self-contradiction. His work develops inordinately and without balance the darker side of Augustine's teaching and his patrismic[7] theology was uncompensated by any of the elements which had developed within traditional Catholicism. 'The basis of Calvinism in father-identification needs a little stressing. We find it in the marked authoritarianism of the movement, in its depression of the status of women, and even in such characteristic details as a fervent belief in witchcraft: extreme Protestants persisted in this belief long after the rest of Europe had abandoned it.' (Taylor, 1965, 158).[8] Consonant with their 'spiritualism', the Calvinists abolished sacramentals, reduced the number of sacraments and tried to dematerialise the two they retained.[9] They naturally abolished the cult of the saints, images and relics, together with customs which seemed to imply a sanctification of the material creation such as pilgrimages, saints days, etc.[10] It seems that every traditional concept of the body had to be abandoned and replaced by a 'utilitarian' rather than a 'sacramental' view. Celibacy and virginity had been conceived as a worthy offering of a good, the idea of offering was replaced by the notion of 'saving' – the untouched property was to be kept intact until it could be used for propagating a family which would be of economic value to the 'godly'. Large families among the poor would tend to produce poverty which became a sign of God's reprobation for sin.[11] In the economic transmutation of values[12] illegal sex becomes the greatest sin and work the supreme virtue, meritorious in and for itself, and leisure, by contrast, was regarded if not actually sinful at least as the proximate occasion for sin.[13] The human body became an instrument only, a tool, and the use of the word 'hands' to describe manual workers seems to originate in this period. The human body was not only an instrument for work, it was also an instrument apt for diabolic utilisation and therefore all its activities and manifestations required strict policing and censorship. In the 'school of Christ', which Calvin established by his autocratic rule of Geneva, bridesmaids were arrested for decorating a bride too gaily and punishments were inflicted for the sins of drinking, dancing and eating fish on Good Friday.[14] Pierre Ami, who was one of those who invited Calvin to Geneva, doubtless regretted his enthusiasm when he was imprisoned for dancing with his wife at a betrothal party.

Church attendance on Sundays and Wednesdays was enforced by the police, but it was also an offence to go to church at times unsanctified by the preacher.[15] The old religious acts of rite and ceremony, sacrament and sacramental were replaced by the less material 'Word' as proclaimed and interpreted by Calvin and those rare spirits on whom he bestowed his approval. Parallel to the reduction of the Incarnate Word of God to Scripture was a new preoccupation with words – the propriety of non-Biblical words, especially those found in novels, plays and 'profane' songs. Here we find the severing of sacred and secular and the origins of 'obscenity'. Certain words were proscribed, particularly those relating to fundamental activities of the body, and it was a logical development of this unnatural and artifically induced horror of anything associated, however remotely, with sexual or evacuatory activities, that led to the Victorian concealment of even the legs of their pianos.

In England, the Puritan disciples of Calvin forebade Sunday games in opposition to the mediaeval tradition that holy days were for the recreation of body and soul: the proper and normal times (after Mass of course) for sports, fairs, drinking, archery, dancing, feasting, music, dramatic representations and other celebrations.[16] The high tide of Puritanism, after it had swept away the Royal (and Catholic) cause in the Great Rebellion and the subsequent military dictatorship (1642–60) brought Calvin's vision of the Christian school to England. Maypoles were prohibited, iconoclasm was encouraged, churches were desecrated and Christmas, Easter and Whitsun were abolished as pagan festivals. Playing football, travelling or even walking on the Sabbath (as Sunday was inaccurately renamed) incurred the penalty of excommunication, and there was a specific ban against 'idle sitting at doors and walking in churchyards'.[17] Indeed, 'idleness' replaced pride as the new capital sin and the alleged mother of all vices.[18] Puritan extremism represented one aspect of the lost balance and ordering of the psychosomatic unity. Another, and apparently opposite tendency, overemphasised (and paradoxically degraded) the body by dissociating it from reason and the contemplation of goodness, beauty and truth. There was an outburst of sadism and other perversions which, while certainly not previously unknown, seem to achieve a new status in the upper strata of society where bodily desires are cultivated as a total and circumscribed end in themselves.[19] This 'anti-Puritan' movement, while perhaps psychologically close to its antithesis, expressed itself in eroticism in art and pornography in literature: a double attempt at the deliberate stimulation of sexual impulses dissociated and detached from the total humanity of their object.[20]

Denigration of the human body

The definition of both pornography and eroticism is difficult to free from subjectivism,[21] but it could perhaps be satisfactorily attained along teleological and aesthetic lines. My own identification of both these aberrations would probably depend on the non-totality of response in the subject and the object-thing concept of the object as distinct from a personal one. Clark (1956)[22] has usefully distinguished between the 'naked' and the 'nude' and makes the following point:

> Although the naked body is no more than the point of departure for a work of art, it is a pretext of great importance. In the history of art, the subjects which men have chosen as nuclei, so to say, of their sense of order, have often been in themselves unimportant. For hundreds of years, and over an area stretching from Ireland to China, the most vital expression of order was an imaginary animal biting its own tail. In the Middle Ages drapery took on a life of its own, the same life which had inhabited the twisting animal, and became the vital pattern of Romanesque art. In neither case had the subject any independent existence. But the human body, as a nucleus, is rich in associations, and when it is turned into art the associations are not entirely lost.

Concern about the representative character of Clark's examples or about the omission of the dominant subject of mediaeval art (man's total salvation) does not inhibit agreement about the cosmic or symbolic significance of great art whatever its 'pretext'. Great art centring on the human body is open-ended and expansionist, cerebral and imaginative; 'erotic' art is narrowing and reductionist – the human body is only a conveyance for genitalia and response is a conditioned reflex. Though Clark dismisses Alexander's statement that 'if the nude is so treated as to raise in the spectator ideas or desires appropriate to the material subject it is false art and bad morals', it would seem undeniably true if 'only' was inserted before 'ideas'.

'Erotic art'[23] is characterised by its single aim to arouse depersonalised physical desire and it appeared first in Italy[24] and, with the usual cultural lag, reached England about a century later.[25] The process of sexual commercialisation through art had begun and would degenerate into the 'dirty postcards' and 'exhibitions' of the modern trade.[26] This development shows increasingly derogatory attitudes to the body, but their seeds seem already visible in the engravings which Melville (1973, 19) finds remarkable 'for their pagan, celebratory and guilt-free attitude towards sexuality'. To other eyes they may give the impression of aggression, if not sadism, and there is little indication of love or tenderness in any of them and the fact that in many of the drawings (e.g. 8, 12, 16, 19, 20) the male protagonist is a beast or satyr is significant. Though the nude in art is often presented as an admirable expression of the European spirit it seems almost immediately after the Renaissance to have shown signs of disorder and disintegration.[27] Berger (1972, 62ff) derives this from an irresolvable contradiction between the individualism of man, be he painter, patron or owner of the work of art, and the depersonalisation of woman 'treated as a thing or abstraction'.[28] This process was to continue and to extend to include the male body, so that in our time painters such as Picasso or Francis Bacon have distorted or entirely disintegrated the human body which was once an icon, the nucleus of the artist's sense of order.

The degeneration of the body which we have traced in the plastic arts was paralleled in writing[29] where sexual activity, from being an aspect of the many-sided nature of man, became central and an end in itself, detached and isolated from any notion of human totality or psychosomatic unity. The result was pornography which rapidly lost even the most superficial refinements of style and became a series of boring and stereotyped accounts of a mechanical or sadistic activity.[30]

These processes may be explained both as the result of the loss of the fine balance barely achieved by Christian thought and imperfectly maintained by the influence of the Church and of a reaction against views which while claiming still to be Christian (or an improved version of Christianity) themselves represented an unbalanced and distorted view of human nature. Much of the character of the Restoration period in England seems to be an overreaction to the enforced austerities of the preceding age of triumphant Puritanism. Conversely, Victorian Puritanism can be explained as a swing of the pendulum from the licence of the Regency.[31] This is not the whole explanation and there is some evidence in the Reformation period of diabolism,[32] by which I mean a deliberate rejection of those values which had hitherto been common to the best minds, a deliberate asseveration of the principle 'Evil, be thou my good'[33] and the calculated acting-out of a moral anarchism emphasising perversion where sadism and masochism become desirable norms.[34]

The development may be typified by Don Juan or Casanova, but many real people actually operated with the same or greater callousness without entering literature. The association of blasphemy with cold viciousness is found in de Sade and such English aristocratic institutions as the Hell Fire Club and the Medmenham 'Abbey'. The connection between sexual libertinism and general physical violence[35] is exemplified in such other eighteenth-century phenomena as the Mohacks and the sport of seduction in which far more points were scored for the corruption of an innocent than for success with more worldly women. To such people physical love was much less 'an affair of passion than one of pride and the gratification of their consciousness of power'.[36] The cult of virginity for privileged destruction is a particularly perverse expression of this attitude.[37]

The final remains of mediaeval order and synthesis seem to have disappeared in the course of the eighteenth century which, rather than the sixteenth, marks the real beginning of the modern world. This was the age that saw, not so much the beginnings of modern science (which were much earlier) but the hardening of its outlines and direction, it saw the establishment of a mechanistic view of the universe and of man, the return of both formal and informal slavery, the first victories of a triumphant and largely unopposed capitalism, the introduction of mass production with the consequent subordination of human nature to technology, the application of statistics to human organisation and the beginning of total war. It was an age of revolution in thought, technology and social order, and in it the thought and attitudes of the Church generally followed slavishly the contemporary fashions (or the just outmoded ones). It was an age which its aristocratic beneficiaries knew was a turning-point as Talleyrand, one of its most cynical representatives, said: 'No one who did not live before 1789 knows the sweetness of life.'

That sweetness was, naturally, an aristocratic perquisite; lesser mortals had become the *mobile vulgus*, the undifferentiated mob who were, in France at any rate, shortly to exact revenge for their depersonalisation. Hauser (1962, III, 30) comments on Talleyrand's remark:

> The 'sweetness of life' is, of course, taken as meaning the sweetness of women; they are, as in every epicurean culture, the most popular pastime. Love has lost both its 'healthy' impulsiveness and its dramatic passionateness; it has become sophisticated, amusing, docile, a habit where it used to be a passion. There is a universal and constant desire to see pictures of the nude; it now becomes the favourite subject of the plastic arts. Wherever one looks, whether at the frescoes in the state apartments, the gobelins of the salons, the paintings in boudoirs, the engravings in books, the porcelain groups and bronze figures on mantelpieces, everywhere one sees naked women, swelling thighs and hips, uncovered breasts, arms and legs folded in embraces, women with men and men with women, in countless variations and endless repetitions.

Such art was directed at the jaded senses and idle bodies of an aristocratic[38] clientele or the rich bourgeois aspiring to the trappings of aristocracy. Since the Middle Ages there has been little 'high art' for the people (the Renaissance was an aristocratic movement) and increasingly it has become restricted and privatised; mercantile capitalism has increasingly brought both art and its subject-matter into the realm of private ownership through the exchange and mart. The real human body was a reminder of the truth of the human condition, its artistic representation has become a symbol of wealth and power and possessions. This new art also represents a male chauvinism beyond that of mediaeval preachers which is described by Berger (1972, 63). 'In the art-form of the European nude the painters and spectator-owners were usually men and the persons treated as objects, usually women. This unequal relationship is so deeply embedded in our culture that it still structures the consciousness of many women. They do to themselves what men do to them. They survey, like men, their own femininity.'

This is the age of rococo, of the theatrical, centring on a sensual cult of beauty an artistic style which was 'an erotic art intended for rich and blasé epicureans[39] and it represents the last stage in the 'culture of taste' that began at the Renaissance. Rococo is the last universal style of Western Europe – the last glitter from the shattered synthesis.

The elegance conceals a growing hollow of reductionism: art has been reduced to taste, its social significance to the delectation of a male élite and cosmic significance itself to the working of an engine. When the human body is not being considered as an instrument for sensual gratification it is being thought of as a machine, and since the two attitudes rested on the same basic notions they could easily be combined. Novelty, amorality and entertainment may lie almost equally beneath scientific and sado-sexual experiment at the beginning of the development in the eighteenth century.[40] Towards its end, a Victorian pornographer, running out of imaginative steam after describing the 'delicious transports' and 'ecstasies of the senses' experienced by a woman 'in that favourite part of her body which was so luxuriously filled and employed' summarises the situation in a mixed metaphor dominated by mechanism: 'In short she was a machine (like any other piece of machinery) obeying the impulses of the key that so potently set her in motion, till the sense of pleasure foaming to a height drove the shower that was to allay this hurricane.'[41] This is nearly the end of a process which began with Newtonian physics and, supported by Cartesian metaphysics,[42] reflected the triumphs of a technology flavoured with Rousseauian naturalism. When the mirror of Divine Love had been reduced to cogitation[43] and human love to a mere game (whether the high sport of Duclos' *Les Liaisons dangereuses* or the maidenhead counting of the less stylish), it was consonant that man should be reduced to a tool, either as a 'hand' in a factory or a conveyance for his penis which is in the new order becomes personalised and the reason for his existence.[44]

The rococo art which embellishes (and to some extent conceals) the second stage of this development was the last artistic style to cover Europe as an accepted fashion, roughly contemporaneous in all countries. Essentially aristocratic, it reached the people in one area – in the decoration of churches, particularly those of Austria.

Conflicting images

This partial persistence of Christian tradition was one of the effects of the movement known as the Counter-Reformation or Catholic Reformation. Though somewhat taken by surprise by the force and destruction of Protestantism, the Catholic Church was aware of explosive tensions and the urgent need of reform and had, indeed, begun to meet this need.[45] It failed, however, to assess the significance of Luther and the response he would release, for a variety of reasons, among the Germans. When the magnitude of the crisis became apparent and the situation almost desperate, the Council of Trent which, initially, was intended to be both reforming and ecumenical, adopted a siege mentality and produced a Roman Church embattled and fully armed against all adversaries. Reaction became associated with reform and this reaction affected both artistic and intellectual spheres.

A modern Catholic historian has said that 'the work done at Trent consisted in breaking with the traditions of the Renaissance' (Janelle, 1972, 159) and though this is hardly adequate it does indicate some results. Perhaps the following is a more interesting and relevant comment:

> The period of the Council of Trent has been described as 'the birthday of prudery' . . . neither the aristocratic society of early classical antiquity nor the Christian society of the Middle Ages was 'prudish'. They avoided the nude but were not afraid of it. Their attitude to the physical was much too clear-cut for them ever to have wanted both to conceal and to stress the sexual by introducing the 'fig-leaf'. The ambivalence of erotic feelings does not arise until the onset of Mannerism, and it is bound up with the whole dichotomy of this culture in which the greatest polarities are united: the most spontaneous feeling with the most intolerable affection, the strictest possible belief in authority with the most arbitrary individualism and the most chaste representations with the lewdest forms of art. Prudishness is here not merely the conscious reaction against the provoking lasciviousness of the art

produced independently of the Church, such as is cultivated at most courts, but it is also itself a form of suppressed lasciviousness. (Hauser, 1962, II, 112.)

Nudity was proscribed in religious art and an attempt was made to prevent the painting or carving of pagan or lascivious images (the two categories tended to be identified).[46] Catholic puritanism tended towards the same effect as Protestant iconoclasm in the rejection, though for different reasons, of images and pictures of the saints. But the weight of tradition and the necessity of meeting heretical attacks on popular piety brought a reaffirmation of Catholic practice,[47] including 'the legitimate use of images', though care was taken that such representations adequately communicated to the unlearned the orthodox doctrines of the Church. Artists were to return to the service of truth, to body forth as best they could the forms of things unseen and to abandon the irresponsible personality-cult and the self-indulgence to which too many had succumbed in the disordered enthusiasm of the late Renaissance which Possevinus, at least, saw as a diabolic counter-attack against the Church's latest successes in the newly discovered Indies. This attack was double-pronged: on the one hand, through unchaste books and lewd philosophy and, on the other, through

> outrageous images of nude women, of Fauns and Satyrs, infamous statues, and even fragments of idols dug out of the bowels of the earth; the which being placed on the fronts of houses, on towers, on the mansions of noblemen, in the innermost parts of their dwellings, renew the memory of those who were confined, restoring whatever was most pagan. Meanwhile, the images of saints and holy mysteries of our Lord were being painted either without dignity, or for the sake of fancy rather than piety, or were placed among the images of false gods, so that religion itself was gradually removed from the souls of many. (Cited in Janelle, 1972, 162).

Though there was some recrudescence of paganism there was more over-reaction, and liberal attitudes, as always in times of crisis, became more difficult to retain. The pressure against them can be charted in the contemporary official attitudes to such a masterpiece as that of the convincedly Christian Michelangelo's *Last Judgment* (1541) which glorifies the east wall of the papal Sistine Chapel. It is said that an illiberal cardinal complained about the total nudity of the figures in heaven and hell and asked for it to be modified. The pope refused, ironically commenting that his jurisdiction was confined to the Church Militant, i.e. to Catholics still in this life.

But, as early as 1559, within Michelangelo's lifetime, Paul IV had some of the pudenda concealed. The process was continued by Pius V in 1566, while Clement VII (1592–1605) was only prevented from covering the entire fresco by the powerful intercession of the Academy of St Luke, the guild of the Roman painters.

Such reactions seem to have stemmed more from individual feeling than from the objective application of Tridentine principles, for as Hauser (1962, II, 113) says: 'In spite of its moral rigorism and its anti-formalistic attitude, the Tridentinum was, in contrast to the Reformation, by no means inimical to art. Erasmus' well-known saying "ubicumque regnat Lutherismus, ibi literarum est interitus" (wherever Lutheranism reigns culture is destroyed) cannot be applied in any way to the enactments of the Council of Trent.'[48] But in spite of some successful rearguard actions of the Church, the unity that the Middle Ages had almost within its grasp was gone: the disintegration continued and the disorder increased. Though Tintoretto was to take up the cloak of Michelangelo and express the religious rebirth of his own age and though he was succeeded by El Greco, the most deeply religious artist since the Middle Ages, such visions were increasingly those of a minority as, for the majority, the body was divorced from soul, morality from intellect,[49] and man from his ordered place in creation. Concepts of stewardship and mediation retreated before the aggressive forces of exploitation and separation while organic notions were replaced by mechanistic ones. In art the body of an attractive girl was transposed from an image of intellectual virtue[50] to an object of physical lust. Previously, both male and female bodies had been presented as unifying symbols of cosmic order: the Christian God and Redeemer had a male body, Michelangelo's most powerful images are male, the proportional drawing entitled *Vitruvian man* occurs frequently, but the situation changes as the roots of Christian Humanism are forgotten, every kind of chauvinism increases and cultural order and common concepts are dissolved from the European picture.

It is not an accident that the rococo is the last 'universal style' in the West, nor that the eighteenth century is the real divide between the old world and the modern world with its mechanism and capitalism, its characteristic institutions of prison and asylum, its lust for aggressive action and its contempt for contemplation. Descartes' divorce of body and mind[51] led to the philosophy of Locke, and La Mettrie's concept of man as machine had been allied to the notion that maltreating the body improves the mind,[52] and this in turn produced the disordered reaction of Rousseau whose ideas are summarised by Maritain (1941, 147) as 'a complete realisation of the Pelagian heresy through the mysticism of sensation'.[53]

Most philosophers and most artists have hitherto been men and therefore concepts and representations of the human body generally show a masculine bias. When men consider or portray a woman's body this can either be positive, an expression of their deepest ideals or negative, an indication of aversion and contempt. Christianity presented 'embodiment' as the linchpin of the created order and the mediaeval cult of the Virgin Mary had projected woman as the intermediary between both God and man and man and the world, incarnating life and will and intellect and also concealing the mysteries of this process.[54] In the later Renaissance there is the beginning of a shift from the thing symbolised to the symbolising thing and afterwards we see the growing concept of woman as a thing to be possessed and therefore her body is increasingly represented with the inertia and passive qualities of an object. By the eighteenth century, the apogaeic age of extravagance, of status through possession and conspicuous expenditure, the degeneration and dichotomy is manifest. 'When a woman is given over to man as his property, he demands that she represent the flesh purely for its own sake. Her body is not perceived as the radiation of a subjective personality, but as a thing sunk deeply in its own immanence; it is not for such a body to have reference to the rest of the world, it must not be the promise of things other than itself: it must end the desire it arouses.'[55] Thus, it is no surprise to find that a book entitled *Woman as Sex Object*[56] begins its study in 1730. All kinds of reductionism meet here: persons to things, agape to eros, erotic to 'erotic for men', creativity to sensuality,[57] and bodies to genitalia-porters.

We began with the idea of Man[58] made in the image of God, with a world-view in which human persons were coadjutors with a personal God, with humanity at the centre of a created order in which every man was a particular kind of artist (like his Creator). The Renaissance produced the inverted idea that the artist was a special kind of man, while the eighteenth and subsequent centuries produced the idea that the artist was a peculiar form of God, arrogating divine attributes and fashioning through self-expression 'from inert matter an ideal erotic object for himself, a woman cut to the very pattern of his desires'.[59] By a similar development, the Renaissance had seen women's bodies (and to a lesser extent, men's) as expressing spiritual ideas, whereas more recent art more commonly uses material things to point not only to the human body in general but, more narrowly, to its copulative functions.[60]

This process was neither even nor continuous, nor did it lack Christian influence either by positive inspiration or negative reaction. Henry Fuseli's recurrent obsession from the 1780s with *The Nightmare* can be enjoyed as the private joke of a lapsed Protestant minister against martyrology in art.[61] In the nineteenth century, Ingres could go to Giulio Romano for his 'fount of erotic inspiration' as well as concerning himself with the nude as an allegory of the senses[62] and with the representation of the spiritual world of form. In our own times, Dali can produce the satirical masturbatory fantasy, *Average Atmosphero-cephalic Bureaucrat in the Act of Milking a Cranial Harp*, alongside such religious images as *The Christ of St John of the Cross* while Francis Bacon, whose simile of life is 'a heap of dog-shit'[63] can at least find a point of departure for his fecal vision in representations of the Crucifixion and Velázquez' magnificent portrait of Pope Innocent X.

SUMMARY

This rather miscellaneous and general chapter has tried to indicate some aspects of what I have called the disintegration of the Christian position. The Catholic Church which once had fostered European culture has suffered both internal and external effects from the fifteenth-century Renaissance and has been dismembered by the complex movement called the Reformation. The increasing secularisation which was both a cause and effect of these movements and the growing influence of the 'scientific attitude' resulted in the divorce of sacred and secular, the reduction of the physical to physics, and the narrowing Christian culture merely to pietism, and the degradation of art from iconography to a status symbol and investment for the aristocracy (or those aspiring to that state). There is an increased mechanism flowing both from 'science' and unbalanced intellectualism, resulting in a contraction of the ideas flowing from 'sacramental incarnationism' which accepted materialism and embodiment as a medium of the divine. Examples have been given to indicate how 'high art' and literature alike witness to this change and how the early stages of this movement affected the Catholic Church in the enactments of the Council of Trent. The Church, having lost its central position, tends to turn in on itself and becomes nervous of admitting anything which it has seen grossly abused or which appears contributory to the disintegration of Christian culture that is everywhere apparent. The effect of these general movements on the value and symbolism of the body is indicated and the evidence of art called to witness.

Much of our contemporary attitude towards the body, its artistic representation, together with its use and abuse, may spring from a confused reaction[64] against what has been subjectively conceived as an enslaving or derogatory attitude to the body which has been identified as Christian. Though Christians have been far from guiltless, their opponents do not always seem to distinguish substance from accident, the central tradition from its perversions, or culture from religion. It remains to attempt the difficult task of summarising what we believe that tradition to be, to assess its present position and perhaps outline possible trends in its future development.

11

A BACKWARD LOOK

In general, the writers of the ancient world seem either to have despised or to have feared the human body. The central and persistent teaching of those who were considered 'the best minds' was that all man's troubles, sins and sufferings arose from the fact that he had a body. Plato described it as 'the prison-house of the soul', Seneca spoke of 'the detestable habitation of the body', while Epictetus described himself as 'a poor soul shackled to a corpse' and Porphyry, in his panegyric life of his master wrote of him: 'Plotinus, our contemporary philosopher, seemed ashamed to be in the body.'

The poets and artists were not in entire accord with the philosophers: 'Homer, and after him the Greek sculptors, discovered the glory of the human body and gave this – the most beautiful thing they knew – to the gods.'[1] But the poets and artists were themselves inconsistent, for in primitive Greek art the gods seemed to have been clothed in order to 'distance' the numinous from the human. When that veil was removed the gods became humanised and the models for men and woman are drawn from the aristocracy, from athletes[2] and hetaerae, and eroticism enters classical art. This erotic element primarily centred on Dionysius and portrayed satyrs copulating with nymphs and animals while its second source was the love-life of the humanised Olympians: the episode of Leda and the Swan being particularly popular. Then, in the early sixth century B.C., artistic interest shifted from myth to reality with the portrayal of brothel scenes along with elegant orgies involving hetaerae. Henceforth, vulgarity marched hand in hand with decadence so that by the Hellenistic period there is a manifest mechanical element in intimate body-relations and the ubiquitous phallus becomes a monstrous tool which dominates its user.

Some critics have seen this development as an example of the alternating 'patrist' and 'matrist' cycles of history: the classical Greek idea of beauty being essentially feminine, while the characteristic Roman work of art is the unidealised portrait-bust of the masculine man of action. But there were other elements in the cultural change as diverse as the example of Alexander[3] and the influence of Plotinus.[4]

The Roman contempt of the body was more obvious than that of the Greeks: not only in the writings of Seneca (based on Greek philosophy) but even more obviously and generally in their characteristic institutions. Some of these, like their philosophy, were an inheritance from or shared with the Greeks, e.g. athletics, theatre, slavery, but by the time of the Empire, if not before, the Romans seem to have added a peculiar and dominant element of callousness and sadism. Bodies are depersonalised and, as either single units or conglomerates, are reduced to instruments of power, objects of lust or raw material for savage entertainment. They anticipated by almost two millenia many features of contemporary society: admass man, mindless spectator sports, doles and State charity, a top-heavy bureaucracy and reification of the State, and only failed of our achievement through deficient technology.

This was the world that the Christian Church entered with its extensive Jewish inheritance, and its horror and alienation was only mitigated by the conviction that this world was shortly to perish and be replaced by a new one of ideal human dimensions. So it contented itself with preparation for better things in the eschatological future by present dissociation, particularly from the demonism of pagan practices which it saw as the supernatural power-house of cosmic corruption. Its central belief was in restoration: the restoration of human nature from its fall to a risen posture, the restoration of reason and order in human society and the whole of nature. This belief was centred on and expressed in the resurrection of Christ and the dependent resurrection of each individual member of His Body. Consequently, Christians prayed with their bodies erect on all Sundays and throughout Eastertide in allusion to the mystery of the Resurrection, and the Council of Nicea (A.D. 325) positively forebade kneeling on Sundays and every day from Easter to Whitsuntide.

It was natural for paganism and its associations to be seen as the antithesis of this faith, and some critics have seen the earliest Christian art as reflecting this attitude with an apparent deliberate rejection of 'earthly' values and with its expression of a new type of spirituality. Others[5] have explained the quality of primitive Christian art as due to mere amateurishness. Whatever the reason, it seems agreed that the human figure did not disappear from Christian art but the nude did. There were probably two motives: the nude was associated with paganism and depersonalised eroticism on the one hand, and on the other, clothing showed respect, detachment and honour.

Certainly, the earliest Christians showed no lack of respect for the body, its dignity and significance: they believed in a total redemption, a sanctification of body and soul expressed through material rites and sacraments applied to the whole man.[6] They believed that they were saved in and through the body which was of such a nature as to be a worthy offering to God. Both the founder of Christianity and its greatest missionary were fond of using as exemplars such contemporary figures as soldiers, athletes and charioteers which could hardly be regarded as ideal 'spiritual' types. There was certainly no glorification of the body at the expense of the 'soul', but there was a clear implication that it must be treated realistically and its natural needs met. Indeed, one gets the impression in the earliest centuries that to misuse or neglect the body is some kind of sin: to allow it, through carelessness, greed or sloth, to become weak, ill, inefficient or flabby is to show a lack of proportion or order. There are times both for feasting and fasting, but in the latter exercise there must be particular attention to the toilet so that the effects of fasting are more inwardly than outwardly apparent. [7]

It is perhaps worth mentioning at this point that Christianity, unlike many other religions, required no kind of bodily mutilation or marking such as caste-marks, tattooing, or the like, and it did not (in spite of its significance in the Jewish religion) continue the practice of circumcision. Some religions castrated their priests, but serious bodily blemish or mutilation could be an impediment to ordination in the Christian ministry. [8] On the other hand, respect for the body included keeping it in order in every sense of this phrase and we remember that 'ascesis' means 'training'. Rational fitness and good appearance seem to have been regarded as a respectful duty. Christianity is social as well as individual and its teaching demands that the bodies of others should be cared for and respected. The practice of the 'corporal works of mercy' seems to have been contemporaneous with the acceptance of Christian doctrine.

The essence of Christianity lay in the 'enfleshing' of God, belief in the Incarnation which was the full and complete union of matter and spirit, of God and man, in the historical person of Jesus of Nazareth. This doctrine as Athanasius was to affirm against the world, [9] was an extension of the doctrine of Creation – a work which was wholly good, but perverted by man's self-will, was restored by the obedience of a perfect man who closed the gap between God and his creation. Creation was not merely good, but a manifestation of God; His beauty and truth and goodness shone through it. The Incarnation was a renewal of creation – a re-creation which, thus renewed, provided through the material sacraments and historicity of Christianity a universal means of personal restoration in that ecclesiastical Body of Christ which continued the work begun in the original 'embodiment' of God.

Such a religion was too materialistic for the Gnostics and others, who set an antithesis between God and matter, between body and spirit. This 'spiritualistic' rejection issued in one of two extremes. It could take the form of a complete and inordinate asceticism in which the body was despised and neglected and all its impulses stifled, where everything to do with the body and its reasonable care – nature, marriage, sex – is regarded as incurably evil and must be ruthlessly excised with the possible exception of a minimal area necessary to maintain life. Alternatively, if the body is already utterly evil nothing can make it worse and contempt may be expressed in complete indulgence – in the satiation of its appetites and the fulfilment of all its impulses so that the soul is freed from the demands of its unworthy vehicle. Gnosticism assailed the Church without and within; even in the more orthodox forms of Christianity the two strands of 'world-affirming' and 'world-renouncing' are often inextricably intertwined and in Christian enthusiasts it is sometimes impossible to distinguish between the exaltation of the higher potentialities of man and the denigration of his mortal body.[10]

The fall of the Roman Empire and the resulting Dark Ages made the maintenance of this delicate balance impossible as men's minds became increasingly obsessed with survival and the transience of all earthly things, including the body. Efforts were made to preserve order and priority and though there is a great paucity of written evidence from this period, Sidonius Apollinaris (c. 430–c. 480) deserves honourable mention. He was an aristocrat, courtier and littérateur who became bishop of Clermont around A.D. 470. He inspired his flock through many barbarian sieges and laboured tirelessly to mitigate the evils of the time. He was canonised and one of his poems, written a few years before he became a bishop, gives us a last glimpse of the aristocratic Roman amusements, including a pantomime and an amateur chariot-race.[11]

Half a century later, St Benedict (c. 480–c. 550) produced his *Rule* of monastic life, remarkable for its common sense and humanity[12] in any age, but particularly so considering it was written during a period of almost incessant wars, massacres, pestilence and famine. More lasting than the buildings in which it was conceived, this little book was the greatest single influence in the restoring of order and stability and the re-creation of European culture. Nevertheless, life remained extremely precarious and the body only too obviously vulnerable and mortal,[13] so thought remained polarised between the immediate and the eternal. The Benedictines became the victims of their own success, but the idea was self-renewing and the twelfth century saw the prodigious success and influence of the Cistercians who practised work and prayer in equal measure for the benefit of both soul and body. (Zarnecki, 1972, 71).

As order was toilfully and slowly established, new instruments aided the process: towns, often growing under the shelter of Benedictine walls, and the secular power of kings and aristocrats converted to the defence and extension of Christian civilisation. 'The Church encouraged the formation of the new chivalric nobility with all the means at her disposal, consolidated its social position by a form of consecration, charging it with the protection of the weak and oppressed, recognising it as the Army of Christ, and so raising it to a kind of spiritual dignity.' (Hauser, 1962, 187.) None of the knightly virtues were accessible apart from physical strength and long bodily training, and their religious encouragement provided a balance to the monastic near denial and actual mortification of bodily excellencies. A new knightly education developed alongside the academic education of the clerics, an education whose main elements were bodily fitness and social skills. Hauser (1962, 190) comments: 'Leadership, especially in poetry, now passed from the clergy, with their one-sidedly spiritual outlook, to the knights; monkish literature loses the leading role it had formerly held and the monk is no longer the representative of the age; its typical figure is the knight as he is portrayed, for example, in the "Rider of Bamberg", noble, proud, intelligent, the fine flower of spiritual and bodily training.'[14]

This growing balance and order of the later Middle Ages is not only represented by the combination of 'religious' and 'secular' roles, the association of realism and naturalism with the highest spirituality, but also by a real merging of masculine and feminine elements. The courtly culture is markedly feminine, women take a full part in intellectual and aesthetic life, the sensibility of the men is in many respects feminine and women achieve a position which at first sight seems incomprehensible (Hauser, 1962, 190f.).

Of course there were backslidings and persisting imbalances and for far too many life remained nasty, brutish and short, but the period shows a clear love of nature, a full and honest acceptance of the body with all its shortcomings, together with an aspiration towards the divine heights. These attitudes are manifested throughout contemporary art:[15] in illustration and painting, in sculpture and architecture, in poetry and drama, as well as in the great theological syntheses characteristic of the age. Human personality has been discovered, together with the possibilities of the deepest love and friendship.[16]

At this time there seems to have been little consideration of the human body as an entity in itself. The mediaeval mind tended to synthesis more than to analysis, and the body was seen as part of the totality of man who himself was part of an interlocking cosmos[17] in which the powers of Heaven and Hell, of Being and Not-being, of Order and Disorder, of Balance and Chaos were locked in a determined struggle with man's body and soul as a battleground and prize. Amid the confusion and stress man could only see the predetermined end through the theological virtues of faith, hope and love. There was no cult of the nude because of its associations with poverty, weakness and paganism, but there was a sense of the reality of the body and a notion that the body was well enough if left alone: it could speak for itself without the aid of make-up or excessive or disproportionate apparel. The sin of *luxuria* extended far beyond erotic sensuality and it is not insignificant that gluttony was also considered a deadly sin and that the most deadly of them all was pride.

Perhaps the mediaevals were too rational, too logical, too prone to see consonances and unitative symbols, orders and analogies in a world-vision that was as precarious as their cathedrals, but we can envy their optimism and their struggle to find and create order, balance and unity. Their achievements included the exploration and development of friendship between men and women and of love between men. They even made love an element in marriage.[18] The Middle Ages firmly asserted the unity of the cosmos in spite of appearances and thus laid the foundations of Western science.[19] They sought for order in the passions and the supremacy of reason in all things and left a lapidary statement of this faith in the soaring cathedrals which were a symbolic expression of total unity and order and of the divine image in man. Notions of order and proportion penetrated all areas of life, art and thought, to physical beauty and the human face. They were fond of 'mystic numbers' of which the holiest and most perfect was thought to be seven. They believed that the proportions of the ideal face should be related to sevenths: hair one-seventh, forehead two-sevenths, .nose to mouth one-seventh, mouth to chin one-seventh. (This aesthetic principle persisted into the age of Hogarth and Reynolds.) In some areas mediaeval thought followed the circle which they believed to be a perfect form. They were convinced of the truth that 'in my end is my beginning', that a re-creation had taken place which subsumed the original, that Christ was both Alpha and Omega, that all things were brought to a Head in Him and that His Body had many meanings. They also believed that all meanings and connotations were incorporated in one 'mega-meaning' which is why they were so facile with allegory, symbol, emblem, sacrament and image.

The Renaissance proved both the reality and the fragility of this total synthesis. Though it was not the liberation movement against monkish dogmatism that the unhistorical nineteenth century believed it to be, and though its art was an 'expression of ancient wisdom rather than of modern sexuality' (Gombrich, 1972), the Renaissance did tend to find its reference in man and time as against

God and eternity, and it diverted attention from the image to the image-maker and from the social body to the cult of the individual. Even its interest in the human body became progressively more and more superficial in the strict sense of the word. The obsession with perspective and preference for the medium of paint are both expressions of this tendency.[20] Artistically, the body was a medium for the reflection of external light rather than an expression of the inner light of the soul. It became more the object of the artist than the subject of its associated spirit. Detached and detachable art was part of the revaluation of creativity in monetary, instead of spiritual, terms.[21]

The process of representation moved from 'What is this?' through 'Who is this?' to 'What is this worth?'. Instead of being publicly possessed icons, works of art became private possessions, objects that could be exchanged for monetary counters as a hedge against inflation. They represented a new medium of material exchange instead of their former bridging function as a corporeal representation of the immaterial – the expression of an idea, a virtue, a religious and eternal truth. *Objets d'art* replaced the bodies of the saints as new and secularised 'relics' – the material remains divorced from a spirit that once gave them life and purpose. It is significant that modern man takes as much care about the authenticity and accompanying stamp of approval from the appropriate authority for the validation of these relics as ever mediaeval man did for the bones of saints. The denatured images of the late Renaissance become the reference-point for other denatured images and so the process is cumulative. Body was divorced from spirit in art long before Descartes separated them in his philosophy.

Another separation, or rather distinction, associated with the Renaissance is that between the naked and the nude.[22] To be naked is to be simple, oneself, without disguise, vulnerably human. To be nude is to be seen as a naked object, a thing displayed (and normally for the benefit of the man who owns the painting). The body has been depersonalised, its meaning limited and its significance reduced (often to a function). In spite of all the male chauvinism of mediaeval preachers, this reductionism had not occurred in the previous age: indeed, the anti-feminism of sermons was probably a rearguard action against overdeveloped personality.[23] The mediaeval balance had not been lost by the early Renaissance where Apollo or Mars appeared equally with Venus.[24] Even after this period, paintings appeared which were not manifestations of total exteriority or of a implicit contempt for the body: one might instance works of Titian,[25] Giorgione, El Greco, Vermeer, Rembrandt and Turner; 'yet if one studies these in relation to the tradition as a

whole, one discovers that they were exceptions of a very special kind'
(Berger, 1972, 87).

The loss of a balanced attitude towards male and female seems
related to the new divorce between body and soul and the
dethronement of reason[26] whose main function, in mediaeval
thought, was the provision of stability and order. Erasmus, writing
on the eve of the Reformation, remarked that the 'gods had confined
reason to a narrow corner of the brain and abandoned the rest of the
body to our passions', especially anger which takes possession of the
heart and lust which stretches its empire everywhere.[27] When the
Reformation came it brought an unbalanced approach to all nature,
exemplified in its rejection of the material in sacramental religion, in
its attack on art[28] and in the recrudescence of Gnostic and
Manichaean notions. In the face of the crisis which it interpreted
both as schism within the Body of Christ and an external assault of
reborn demonic paganism, the Catholic Church lost its own balance
as it struggled to maintain its tradition against differing interpretations of Christianity and also against a variety of 'secular'
movements: naturalism, scientism, hedonism, aggression and
brutishness.[29]

In spite of the proclamation of the expansive nudes of Rubens[30]
(who was not only a painter but a propagandist of Roman trium-
phalism and a papal special agent), Church authorities tended to
view the contemporary scene with undifferentiated suspicion and
regressed to an uncritical conservatism. A siege mentality developed
which withdrew from the 'world', conceived as anything outside
contemporary orthodoxy and clerical authority, and the 'world' thus
abandoned inordinately developed tendencies endemic in the
Renaissance towards increased superficiality, mechanism and
reductionism.[31] The disintegration was slow and uneven and
Pascal[32] illuminated the seventeenth century as he struggled to
produce a synthesis involving God, science and the world in accordance with tradition:

> Our intelligence stands in the order of intelligibles just where our
> body does in the vast realm of Nature. Confined as we are in every
> way, this middle state between the extremes figures in all our
> faculties. Our senses perceive nothing extreme: too much noise
> deafens us, too much light blinds, too great distance or too great
> nearness hampers vision, too many words or too few obscure
> speech, too much truth baffles us. . . .
>
> Man is to himself the most abnormal object in Nature, for he
> cannot conceive what body is, still less what is mind, and least of
> all how a body can be united to a mind. This is man's crowning

difficulty, and yet it is his essential being. How the spirit is attached to the body is incomprehensible in man, and yet this is what man is.

If a man will look at himself . . . seeing himself suspended between the two abysses of Infinity and Nothingness, he will tremble beholding these marvels.

Give a man no wine and he cannot find truth; similarly, if you give him too much.

But the spirit of the times was adverse and it was the ideas of the earlier Descartes[33] which were to prevail, divorcing body and mind and reducing human existence to cogitation. The process continues with Locke, La Mettrie[34] and the Abbé de Condillac and naturally art abandoned metaphysical communication, retreating further into the superficial, fragile and aristocratic world of Boucher and Fragonard and concentrating even more narrowly on matter (including the body) divorced from spirit.[35] When the human body had been reduced to a depersonalised thing: a machine to be used or a status-enhancing possession for adornment or exploitation,[36] sensitive artists searched for another subject suitable for the conveyance of symbolic or sacramental meaning. They found it in landscape which expressed the continuing love of nature and the traditional notion that nature was a source of revelation. Landscape thus became the new location for innovation in art[37] and this new vision led progressively away from the substantial and tangible to the insubstantial and intangible. This development led, through the 'picturesque' (i.e. 'suitable for a picture') to Romanticism and nature-mysticism. The sensitive, having lost the God of nature, strove to find a god in fallen nature. The loss of balance between reason and revelation, between intelligence and feeling, between body and spirit, found expression in Rousseauism and all the hypocrisy and unreality of that heresy.[38]

Artistic expression, whether in poetry or painting,[39] became a refuge from the horrors of the world. In the sciences, analysis replaced synthesis, disciplines disintegrated. Cosmology and anthropology escaped from theology, psychology lost contact with anthropology so that by the nineteenth century it not only could be said to have lost its soul but gone out of its mind. By the twentieth century its subject-matter was modelled on a machine or electrochemical processes. Generalised and increasing reductionism is characteristic of our century. Man is but a naked ape, love is only a matter of chemistry, mysticism and athletic achievement are alike induced by drugs. Human bodies, in their millions, have been reduced to cannon-fodder or soap. If they have escaped this fate and prison-camps they have been reduced to 'hands' for material production or voices for unison slogans. The mind or soul has been reduced both concomitantly and separately, assaulted not only by hidden persuaders and open propagandists but also by an artificial, mechanistic and not merely physically polluted environment.

Women[40] suffered even more than man in the depersonalising and consequent reduction. She was not only reduced to a body (or less than a body[41] as a mere sex object) but her detached body became a means, an advertising instrument, to expedite the sales of material objects.[42] It was seen as a machine and most frequently portrayed through a machine (the camera) – a detachment that began with Manet. Man's body was not only increasingly dissected and experimented on and tortured in the interests of the body politic[43] but it is increasingly regarded as a source of spare parts.[44] Its actions and reactions have been isolated and distinguished by an army of researchers extending from sociologists to athletic coaches.[45]

The fragmentation associated with reductionism is reflected in modern art which combines, in its treatment of the body, sensationalism[46] (the last stage in sensualism) with distortion. Picasso's Cubism[47] is an obvious example and the whole process may be observed in the successive stages of his *Deux femmes nues*.[48] The work of Francis Bacon, in whom 'eroticism has been turned into a sort of fetishism with deformity as its outstanding feature',[49] is perhaps even more significant. His work is characterised by distortions of ancient themes: a Velazquez portrait, a Michelangelo drawing or a representation of the Crucifixion, and it seems significant that one of his favourite sources of inspiration is the chemico-mechanical images of Maybridge and other photographers. His intention can be gathered from his words[50] as well as his works:

> I want a nailing of the flesh on to the bed. . . . I manipulate the Maybridge bodies into the forms of the bodies I have known. But, of course, in my case, with this disruption all the time of the image – or distortion or whatever you like to call it – it's an elliptical way of coming to the appearance of that particular body. . . . I do see in these images the way in which the mouth, the eyes, the ears could be used in painting so that they would be there in a totally irrational way but in a more realistic way. . . . (Sylvester, 1975, 78, 114, 117f.)

The association of utilisation, dismemberment, irrationality and reality seems the antithesis of the process which begin during the Renaissance and yet it is observably the result of that process. Bacon, like all artists, reflects his times and, like all post-Renaissance artists, he projects his personal emotions. His is a world of terror, isolation and anguish – of screaming popes and distorted figures cowering in glaringly lit but uninhabited rooms. For him, man is not merely isolated and desocialised but abject and humiliated, stripped of everything including even his bodily shape and consistency. This is the Nietzschean world where God is dead and the Sartrian world where existence precedes essence. It is also the consumer world of mass machine-production, a world where all distinctions are merely fashions – in short, a world of disintegration. Assertion of the psychosomatic unity of man is the expression and symbol of an integrated world and therefore man's mind and body in separation are the prime objects of contemporary attack, whether in political or other theory or in the practice of art. This attack involves an onslaught on those traditions in thought or art which represent the Christian humanism achieved at so much cost and effort in Western Europe. Examples may be drawn from a variety of sources, but one may instance the biomorphic art of Miro or Tanguy where repulsive abstracts hint at a resemblance to natural parts of the human body – usually breasts, buttocks or sexual organs, so that 'often the spectator is conscious of a sort of hostility towards the achievements of the past: some of the variations might almost be described as rapes or dismemberments'.[51] Of his grotesque series *Corps de Dame* which combine adult degeneration with pseudo-naïveté, Dubonnet said: 'It pleased me (and I think this predilection is more or less constant in all my paintings) to juxtapose brutally, in these feminine bodies, the extremely general and the extremely particular, the metaphysical and the grotesquely trivial. In my view, the one is considerably reinforced by the presence of the other.'[52] Similarly, there is a tendency to use brutal materials and machine-derived images in contemporary artistic representation of the human body and one might instance the nudes of Tom Wesselmann which are arbitrary, flat silhouettes – bodiless, 'of no substance' and, consequently, inhuman.[53]

Since the eighteenth century, the Western world has detached itself, with increasing acceleration, from the thought and tradition which nurtured it. Nevertheless, even the neglected theologians and Christian thinkers would admit that though the world may ignore theology its very existence depends on God and His Spirit is not confined to the Church. Consequently, though there were obvious losses as polarisation increased between secular and sacred, there were also manifest gains. In the nineteenth century there was a slowly growing belief that maltreating the body rarely improves the mind (though the very superstition that was being abandoned seems to have become popular in the seventeenth century). Our own times have seen the beginnings of a return of humanism in the independent discipline of psychology and a growing recognition of psychomatic unity in medical theory. Ecclesiastical religion seems to be opening its barricades to the breath of the Spirit even when it blows from outside the Church, and there is an increasing acceptance of insights from medicine, philosophy,[54] psychology,[55] sociology and biology.[56] 'The Resurrection of the Body means the whole body. The draperies that Pope Paul IV had painted on Michelangelo's *Last Judgment* have been removed. All body parts, as in the David or the Sistine ceiling, are equally beautiful, equally worthy. The "resurrection of the body" means "an erotic sense of reality".'[57]

Much remains to be done to recover a contemporary equivalent of the mediaeval synthesis and *a fortiori* to go beyond that achievement. There is still no adequate theology of sex[58] or systematic consideration of the body in Christian terms.[59] But there are signs of a realisation that the extended use of the word 'body' is not a mere metaphor. Worries about pollution may well represent a reassertion of the organic against the too-long-dominant mechanical view of nature. Ivan Illich has shown the evil of institutions[60] when they are bodies from which the spirit has departed. He pointedly draws attention (Illich, 1975, 154f.) to the implicit and often explicit assumption that the human body is the possession of a professional corporation which alone may decide when it is healthy, diseased or dead and to the seminal fact that the hubris which characterised the aristocrats of the Italian Renaissance has now spread to all men and to all human activities from art to politics and industrialisation. Against this, he stresses that it is the body which is the seat and memento of man's fragility, the expression of his individuality and the source of his relatedness to both his fellows and to nature. This 'consciously lived fragility, individuality and relatedness make the experience of pain, of sickness and of death an integral part of his life. The ability to cope with this trio autonomously is fundamental to his health.' (Illich, 1975, 169.) Words such as these lead the historian of Christian attitudes to the body to the belief, that, after a long sojourn in the desert, he is at last in sight of an oasis.

12

THE WAY AHEAD

Though it is true that many religious people fear the body and though in modern times there has been much talk about the 'anti-body attitude of religion', it seems that some extreme attitudes within the Church have been taken by outsiders as expressing the normal approach without even considering the basis of these extreme attitudes, and consequently what has begun as a sound reaction against unbalanced views within the Church has hardened into an indiscriminating prejudice against her attitudes.

I have tried to show by picking up hints and signs that the fundamental religious experience is the total response of man as an embodied person to religious reality and value and from this, as Davis (1976) says,[1] 'it would follow that we should encourage and train the bodily component of our affectivity, direct and refine it so that it becomes a medium of spiritual meaning. The body is not only a manifestation of the Spirit, it could well be for some people the manifestation'.

For this reason, the contemporary use of the body (particularly, of course, the feminine body) as a means of advertising anything from cosmetics to cars, from beer to bathing suits, is not a manifestation of an adjusted attitude towards the body or of an advance in its valuation. On the contrary, it is an exploitation akin to that of the exploitation of slaves. There are many kinds of prostitution and the exchange of money for the use of a body represents price not value.

Another indication of the complete failure of modern developments (and perhaps a sign that the 'advance' is on the wrong road) in adjusting to 'bodiliness' is seen in the rather peculiar cult of the (feminine) naked body at that fleeting stage when adolescence has just passed into maturity. If we had a real acceptance of the body in its essential nature we would accept and reverence all bodies at all stages of their development – at different ages, of all shapes and sizes, bodies which bear the marks of their fragility, of the pain and struggle of human life, bodies which are prone to accident, disease, ageing and death. The body should evoke compassion, pity, love rather than lust (with its variants of sadism and masochism), greed and possessiveness. A simple aesthetic approval of the body is to some degree an abstraction, an objectification and therefore a dehumanisation.

The most 'communicative' area of the body is the human face and we do not normally apply aesthetic canons of perfection here. A face can be hateful even though it has firm flesh, finely textured skin and perhaps perfect physical proportions. There is, if not a greater beauty, a greater stimulus to love in a face which presents the total expression of a lovable personality. Similarly, a fully human response to the body would be to its manifestation of a real, fully human (and therefore suffering) human being. Its living beauty is never exclusively physical.

Nudity, therefore, can express a rejection of the human body and this is something which the Middle Ages appreciated – that the centrally spiritual can be reduced to the pure physicality of the sensual and that clothes are important. They allow levels of expressiveness: they amplify the body-language of bearing and gesture, of stance and movement, even of personality, value and commission.

Again to quote from Davis:

> It would be a mistake to interpret the sensuality of our day as an acceptance of the body when women, at great discomfort, force their bodies to conform to an ideal of young and changeless beauty. They are denying the reality of their actual bodies and men who engage in phantasies of sexual athletics and perhaps even try to live them out are refusing their sexuality as an organic, living and ageing bodily power and are conceiving it as a machine. 'La Sexe Machine' is the apt name of a Montreal topless night-club. Sensuality is a rejection of the body because in sensual indulgence the body is driven by the mind against its own spontaneous rhythms and this rejection of matter, in particular of the living matter of the body, is characteristic of our culture today.[2]

There can be no doubt of the appreciation of the body in the sense of a loving care in the periods of the Church's strength and influence. It is not without significance that the 'corporal' works of mercy were the epitome of love of one's neighbour flowing from the primal love of God. It is not an accident that the mediaeval Church created hospitals, refuges for the sick and the lame, almshouses and bede-houses. There was a real care, an undoubted sacrificial care, for the body. There was a real care and appreciation of 'bodiliness' which was also expressed in the character of mediaeval art and symbolism[3] and the closeness of mediaeval life and spirituality to natural rhythms, natural forms and natural processes.

One of the central signs of the body's nature is its need for food for it becomes what it consumes, and perhaps a more significant sign of modern attitudes to the body may be seen not in its attitude to nudity or sex but to food – its production, preparation and presentation. Its production has been mechanised and standardised, its preparation has been reduced to processing and its presentation is 'a matter of utility and speed instead of ritual and recreation.

The implications of attitudes to the body and the material could be worked out in a number of contemporary applications including the asphalt jungle and the concrete wilderness. It is undoubtedly true that the modern city is not designed as a material environment but is the result of a cerebral nightmare. It is the result or ratiocination, of 'planning', the application of brain or intellect without regard to emotion, sensibility or any kind of consideration for sensuous factors. There is no respect either for the materials used or for the nature of man. The preferred materials are concrete or plastic which possess not so much a 'thisness' of their own but a 'thatness' which can be manipulated or imposed upon them by the planner or so-called architect. One has only to look at the living remains of a mediaeval city such as York or Siena or Albi and compare them with such an abomination as Birmingham to see this point most clearly exemplified. To quote again from Davis: 'To call our age materialistic is a false interpretation. The dominant culture of our time has no love or appreciation of matter, no feel for it, especially not for living matter with its organic rhythms, its processes of growth and decay. Plastic Flowers may serve as a typical symbol.'[4]

A more accurate name for our age would be the Machine Age, for the machine is matter when overcome and subordinated to the mind. It is a significant boast when one set of city fathers describe their creation as 'the motorway city of the future' or when 'spare-part surgery' is seen as the shape of things to come. 'Spare parts' belong to machines, to exploitation, to mass-production, to mechanistic thinking (one might also note the application of 'processing language' by the D.E.S. to what used to be institutions of learning – they talk of 'input', 'output' and 'throughput', 'full utilisation of plant', 'unit cost-effectiveness', etc.).

When the machine becomes the model, the machine takes its revenge by subduing, in the end, man's natural requirements to those of the machine. (Corbusier spoke of a house as 'a machine for living in'; modern planners speak of both houses and their inhabitants as 'units' – the next number below one is zero.)

The danger of the machine was long recognised by those educated in what rightly were called 'the humanities' and by the artist and novelists. The distinction between machine and tool was made a long time ago, and in the 1930s, Eric Gill and others, defined a tool as a development of man's limbs and senses by extending the body, while a machine is something that envelops the body. One increases the power of the body, the other enslaves it (and perhaps its accompanying mind and soul as well).

Parallel to the distinction between tool and machine is the distinction between sensuousness and sensuality. The roots of this distinction are perhaps as old as St Paul, distinction between *sarkinos* and *sarkikos* but, to quote a more recent Christian, Davis distinguishes as follows:

Sensuousness is when we participate in the spontaneous rhythms and responses of the body and are open to the joys and delights, pain, suffering and stress of bodily experience. It implies an ability to relax which I understand as allowing the spontaneous responses of the body to hold sway and suspend the controlling and driving impulse-impetus of the rational mind and will. Sensuality, in contrast, is what happens when the body is driven by the mind and used as an instrument of pleasure for reasons found in man's mental and spiritual state. The roots of sensuality are not in bodily impulses but in man's mind as John Wren-Lewis writes:

The body itself seems to know that it does not want sensual indulgence. It takes only a small amount of real sensory awareness to waken the body to the fact that it is being biologically maltreated by the way mind organises life and this maltreatment happens as much when the individual wallows in self-indulgent sensuality as it does when he strives neurotically for wealth and power, regiments himself to mechanical work-routines or suffers extreme poverty' (*What Shall We Tell the Children?* (London 1971), p. 152).

Sensuality is the submission of the body to the driving, straining consciousness of a mind alienated from its bodiliness. It is not, despite the traditional view, the subjection of the mind to bodily impulses. In sensuality, the body does not enslave; it is enslaved.

I would further argue that sensuousness accompanies a sacramental, mystical view of the world, in which the body and physical nature are mediatory of the spirit, whereas sensuality implies a destruction of the mediatory, symbolic character of the physical world and the reduction of that world to pure physicality.[5]

Sacramentalism attributes meaning and grace to matter. The opposed view of matter is seeing matter, so to speak, as a 'thing-in-itself', as a collection of physical *facts* and their interrelationships. It results from the bifurcation of the so-called 'scientific' way of looking at things from the total humane perceptions. It results from the 'scientific revolution' whose success stemmed from its ability to manipulate nature and resulted in the scientific arrogance symbolised by its total appropriation of the name and nature of 'science' (i.e. knowledge) to itself.

When the body (using the word in a total sense of the material world as the mediaevals would also have seen it) is reduced to physical 'facts', then the sense-experiences become mere physical objects and events, split off from the consciousness of the observer and deprived of any meaning other than their relationships to other, separate, physical objects. Such a world is of course no longer sacramental, it is utterly and fundamentally mechanical. We have tried to show how this manner of thinking which began in the Renaissance and became dominant in the eighteenth century has not only deprived the world of moral and philosophic meaning but has produced an increasingly total alienation.

When, on the other hand, the physical world is seen as related to human living (man as the 'point' of the world), sensuousness and not sensuality, becomes the appropriate key to attitudes of the body. Sensuality is the result of objectifying the body as a physical 'thing' to be *used* and thus stripped of its sacramental meaning and physical associations. (Consonant with this are the approaches of some handbooks of sex education which are concerned with how things 'work' rather than with what they 'mean'. They result in good mechanics rather than in good human beings, in skilled technicians rather than human communicators and communicants). Language, as always, reflects the mind – 'switched on', 'turned on', the set of 'making love' is coterminous with the set of applying mechanical stimuli. Value, meaning, total human communication do not fit into this mechanical mode of thought.

Reductionism is characteristic of contemporary 'realism', what may be called the '. . . . is only . . . syndrome' – 'man is only a naked ape', 'the mind is only a computer', 'sexuality is only an appetite like hunger' – and the word 'only' need neither be appreciated nor expressed – 'painting is putting the right colour in the right place', 'religion is the opium of the people'.

Many uses of the word 'body' are a form of reductionism by which the concept is constrained to a physical object, therefore Davis wishes us to use wider words like 'bodiliness' when referring to human personal experience as embodied subjects. 'When we say "body"', he says, 'we objectify and the danger is that we objectify our "bodiliness" only partially as though it were *merely* physical and not the embodiment of spirit. We might also say that "bodiliness" is what we experience when we live sensuously as embodied persons; but "the body" is what we experience when we indulge in sensuality and relate to our own bodies as physical objects alienated from us.'[6]

If we accept this useful approach, sensuality becomes a term for the subordination of the body to the calculating mind. 'It implies a denial of the participatory mode of relating to the body and physical world, an ignoring or rejection of the sacramental meaning and mystical mediation of bodiliness. It is basically a rejection of the body, a rejection of its spontaneous rhythms, of its expressiveness, of its eros – which is an eros towards transcendent values.' Davis continues:

> The puritan, then, who sees the body merely as a sensual obstacle to the moral and religious life, and the libertine who sees the body as a mere instrument of pleasure, have the same conception of the human body and the same attitude to it. Both, in fact, reject bodiliness. Both fear and repudiate the spontaneous, sensuous eros of the body. Both ignore or deny its sacramental meaning and mystical mediation. Both reduce the body to its pure physicality and set it over gainst a rational consciousness alienated from the body. Both shut off their inner self from feeling as the spontaneous, connatural response to value, because they fear its independence of the controlling consciousness of the rational self, its transcendence of established rules and conventions, and its frequent disruption of preconceived and calculated goals. [7]

If support were required for this clear and, to the present author, fairly obvious attitude one can see it in the puritan who has historically rejected the sacramental life. He objects to all matter intruding into the 'religious' sphere. Perhaps the only human creation which they do not resist entirely is that of music, because of its alleged ethereal and immaterial quality. On the other hand, the true tradition seems one of substance, a tradition of the sanctification of the material environment and conditions of the human state. The Catholic version of the Christian religion presents the most material of religions, focusing attention on matter all the time – on bread and wine, on oil and salt, on water, on word and gesture, on life, on the flesh, on the sacramental flesh of Christ, on the flesh of His crucified and resurrected Body, on the dead flesh – on the fragmented dead bodies of saints – in the pervasive cult of relics, on material places where God has walked or revealed Himself through His saints or which has been hallowed by their life or death. These seem to me, whatever aberrations they may carry in their train, are of the very essence of the Christian, *incarnation and sacramental* and therefore material and bodily view of life. The Christian, true to his beginnings and authentic tradition, should not reject the body, but he may have great need of distinguishing between a false acceptance in terms of machines and sensuality from a true acceptance in terms of sacrament and sensuousness.

NOTES

Preface

1. In prose there were the hagiographical accounts of spiritual friendship mentioned later, as well as a number of treatises on friendship. There were also letters between seculars and religious and between nuns and clerics of which Hauser (1962, I, 201) writes: 'It is true that the friendly correspondence between clerics and nuns reveals, even in the eleventh century some curious sentimental relationships which hover between friendship and love, and already betray that mingling of the spiritual and the sensual familiar to us in chivalric love.' It could well be that relationships which hover between friendship and love and are so human that they unite body and soul are 'curious' to a twentieth-century writer, but they could also be seen as an intimation of an ordered and full acceptance of the reality of the human condition. Of the lay productions – romances and knightly poetry – Hauser (1962, 198) comments: 'There is hardly an epoch of Western history whose literature so revels in descriptions of the beauty of the naked body, of dressing and undressing, of bathing and washing of the heroes by girls and women, of wedding nights and copulation, of visits and invitations into bed, as does the chivalric poetry of the rigidly moral Middle Ages. Even such a serious work, as one written with such a high purpose, as Wolfram's *Parzival* is full of descriptions that border upon the obscene' and later (p. 200) he concludes: 'Knightly love poetry is, in spite of its sensualism, thoroughly mediaeval and Christian' (ibid. p. 200). We would not demur with this judgment except perhaps to query 'in spite of'.

2. For the tensions and problems compressed within this aphorism, see Lovejoy (1936). The principle continued to be emphasised long after Aquinas, e.g. in Cardinal Nicholas of Cusa (d. 1464), *De Doct. Ignorantia*, iii, 1. It is found in Blaise Pascal and was maintained into the eighteenth century when it began to disintegrate under the dominant mercantile notions that created things existed only for exploitation, immediate profit and other abuse. Attitudes to the human body, in particular, showed this decay: slavery returned both *de jure* and *de facto* – the body was either treated as a living machine or made to serve inanimate ones and it was not only sold itself but, ultimate degradation, was used as an instrument to sell artefacts: cars, toothpaste, tobacco and sweets.

3. As against the 'spiritual' Platonism which always attracts unworldly minds but which denigrates both the body and (logically) art which it sees as nothing more than an imitation of something which itself is only a secondary reality. (see Plato, *The Republic*, Bk. x and his *dialogue, Phaedo* (Jowett, 1928, pp. 118 – 274) and extract in Gerber (1972, pp. 130–2), cf. also Murdoch (1977).

4. For recent American studies of some aspects of sex exploitation in the public media, see *Journal of Communication* (Philadelphia, 1976), vol. 26, no. 1.

5. A German example of this genre, dated 1320, is illustrated and discussed in de Silva (1968, 28–30).

Chapter 1

1. Cf. the well-known lines from Juvenal's *Third Satire* 62f. (Ramsey, 1965, 37): 'Long since the Syrian Orontes has flowed into the Tiber, bringing with it its language and customs.' The marvels of India were known to the Greeks and Romans of this period and affected their literature, e.g. influence on Achilles Tatius' novel *Leucippe and Clitophon* which probably dates from the turn of the first century A.D. (tr. S. Goulee, London 1961).

2. The lesser deities included Fortuna virilis ('man's luck'), the probable dedication of the little temple still standing near the Tiber. He was commonly worshipped by women of the poorer classes in the male bathing establishments because 'there are uncovered those parts of the male body which seek woman's favour' (*Fasti Praenesti*, Kal. April.). They also included Liber, symbolised by a large wooden phallus, who was later identified with the Greek Dionysius. The phallus (in Latin *fascinum* and the origin of our word 'fascinate') was the most popular amulet or good-luck charm in ancient Rome as it still is in contemporary Naples. It was hung round children's necks, set over shop doors, adorned the triumphal chariot of a general, carved into the structure of a bridge (one survives near the South Tyne) or over a city gate (sometimes with the superscription 'Here dwells happiness'). Cf. St Augustine, *The City of God*, Bk. VII, 29.

Priapus was a similar being, represented with an enormous erect genital organ. His functions included the protection of gardens, the patronage of human fecundity and the solution of sexual difficulties.

It is perhaps worth mentioning that the phallus, besides its happy associations, was often conceived by the Romans sadistically as a weapon or instrument of punishment to inflict chastisement through gross sexual acts. This theme runs through the collection of Latin verse called *Priapeia* which consists of anonymous, obscene doggerel with a strongly sadistic tone. Cf. Kiefer (1969, 259f.).

3. The Christian apologist, St Augustine, takes full advantage of this proclivity when he waxes ironical at the expense of the good pagan whose wedding-night labours require the assistance of the deities Virginiensis, Subigus, Prema, Pertunda, Venus and Priapus (*City of God*, Bk. VI, 9). Venus is a comparative latecomer into the Roman pantheon. Originally, she seems to have been the patroness of gardens and flowers and then coalesces with the Greek importation, Aphrodite. Julius Caesar claimed descent from her and Augustus used her cult to glorify the Julian dynasty. Her worship was ambiguous: she was both the guardian of honourable marriage and the patroness of prostitutes, as well as somehow being considered as the mother of the Roman nation. The ambiguity is such that in later thought there are 'two Venuses'.

4. Cf. St Paul's speech in Acts, xvii, 23.

5. For Cybele, see Ovid's *Fasti*, Bk. iv, 11. 223ff., (tr. J. G. Frazer London

1967), and Catullus' *Poems*, lxiii, (tr. F. W. Cornish London 1966, pp. 91–7. Compare the worship, restricted to women, of Bona Dea (The Good Goddess), a variant of the mother-goddess, which was regarded by Plutarch as a gentle, gay cult and by his contemporary Juvenal as an unrestrained orgy. See also Kiefer (1969, 144f.) and St Augustine, *City of God*, Bk. Vii, 26.

6. The ecstatic Bacchanalian movement, associated with the god Liber, seems to have reached Rome after the crisis of the Punic Wars (264–146 B.C.) when its development acquired such a form as to fill all serious-minded Romans with anxiety and even terror (see Livy's *History*, Bk. XXXIX, xv, 6, 9ff., vol. XIV, Loeb edn. *hoes* (tr. E. T. Sage, London 1965, p. 261):

'The rites had become open to everyone, so that men had attended as well as women, and their licentiousness had been increased with the darkness of night; there was no shameful or criminal deed from which they shrank. The men were guilty of more immoral acts among themselves than the women. Those who struggled against dishonour, or were slow to inflict it on others, were slaughtered in sacrifice like beasts. The holiest article of their faith was to think nothing a crime. The men prophesied like madmen with their bodies distorted by frenzy. The women, dressed like Bacchantes and with their hair unbound, ran to the Tiber with torches ablaze. . . . They said, "The gods have taken them" when certain men were bound to a windlass and snatched away out of sight into secret caverns. These were the men who had refused either to take the oath or to join in the crimes or to be violated. The society had an enormous membership – almost half the population – and included men and women of noble birth . . . fanatics maddened by night-vigils, by wine, by nighly shrieking and uproar.'

This was the situation which produced the Senatorial decree of 186 B.C. which prohibited the Bacchanalia, though the institution returned in a modified form during the imperial period.

7. See Acts, xix, 23 – xx, 1.

8. Acts xvii, 15–34, esp. 18. For another aspect of the syncretism of the late classical world see the wondering crowds' identification of the miracle-working apostles with an epiphany of their gods in Acts xiv, 11–13.

9. On the other hand, it has been said of Seneca (4 B.C.-A.D. 65), the Spanish tutor of Nero, that his letters and treatises are full of sentences which look as though they were written by a Christian. The early Church explained this by producing a spurious correspondence between the philosopher and his contemporary, St Paul. The truth seems to have been rather that early Christianity was Stoicised rather than a late Stoic was Christianised. There can be little doubt that the pervasive Stoic ideas affected Christian thinkers, different as both their origins and deep foundations were.

Stoics cultivated detachment and suspected enthusiasm. They were the first to despise and condemn 'irregular' sexual satisfactions, though they did not value marriage very highly and a contempt, even a rejection, of the world became an essential characteristic of the school.

10. Some mention should, perhaps, be made at this point of Neo-Platonism and its possible relation to notions of asceticism. It was a very ancient Orphic and Pythagorean idea (perhaps derived from India) that the soul 'sinks' out of a pre-existent state of bliss when it enters this life and consequently its bodily imprisonment appears as a punishment or purgation which the soul must endure before – if it completes the process successfully – it returns to the heavenly sphere. The purer the life on earth, the quicker the return to the realms above. Purity means single care for the soul and consequently an aversion from the sensual. It is described as follows in the *Phaedo* (66c.):

'For the body is a source of endless trouble to us by reason of the mere requirement of food; and it is liable also to diseases which overtake and impede us in the search after true being; it fills us full of loves, and lusts, and fears, and fancies of all kinds, and endless foolery, and in fact, as men say, takes away from us the power of thinking at all . . . even if we are at leisure and betake ourselves to some speculation, the body is always breaking in on us, causing turmoil and confusion in our enquiries, and so amazing us that we are prevented from seeing the truth. It has been proved to us by experience that if we would have pure knowledge of anything we must be quit of the body . . . either knowledge is not to be attained at all or, if at all, after death. . . . In this present life, I reckon that we make the nearest approach to knoweldge when we have the least possible intercourse or communion with the body, and are not surfeited with the bodily nature, but keep ourselves pure until the hour when God himself is pleased to release us. And thus having got rid of the foolishness of the body we shall be pure and hold converse with the pure, and know of ourselves the clear light everywhere, which is no other than the light of truth. For the impure are not permitted to approach the pure.' (Jowett, 1928, 186f.)

This development reached its climax with *Plotinus* (tr. H. Armstrong, 3 vols., London 1966), the corner-stone of the Neo-Platonic school, who flourished in the middle of the third century A.D. and who 'conceived asceticism not as a violent annihilation of each and every natural impulse, but as the consistent conquest of the instincts, "the body", by the spirit' (Kiefer, 1969, 153; see also Turnbull, 1934).

11. Cited Perowne, 1969, 79. The whole work is invaluable for the religious background.

12. Horace was a Roman poet whose works became school texts almost in his own lifetime and continued to be used until the death of grammar schools in our own time. He lived from 65 to 8 B.C. and the implied references are to his *Odes*, Bk. i, 11; i, 4; iv, 7 (tr. C. E. Bennett, London 1964).

13. One of the greatest Roman poets, a magnificent craftsman possessed of immense psychological subtlety. His love affairs seem to have brought him more pain than pleasure. He lived from about 87 to 54 B.C. and the references are to ideas expressed in *Poems* 3, 5, 8, 32, 69, tr. F. W. Cornish (London 1966).

14. According to tradition, St Peter played his small part in filling such

an 'interval' by being crucified upside down on the *spina* or central barrier of the race-track in Nero's Vatican gardens.

15. In the Byzantine period, theological factions became associated with specific 'colours' so that supporters' clubs were almost theological schools.

16. Juvenal, *Satires*, XI 193–202. (tr. Ramsay, 1965, 235).

17. The theatre of Pompey, opened in 55 B.C. and in which Julius Caesar was assassinated while the Senate was temporarily meeting there, had a seating capacity estimated at 27,000.

18. The word means 'one who can act any part' or 'mime everything'.

19. Graffiti have been found describing gladiators as 'the maiden's prayer and delight' and 'the doctor to cure girls'. Faustina, wife of the Stoic emperor Marcus Aurelius, was accused of liaisons with gladiators and her depraved son, Commodus, was suspected of being the fruit of one of these unions. Distinguished gladiators were the subjects of many poems and their portraits were to be found on lamps, dishes and pots.

20. 'I chanced to stop in at a midday show, expecting fun, wit and some relaxation, when men's eyes take respite from the slaughter of their fellow-men. It was just the reverse. The preceding combats were merciful by comparison, now all trifling is put aside and it is pure murder. The men have no protective covering. Their entire bodies are exposed to the blows, and no blow is ever struck in vain. . . . In the morning men are thrown to the lions and the bears, at noon they are thrown to the spectators. The spectators call for the slayer to be thrown to those who in turn will slay him, and they detain the victor for another butchering. The outcome for the combatants is death; the fight is waged with sword and fire. This goes on while the arena is free (i.e. during an interlude in the scheduled programme). "But one of them was a highway-robber, he killed a man!" Because he killed, he deserved to suffer this punishment – granted. "Kill him! Lash him! Burn him! Why does he meet the sword so timidly? Why doesn't he kill boldly? Why doesn't he die game? Whip him to meet his wounds! Let them trade blow for blow, chest bare and within reach!" And when the show stops for intermission, "Let's have men killed meanwhile! Let's not have nothing going on!"' (tr. in Lewis and Reinhold, 1966, II, 230 cf. Seneca, *Moral Epistles* tr. R. M. Gummere, 1967, I, 31f.).

21. Juvenal (*c*. A.D. 60–140), *Satires*, VI, 11. 114–32 (tr. Ramsay, 1965, 193).

22. Pompeii, near Naples, was destroyed almost overnight in the famous eruption of Vesuvius in A.D. 79. The nature of the cataclysm has produced a unique mine of information about every aspect of life in a small Roman town in the first century A.D.

23. Petronius, called the 'Arbiter', was compromised in a political conspiracy and stoically committed suicide by opening his veins in A.D. 65. The reference to Trimalchio is from the famous *Satyricon*, lxxv (tr. M. Hezeltine, London 1961, p. 151).

24. A toy survived from this period which is, or was, in the Berlin State Museum. It consisted of a terracotta model of a slave so constructed that it could be hung up and whipped by its child-owner. Children then as now loved to imitate in their games the actions of their parents.

25. Juvenal, *Satires*, XIV, 11, 14–24 (tr. Ramsay, 1965, 267), cf. Seneca (4 B.C.–A.D. 65), *Moral Epistles*, xlvii, (tr. R. M. Gummere, 3 vol., London 1967, I pp. 301ff.).

26. Juvenal, *Satires* VI, 11. 219–23, (tr. Ramsay 1965, 101).

27. Pliny the Elder (A.D. 23–79), a Roman naturalist who died investigating the eruption of Vesuvius. The reference is to his *Natural History*, Bk. XXIX, viii, 17 (tr. W. H. S. Jones, 10 vols, London 1963 VIII, 193).

28. Lewis and Reinhold (1966, II). Index s.v. 'Baths' and especially p. 92.

29. The roman coin *as* is roughly worth four new pence in contemporary money.

30. Cf. Seneca, *Moral Epistles*, lvi, 1–2 (Gummere, 1967 I, 373f.).

31. 'The coarse, sensual character of the nation made it impossible for them to see a naked body as anything but a sexual stimulus. Cicero believes that homosexuality is a natural product of nakedness (*Tusc*. iv, 33) and Propertius and Plautus both show that the naked body of the beloved is admired from purely erotic grounds, but never as a work of art (Plautus, *Most*. 289; Propertius *Poems* II, xv, 13; Seneca, *Epp*. 88). It is very significant that in Latin the word *nudus* (naked) can also mean "rough", "uncouth" (as in Pliny, *Epp*. IV, xiv, 4). The Romans always took nakedness to be synonymous with indecency, impropriety.' (Kiefer, 1969, 161.)

32. Ovid (43 B.C.–A.D. 18) in his poem the *Art of Love*, reduces love to physical intercourse and makes seduction into a heartless game. As part of his instruction to the beginner, he lists the best places for a 'pick-up':

The tiered playhouse gives you amplest scope;
There's hunting richer than you dared to hope.
There you shall find a mistress or a toy
To touch but once or be a lasting joy. . . . (17)

Nor miss the ring where high-bred coursers race,
You'll find much vantage in that crowded place.
Sit next your mistress, none can say you nay,
Press side to side as close as e'er you may;
Thanks to the custom of the crowded bench,
Coy though she be, you're bound to squeeze the wench . . . (19f.)

Such aids to new love will the Circus bring,
Or the grim bustle of the boxing ring.
Love oft in that arena fights a bout.
When 'tis the looker-on who's counted out. (21)

Lesser games also provide opportunities

If with the numbered ivories she play,
Take the first throw, and throw the game away.
At knucklebones ne'er make her pay her loss,
The luckless deuce yourself contrive to toss;
And when the raiding chessmen take the field,
Your champion to his crystal foe must yield . . . (60)

But the baths provide both security and special opportunities:

When, while the lackey guards your clothes outside,
The baths much scope for furtive joys provide (116)

The references are to pages in B. P. Moore (1965), also tr. J. H. Mozley (1962). Martial (*c.* A.D. 40–104) in his *Epigrams*, xi, 47 (tr. W. C. A. Ker, 2 vols, London 1961) mentions men visiting baths not to bathe but to have a convenient opportunity for meeting their mistresses. Mixed bathing became established in the first century A.D. when only the women wore a bathing costume (a sort of short apron). Objectionable incidents marked this practice and reforming emperors, such as Hadrian (117–38), tried to discontinue it but without success. Quintilian, imperial Professor of Literature and Rhetoric under Vespasian (A.D. 69–79) remarks of the men's baths that 'it is characteristic of the adulteress to bath in company with men'.

Chapter 2

1. This section is much indebted to A. Gelin, *The Concept of Man in the Bible* (Eng. tr. London 1968) ch. i, but a much more detailed treatment of the Old Testament material may be found in H. W. Wolff, *Anthropology of the Old Testament* where chs. iii, vi, viii, xviii, xix seem specially relevant to this essay.

2. 'The word *nephesh* occurs 755 times in the Old Testament. . . . Today we are coming to the conclusion that it is only in a very few passages that the translation 'soul' corresponds to the meaning of *nephesh*' (Wolff, 1975, 10).

3. See Gelin (1968, 16), but compare Wolff (1974, 40–58) where there is a detailed analysis of *leb(ab)* 'the most important word in the vocabulary of Old Testament anthropology (which) is usually translated "heart" and which is the source of reason in Hebrew thought.

4. 'When the most frequent substantives (in the Hebrew text) are as a general rule translated by "heart", "soul", "flesh", and "spirit", misunderstandings arise which have important consequences. These translations go back to the Septuagint, the ancient Greek translation, and they lead in a false direction of a dichotonomic or trichotonomic anthropology, in which body, soul and spirit are in opposition to one another. The question still has to be investigated of how, with the Greek language, a Greek philosophy has here supplanted Semitic biblical views, overwhelming them with a foreign influence.' (Wolff 1974, 7).

5. See Wolff (1974, 32–9).

6. See T. R. Glover, *The Conflict of Religions in the Roman Empire* (1923, 37f.).

7. It is possibly worth observing that, in the English language, the words 'wholeness', 'health' and 'holiness' are cognate.

8. This usage is a development of the association of *ruah* with mere physical energy as in e.g. Judg. xv, 19; I Kgs. x, 5.

9. This idea is, of course, not unconnected with the notion of man being 'in the image of God' on which cf. below pp. 23f.

10. The adherents of this school of thought even made puns depending on the similarity of the Greek words *soma* (body) and *sema* (tomb).

11. See Orchard (1953, 135). There also seems to have been some idea that blood was involved in reproduction as well as the significance of the fact that it was the male generative member that was operated upon.

12. See Wolff (1975, 60–2).

13. For the uncleanness of dead bodies, see Lev. xxi, 11; N. ix, 6, 10, x, 11, 16.

14. Works of Flavius Jospehus (tr. W. Whiston, 1865, 1). A more accessible translation is available in the Loeb Classical Library – vol. 186, Josephus; *Life, against Apion* (tr. H. St. J. Thackeray, London 1966). Josephus is describing events *c.* A.D. 50. The antiquity of the cold bath 'cure' is worth noticing as is the near identification of the Pharisees with the Stoics.

15. Perhaps the commonest Greek statue, usually catalogued as 'Apollo', represents the young noble victor in the Olympic Games (which was a preserve of the nobility that alone possessed the means and leisure for training and entry). Hauser (1962, I, 64) suggests that the first statues were 'introduced to spur on the weaker, less ambitious, less spirited generations' who succeeded the golden age of the aristocracy (776–536 B.C. – the latter is the date of the first dedication of a statue of a victor). The statues were not individual likenesses but idealised images, preserving the memory of a particular victory and acting as propaganda for the games. Later, bodies seem to have been mass-produced in factories and 'personalised' by pinning on a particular head (hence the large numbers of headless Greek statues which survive).

The thoughts on the 'image of God' are much indebted to Gelin (1968, 27–39) but cf. also ch. xviii in Wolff (1974, 159–65) entitled 'God's image – the steward of the world'. On the 'image of God' in general see Leeuw (1963, 304–27) a totally excellent and pregnant work with much relevance to anyone concerned with human movement or art.

16. One might draw attention to the classical myths concerning Jupiter's (or Zeus') sexual activities while in the guise of a bull, swan, etc. It is perhaps worth noting that Ovid, who in his *Metamorphoses* (tr. F. J. Miller), retells many of these stories, begins with an account of the creation of heaven, earth and the sea, with birds and beasts and fishes, continuing 'A living

creature of finer stuff than these, more capable of lofty thought, *one who could have dominion over all the rest*, was lacking yet. Then man was born . . . and, though all other animals are prone, and fix their gaze upon the earth, he gave to man uplifted face and bade him *stand erect* and turn his eyes to heaven.' (*Metamorphoses*, Bk. I, 76–88 – the poem was completed in A.D. 7, just before Ovid's banishment by Augustus, allegedly for the immorality of his love poetry but perhaps for more personal and private reasons.)

17. On this, see Jacob (1958, 166ff.) and Wolff (1975, 159ff.). The notion of 'stewardship', continued in Christianity, is not unrelated to modern concerns about ecology, resources, pollution, etc. and is the antithesis of greedy 'exploitation' or thoughtless 'development'.

18. For examples of such interpretations, see B. Ulanov's 'The Song of Songs: the rhetoric of love', in Oesterreicher (1962, 89–118).

19. Some exegetes think it describes either (a) a shepherd girl who becomes a contented wife of King Solomon or (b) a shepherd girl, taken by Solomon, who remains faithful to another shepherd.

20. Among the upper classes in the Near East and in Rome the main (evening) meal was consumed in a recumbent posture. The 'right' hand is associated in the Bible with action, power and honour.

21. The girl has already been described as a garden of delights which the lover longs to enter and enjoy the fruits thereof. It would require a whole book to explore the recurrent theme in Western literature of the delightsome garden. It probably has Persian antecedents but it enters Western thought through the Bible and the Garden of Eden ('Paradise' is the Greek for garden or park). The associations of 'garden' are leisure, delight and love. It is a place of beauty, usually described as 'enclosed' and its dominant flower is the rose (see e.g. Wilkins, 1969). The garden is a setting for both heavenly and earthly love and as such is a frequent image in art. It becomes both a symbol of the soul and of the Virgin Mary who is queen of Love in the religio-erotic poetry of the later Middle Ages (see e.g. Bouyer, 1960; Dronke, 1968; Warner, 1976).

22. It has been observed that the girl's description (v, 10–16) wanders from her lover's head down to his thighs while the man's moves lingeringly upward from her feet to the hair of her head (vii, 1–5). The reader may be interested to compare a description of female beauty from a different culture: 'Shining in her soft and curly long hair, which she had adorned with a great many jasmine blossoms, she strolled along and challenged, as it were, the moon itself by her moon-like face, so attractive through the movements of her brows, the sweet chatter of her mouth, its charm and gentle loveliness.

'Her breasts with her beautiful nipples, scented with an ointment of heavenly scented sandalwood, danced about as she walked, shining under her necklace. At every step the uprising and lively movement of her heavy breasts bent her down* over her beautiful waist, girded by the three folds of her shining belt.

'Below it there shimmered, spread out like a mountain, raised and swelling like the slope of a hill, the temple of the god of love, surrounded by spendour, adorned by the ribbon of the belt, tempting and alarming the heart even of the celestial rishis; the faultless secret parts, veiled by a thin garment.

'The feet with the ankle joints embedded deep into them were hung with little bells. The long red toes and the feet shone like the vaulted back of a tortoise.

'Her appearance was further enhanced by her happy contentment, her loving mood and her coquetry as if she had partaken of some intoxicating drink.' (Description of heavenly nymph Urvashi in *Mahabharata*, tr. Mode, 1970, 39.)

*Cf. description of heroine Drapaudi in op. cit. tr. Mode, 1970, 40 who also has a 'waist bent down by the weight of [her] breasts'.

Chapter 3

1. Though attempts have been made to fill the gaps. Some of these are discussed in Arendzen (1928, 80–93).

2. The interested may care to examine the attempt to place the books of the Bible in the order of their composition made by Rhymer (1975).

3. On Tarsus, see e.g. *Atlas of Ancient and Classical Geography*; Arendzen (1928, 122–35).

4. Both these philosophers were Stoics, whereas Apollonius seems to have been a neo-Pythagorean. Athenodorus Cananites was probably an influence on Seneca and Paul could hardly have been unaware of his teaching. This might explain the close relationship which has been discerned between some of St Paul's ethical teaching and that of the young Seneca (cf. art. in *Expositor* (Sept. 1906) by Sir William Ramsay).

5. For the Biblical use and meanings of the word 'Body', cf. e.g. Richardson (1950). For Paul in particular, see Robinson (1952).

6. Sometimes, however, Paul does seem to slip into a kind of dualistic anthropology in which 'body' is opposed to 'spirit' (e.g. I Cor. vii, 34) and in one case there is the suggestion of a tripartite division of body, soul and spirit (I Thess. v, 23).

7. 'Paul is evidently much more in line with the Old Testament than with Platonism or with Hellenistic ideas; for the word "flesh", as he employs it, represents man in his perishableness, as over against that which is divine, is imperishable.' (van Peursen 1966, 98.)

8. The connection between 'flesh' and 'sin' has 'nothing to do with man's physical nature as such, but with his manner of life in this world. The fact of his earthly existence is not in itself sinful; but it becomes the occasion for sin when man orientates his life wholly and utterly upon it.' (van Peursen, 1966, 99.)

9. Gnosticism makes its full impact on the Christian Church in the second century when it was a totally pervasive element in the intellectual climate,

but it was about much earlier (see, e.g. Barr, 1966, 9–15) and it is apparently warned against in Tim. vi, 20: 'the profane babblings and oppositions of the knowledge [gnosis] which is falsely so called; which some professing have erred concerning the faith'.

10. Paul's teaching on celibacy is offered as a personal 'opinion' rather than as an ecclesiastical 'doctrine' (I Cor, vii, 25) and his argument seems to be twofold. He is expecting the end of the world and in this situation it is best not to accept further responsibilities or even to change one's state (ibid. 26, 29–31) but, even so, it is not sinful to marry though such an action might bring worldly troubles which Paul would like to see his converts spared (ibid. 28). Marriage brings anxieties and a mind divided between the things of this world and God.

11. On the subject of ecclesiastical rules and regulations, Paul comments:

'These have indeed an appearance of wisdom in promoting rigour of devotion and self-abasement and severity to the body, but they are of no value in checking the indulgence of the flesh' (Col. ii, 23).

This remark may be compared with the one in I Tim. iv, 8 where the writer declares that physical (or bodily) training is good but moral training is better. The Greek word for 'training' is *ascesis* – hence 'asceticism'.

12. The concept of the Church as the Body of Christ receives fuller treatment in the Epistle to the Ephesians and those interested might consult Eph. i, 23; iv, 11–16). This Body is the instrument of unity between man and man (iv, 4) and between man and God (ii, 16) and this union in and through the body has anologues: in marriage, especially (v, 22–33) and also in other institutions (v, 21; vi, 1–4; 5–9). There are parallel passages in Colossians (i, 18; 24; ii, 19; iii, 15) and the embodiment of God is seen as restoring psychological unity to mankind which, as a result of the Fall, has become schizoid (i, 22).

13. See I Cor. vi, 15–17 and above p. 35ff. The idea is worked out at some length in I Cor. xii in terms of the multiplicity of organs in a single body. Other usages occur in ii, 17 where 'body' seems equivalent to 'substance' or 'reality' as opposed to 'shadow' and in II Cor. x, 10 where Paul contrasts the weakness of his 'bodily presence' with the vigour of his letters.

14. Only a small portion of animals offered in sacrifice was consumed; the rest went to the butcher's shops and was sold in the normal way.

15. Though the Jews had done much to rid themselves of anthropomorphism and, as we have seen, reversed the process by conceiving man in themorphic terms (cf. above pp. 23ff. on 'image of God'), yet Luke preserves a saying of Christ which might be seen as a reversal of this process, a vindication of Voltaire's cynical remark that God made man in His image and man quickly returned the compliment. After restoring speech to a dumb man, Christ is accused of using demonic power to vanquish demons (Luke xi, 14–23). He replies, according to Luke, that He expels them by 'the finger of God' (the Matthean parallel (xii, 28) has 'by the Spirit of God').

This usage is a recollection of Old Testament imagery whereby the 'finger of God' signifies His power, His operation. Pharoah's magicians had recognised the finger of God in the wonders wrought by Moses (Exod. viii, 19) and the Ten Commandments were 'written with the finger of God' on stone tablets (Exod. xxxi, 18 cf. Deut. ix, 10). The finger is used for demonstration, for non-verbal communication in both Testaments (cf. Isa. lviii, 9; John viii, 6; xx, 25, 27). Uses that Luke has in common with Matthew are found in Luke xi, 34–6; xii, 4f; xii, 22f; xxiii, 52, 55; xxiv, 3, 23; xxii, 19). Cf. also 'The communicative hand', in Benthall and Polhemus (1975).

16. See Richardson (1950), s.v. 'flesh'.

17. For examples, see Gal. iv, 23, 29; vi, 12f.; I Cor. v, 5; Col. ii, 1, 5; Gal. vi, 8; Gal. ii, 20; II Cor. iv, 11; Gal. iii, 3.

18. e.g. Gal. ii, 16; Rom. iii, 20; I Cor. i, 29; Eph. vi, 5–12; Col. iii, 22; II Cor. x, 2f.: I Cor. vii, 28; Phil. i, 22, 24; II Cor. i, 17; vii, 5; xi, 18ff.; Gal. iv, 13f.; Rom. vi, 19; 'Flesh' is associated with 'blood' to signify 'human beings' in Gal. i, 16, cf. Heb. ii, 14; Matt. xvi, 7.

19. Life 'in the flesh' does seem to mean a 'worldly' as opposed to a Christian life in the following texts: Rom. vii, 5, 18, 25; xiii, 14.

20. It is worth noting that Paul's belief in the potential restoration of 'flesh' seems to extend beyond humanity to include the whole of creation, though this is conceived as a potentiality through a dynamic process rather than as an accomplished fact (Rom. viii, 18–25; I Cor. xv, 20–6; Eph. i, 3–14). The idea was continued, especially in Athanasius and Irenaeus, and has been re-presented in modern times by Teilhard de Chardin.

21. Rom. viii, 4–13 where 'flesh' seems equivalent to 'body' as in I Cor. xv, 39, 50. Cf. I Cor. vi, 16; II Cor. xii, 7; Eph. v, 28–31; Col. i, 24.

22. But he also teaches, for example, that defilement can affect the spirit just as well as the body (II Cor. vii, 1).

23. The Revised Version translates 'garment spotted by the flesh'. The Greek text is uncertain but the sense seems to be that charity demands the giving of whatever help is possible, however great the offence to the whole body, the danger of its infection and the consequent proper hatred of their total depravity (mental and physical) whose chief effect is to cause schism in the Body of Christ. The idea is almost that of an infectious cancer.

24. For alternative images and expressions of the primordial unity of man, cf. the Platonic myth of an original bisexual herm aphrodite being related, significantly, by Aristophanes in Plato's *Symposium*, cf. W. Hamilton's translation in Penguin Classics (1951), pp. 59–65 and the discussion in Crawley, 1932, 200–23.

25. i.e. the mingling of human generative cells. Blood was thought to be the instrument and medium of life.

26. K. Grayston in Richardson (1950, 84).

Chapter 4

1. Two Roman monuments survive which have associations with the destruction of Jerusalem: (a) The triumphal arch of Titus, erected in A.D. 81 in commemoration of his victory over the Jewish insurgents. The interior sculptures portray the carrying away, as loot, of the sacred instruments from the Temple in Jerusalem whose inner sanctum had been closed to Gentiles on pain of death. (b) The Flavian amphitheatre (the Colosseum) built A.D. 72–80 by the forced labour of some 12,000 Jewish prisoners of war. Its inauguration lasted 100 days and involved brutally realistic sea-fights, the slaughter of 5,000 wild beasts and an uncomputed, but probably larger, number of human victims.

2. One of the earliest recorded liturgical acclamations was the Aramaic 'Maranatha' (I Cor. xvi, 22) signifying the impending Second Coming of Christ with an associated notion of final judgment.

3. These were standing and persisting calumnies, associated with a zealous hope for the total destruction of humanity by fire. The last may have resulted from Christian ideas about the end of the world, cannibalism may be a misunderstanding of the Eucharist and incest may have originated from the Christian practice of calling each other 'brother' or 'sister'. It is difficult to account for the accusation of infanticide, except that this enormity has been postulated by mobs of other minority groups, especially the Jews.

4. That Christianity was originally, and perhaps even essentially, a city religion is indicated not only by the fact that the first congregations were named after the city in which they lived but also by the etymology of the word 'pagan' which is derived from the Latin *paganus* which means 'a countryman'. Romantics and sentimental followers of 'the simple life', please note.

5. This and other writings of the so-called 'Apostolic Fathers' are easily available in the two volumes with this title in the Loeb Classical Library, (tr. K. Lake, London 1930 and recently reprinted).

6. See the *Letters* of the Younger Pliny (Penguin 1963, etc.), Book x, nos. 96, 97.

7. Hence the name 'Docetists' (from the Gk. *dokeo* – to appear) given to one group of 'Christian' Gnostics. Note that Ignatius uses the expression 'without God' of people who believe in God but not in Him as He actually Is.

8. There may be a play on the word *agape* which means 'love' and also 'love-feast' – applied to the Eucharist or a common meal closely associated with it, sometimes an occasion of scandal (cf. I Cor. x, 20–2). Notice also that 'blood' which in Jewish symbolism equals 'life' is here equated with 'love' thus associating 'life' and 'love'.

9. Hadrian was nicknamed *graeculus* ('the little Greek') because of his passion for the Greek way of life, including pederasty.

10. Many of these survive and portray Antinous in the nude and possessed of a superb and highly idealised body.

11. Tradition identifies the author with a Hermas who was brother of Pius, bishop of Rome (c. A.D. 140–54).

12. This is a development of the concept of the 'two cities' which, probably originating with St Paul reached its climax in St Augustine's masterpiece, *The City of God* which was so influential in the Middle Ages and beyond.

13. The possibility of forgiveness for the sins of the flesh is one of the main themes of the book and seems a deliberate attempt at a balanced approach against an extreme Puritanism which regarded such offences (after baptism) as practically unforgivable.

14. For a vivid (and near contemporary) account of the martyrdom of Polycarp, see K. Lake (1930, II, 309ff.)

15. Barr (1966, 19). It is interesting that Justin the Apologist's witness in both life and death was apparently so distinguished that he earned the soubriquet 'Martyr' which became almost a surname.

16. Preserved in Eusebius, *History of the Church*, Bk. V (pp. 193–203 in the Penguin translation, London 1965).

17. If this philosophic opinion about the rationality of animals was general, it has implications for the passage from Athenagoras (*On the Resurrection of the Dead*) cited above, p. 52. It would mean that man's stewardship and responsibility extended beyond his fellowmen to the animal kingdom.

18. Tatian seems to be making the interesting point that man is born with only the potentiality of 'true humaneness' which means developing from the highest animal to some partaking of the nature of God. The notion that 'humanity' is an achievement and not innate is worth pursuing.

19. Tatian seems to be implying that there is mutual interdependence between the 'elements' which constitute man. The soul is the agent which holds the flesh together against its natural tendency to dissolution, while the flesh (which he has already said is 'the essence of man') is a kind of integument of the soul.

20. Cf. the previous passage and n. 18 above. Taken together, they apparently indicate that the developed actuality of 'true humanism' as distinct from the mere natural possibilty of superior animality requires the assumption of the indwelling Spirit. Does he imply that man is a sort of 'little trinity' and this is the essence of his 'image of God'?

21. For the importance of 'truth' and 'single-mindedness' in Christian formation: (cf. St John's Gospel, *passim*; Ignatius cited p. 47 above and n. 7; Shepherd of Hermas, *Mandates*, III, parable vi, etc.

22. It is necessary to remember that the classical usage of pious and impious has little in common with modern notions of 'piety'. The basic meaning of 'impious' is 'irreverent', 'lacking in respect', 'not giving the honour which is due', 'not performing human obligations', etc.

23. Translation from Ante-Nicene Christian Library (Edinburgh 1968–70) *Writings of Clement of Alexandria*. For this idea, cf. the similarly mysterious passage in St Paul: I Cor. xi, 10–15. It is noteworthy that a superstition associating (bodily) hair with strength and sexuality is by no means dead in contemporary culture.

24. A heresy instigated by the 'prophet' Montanus of Asia Minor in the second century. It encouraged a state of ecstatic madness and claimed that the words spoken in this state were a final revelation of the Holy Spirit. They believed in the imminent Second Coming of Christ and taught a legalistic moral rigorism which included increased fasting over long periods, a prohibition against fleeing from martyrdom and forebade second marriages (after death of partner) and were far from favourable towards any marriage. Its most illustrious convert was Tertullian (in 212) who modified the ecstatic element, but retained the claim to private inspiration and denied that sins of adultery and fornication could be forgiven. The Church opposed tradition and the authority of bishops against what it saw as charismatic anarchy.

25. The heretical tendency to use words like 'self-control', 'moderation', 'temperance' to mean 'self-control in particular areas' (such as sex or drink) or, actually, 'total abstinence' is continuous in Christian thought.

26. Clement of Alexandria, a doughty ascetic, convinced celibate and redoubtable opponent of Encratism, though he taught that Christian virginity was a higher vocation even than christian marriage, yet condemned a virginity which was rooted in a disdain for marriage, declaring that virginity (either male or female) was only a divine vocation when it was embraced from the simple motive of love of God.

27. Op. cit. (1966, 18). There is, at last, an increasing tendency of Christian theologians to respect sexuality. Cf. e.g. Blenkinsop, 1970.

28. It is often forgotten that the word 'martyr' is simply the Greek word for 'a witness' to the truth, cf. n. 15 above.

29. The 'mantle' or 'cloak' was the distinguishing garb of the professional philosopher in classical times in much the same way as academic dress once distinguished teachers.

Chapter 5

1. This is the thesis of *De Praescriptione Haereticorum* which is among the last works which Tertullian wrote before he himself, as a result of his Montanist views, came into conflict with the Catholic Church. There is an English translation of this work at the beginning of volume II of the *Writings of Tertullian* in the Ante-Nicene Christian Library (Edinburgh 1870).

2. See his early work *Ad Martyres* printed at the beginning of volume I of the *Writings of Tertullian* in A.N.C.L. (Edinburgh 1869).

3. Tertullian attacked both Pope Callistus and the Roman 'Shepherd of

Hermas' because of their alleged 'easy absolution', though his objection seems really to have been against the granting of any absolution at all.

4. See *On the Flesh of Christ*, xvi (pp. 197ff. in volume II, ed. cit.).

5. Elsewhere, he explains in what sense 'flesh and blood cannot inherit the Kingdom of God' (*On the Resurrection of the Flesh*, xlvi f. tr. pp. 295 ff. in vol. II ed. cit.) For similar teaching which defends the substance of the flesh cf. *Five Books in reply to Marcion*, IV, xxxvii, tr. Vol. IV (1868) ed. cit. pp. 336f.

6. For Tertullian's teaching that the flesh is an essential element in our human nature, see: *De Anima*, xxvii, cf. *De Res. Carnis*, xlØ *De Anima*, xl; *Adv. Marcion*, V, xv, cf. *De Res. Carnis*, xlvii; *Adv. Marcion*, V, vii; *De Poenitentia*, iii. It will probably suffice to quote the translation of the last (ed. cit. vol. I, pp. 260f.) '. . . of sins, some are carnal, i.e. corporeal; some spiritual. For since man is composed of this combination of a twofold substance, the sources of his sins are no other than the sources of his composition. But it is not the fact that body and spirit are two things that constitutes the sins mutually different – contrariwise, they are on this account rather equal, because the two form one thing – lest anyone make the distinction between their sins proportionate to the differences between their substances, so as to esteem the one lighter or, alternatively, heavier than the other . . . both flesh and spirit are creatures of God.'

7. Cyprian, who was martyred in A.D. 258, has been credited with the invention of Catholicism. For a study of the interrelation, in his thought, of the doctrines of the Incarnation, the Sacraments and Ecclesiology see Bottomley, F., St Cyprian and the Body of Christ' (unpublished Ph.D. thesis, University of London, 1958). *The Writings of Cyprian* are translated in two volumes in the Ante-Nicene Christian Library (Edinburgh 1868–9).

8. Berkhof, cited Heer (1966, 15), says: 'Origenism and Arianism were, fundamentally, attempts to give the Gospel a theological form capable of satisfying the natural perceptions of contemporary pagan intellectuals.'

9. Heer (1966, 17) quoting from Buonaiuti. It is only ignorance of history in general and of the history of thought in particular that has allowed the contemporary abusage of the word 'theology' in the sense of 'ineffective and irrelevant theory'.

10. A bronze statue of Ambrose provides one of the four supporters of Bernini's baroque *Chair of St Peter* which dominates the apse of St Peter's Basilica in Rome.

11 +i.e. of the four elements of which all matter was believed to be constituted: earth, air, fire and water. Man is a meeting point: he is composed of the elements and he is lord of the elements. The passage is pregnant with ideas which are usually attributed to the so-called Renaissance and to the literary movement called Humanism.

12. To my knowledge, this is the first occurrence in Western thought of

the ideas of the microcosm and the macrocosm, twin notions which were to have a long (and fruitful) history. See Lovejoy (1936), Tillyard (1943), Lewis (1967a) and *infra*, ch. 9.

13. We are reminded that Ambrose was a witness of the increasingly rapid decline of the Roman Empire, not only the largest empire hitherto known but one whom its inhabitants felt to be under some special Providential dispensation. Yet this quintessential Roman is aware that all things pass, even the greatest human achievements, whether of individuals or societies. He has an almost Jacobean awareness of the inevitability of decay which is curiously absent in contemporary sensibility. Yet Ambrose is a Christian too, and therefore believes in Resurrection (he even believed in the resurrection of Rome.) There is also a powerful dialectic element in his thinking: he sees struggle as endemic in the human condition and hence the need for an interim period of rest. This consciousness is the origin of the early Christian concept of death as renewing rest and of the prayer that the departed may, in their intermediate condition, 'rest in peace'.

14. The discipline and control that comes from training was an antique virtue admired and respected by Paul and Christ Himself, and Ambrose was not without Stoic affinities. He was convinced that the body had to be disciplined if we are not to be its slaves, just as the vine has to be pruned and trained if it is to produce grapes and not luxuriant but unfruitful foliage: 'Let us then tend this body of ours, let us chasten it, let us reduce it to subjection, let us not neglect it. Our members are "instruments of righteousness" as they are also "instruments of sin" (Rom. vi, 13). If they are lifted upwards, they are instruments of righteousness, that sin should not reign in them: if our body has died to sin, transgression will not reign therein, and our members will be free from sin. Therefore, let us not obey the body's lusts, nor "yield our members instruments of unrighteousness unto sin". If you have looked upon a woman to lust after her, your members are the instruments of sin. If you have spoken and solicited her, your tongue and your mouth are the instruments of sin. If you have removed the land-marks which your fathers set up, your members are instruments of sin. If you have hasted 'with swift feet to shed the blood of the innocent', your members are instruments of sin.

On the other hand, if you have seen a poor man and taken him into your house, your members are instruments of righteousness. If you have rescued one who was suffering wrong, or one who was being led to execution, or if you have cancelled the bond of a debtor, your members are instruments of righteousness. If you have confessed Christ . . . , your lips are members of righteousness. He who can say, "I was eyes to the blind and feet to the lame, I was a father to the poor" (Job xxix, 15) – his members are members of righteousness.' (Ep. xxxvii, 43f.)

15. The problem of how the soul was 'connected' to the body was (and is) a long-standing problem, cf. Lewis (1967a, 166ff.) van Peursen (1966), Vallentin (1939, 440ff.).

16. Commenting on the difference between the Old and New

Testaments, Ambrose remarks: 'Rightly, therefore, does St Paul say that "the letter killeth but the spirit giveth life." For the letter circumcises a small portion of the body; the understanding spirit keeps the circumcision of the entire body and soul; so that when the superfluous parts are cut off (and nothing is so superfluous as the vices of avarice and the sins of lust, which do not belong to nature but are the results of sin), chastity might be observed and frugality loved. Thus the sign is bodily circumcision, but the reality is spiritual circumcision: the one cuts off (part of a member), the other excises sin. Nature has created nothing imperfect in man, nor has she commanded (any part of) it to be removed as superfluous, but (the sign was instituted) so that they who cut off part of their body might understand that sin was to be totally cut off, and that those members which led to offences were to be retrenched, even though they were joined together by the unity of the body, as is written: "If thy right hand offend thee, cut it off . . ." (Ep. lxxiv, 4)

17. Cf. 'For that is true piety which puts divine things before human and prefers the eternal to the temporal.' (Ep. lxvi, 7.)

18. The four elements were to have a long history in Western thought and literature, see e.g. Lewis (1967a, 94ff.).

19. The image is derived from (or associated with) the curious antique practise of diluting wine with water. There may be associations with the mixing of water and wine before the blessing of the chalice at the Mass. This mixture was understood as a symbol of the combination of divine and human natures in Christ or of the union of Christians with Christ at least from the time of Cyprian (Fortescue, 1937, 306). The accompanying prayer is not without significance for the Church's attitude to the body: 'Oh God, who wonderfully created the dignity of human nature and even more wonderfully refashioned it, grant that by the mystery of this water and wine we may be granted a share in the divinity of Him who vouchsafed to share our humanity, Jesus Christ. . . .' This is an adaptation of a Christmas prayer found in the Leonine Sacramentary, a collection of Roman prayers which may go back to the fourth century.

20. Further examples of this often-repeated statement may be found, e.g. in: *De Instit. Virg.* 11; *De Cain*, i, 41; ii, 36; *De Noe*, 38; *De Isaac*, 4; *De Jacob*, i, 4; *De Nabuthe*, 64; *In ps.* xliii, enar. 4; *Ep.* xxxiv, 5; xlii, 14). This repetition, which is often *ad hoc*, should not obscure the fundamental balance of Ambrose's outlook which is concerned with the restoration and perfection of creation, including the psychosomatic unity which is man. Commenting on Isa. lxvi, 22–4, he says: 'If earth and heaven are to be renewed, how can we doubt that man (on whose account both heaven and earth were made), can be renewed? . . . Now shall the flesh of the righteous perish . . . for the essential concept of resurrection is the rising again of what has fallen . . . .
'The very course and ground of justice demands that, since the action of body and soul is common to both (for what the soul conceived the body carried out), each should come to judgment and each should either be surrendered to punishment or reserved for glory . . . it would be in-

consistent for that which had not sinned alone to suffer alone or one element to attain solitary glory when it had not fought by itself.' (*On Belief in the Resurrection*, II, 88f., available in the translation of de Romestin, H. et al. in *Some of the Principal Works of St Ambrose* which forms vol. x in a select library of Nicene and Post-Nicene Fathers (Oxford, 1896).

Ambrose is emphasising the specifically Christian doctrine of the Resurrection as against the pagan notion of the immortality of the soul. Man is body-soul; if man perishes, he perishes completely in body and soul; if man attains eternal life and glory, it is the glory of both body and soul. It cannot be too frequently emphasised that the doctrine of the Resurrection implies the highest possible concept of the body.

21. Thus anticipating Prudhomme by a millennium and a half. For the Communism of St Ambrose, see Lovejoy (1948, 296–307).

22. Consequently, slavery is no part of the natural order but the unhappy result of human sin and folly. However, although the Church recognises the essential equality of all men, Ambrose does not advocate the abolition of slavery (which may serve a useful purpose in an imperfect society), much less does he encourage slave revolts. He follows St Paul (Philemon) in admonishing masters to remember that slaves are human beings like themselves and to treat them kindly as 'sons'. He vehemently denounces the heartless and cruel treatment which slaves too often suffered, yet he exhorts them to patience and willing obedience even to bad masters.

23. Duty is a central concept in the thinking of this former Roman magistrate and ex-Stoic but, to Ambrose as a Christian, duty meant obedience to the will of God as revealed in nature, reason, conscience and, above all, the Scriptures. For Ambrose's 'Stoicism' see Dudden (1935, II, 551–4).

24. The concept of natural law or of the law of nature was to have a long (and not always fruitful) history in the moral thinking of the Western Church. It still affects the Roman Catholic attitude to contraception and other sexual practises, and entirely colours its evaluation of sexuality. For the history of this concept, see e.g. 'Nature as norm in Tertullian' (Lovejoy, 1965), Buchanan (1962) O'Connor (1967), Lewis (1967b). For a short account of Natural Law, see the articles by B. F. Brown, T. A. Wassmer and J. C. H. Wu in *The New Catholic Encyclopedia* (1967).

25. The connection of sexuality with marriage and the extension of its prime end to its entire end or one of its consequences to its fundamental meaning is constant in the Western Church, leaving the need open still for an adequate theology of sex and the body. There have been an increasing number (of still inadequate) attempts to fill this gap, see e.g. Piper (1942), Le Trocquer (1961), Blenkinsop (1970), Davies (1976).

Chapter 6

1. Cf. *supra*, p. 70. For Jerome's similar attitude, see Letter, 4–5 xiv, conveniently available in Loeb edn. (tr. F. A. Wright, London 1933, pp. 35, 37). Ambrose's sister, Marcellina, for whom he wrote his famous treatise *On*

Virginity, was a founder-member of Rome's first convent for women which was established *c.* A.D. 350.

2. Heer (1966, 20).

3. This version, called the Vulgate, since it was in the common tongue of the Western Empire, was translated from the original Latin and Hebrew. Its authoritative scholarship made it the official Bible of the Western Church for some fifteen centuries.

4. Jerome's passion for the Classics led him to describe himself as nearer to Cicero than to Christ. See the famous Letter to Eustochium (*Ep*. xxii, 30) accessible in Wright (1933, 125, 127, 129).

5. Heer (1966, 20) cf. Appendix I in Wright (1933, 483–97).

6. Heliodorus who subsequently became a bishop, had served in the Roman army and this transition from the military to the ascetic life seems to have been not uncommon. Cf. Jerome's Letter to Nepotian, nephew of Heliodorus, who also 'renounced service in the world's army to become a monk or clergyman' (*Ep*. lii, 1). Jerome warns him not to think 'that clerical orders are but a variety of your old military service, i.e. to not look for monetary reward when you are fighting in Christ's army (ibid. 5). Later, after Nepotian's untimely death, Jerome wrote to console his uncle and recalled how the nephew 'while he was still a soldier at court, beneath his military cloak and white linen tunic his skin was chafed by sackcloth; how, while he stood before the powers of this world, his lips were pale with fasting; how, while he wore one master's uniform, he served Another; how he only wore a sword-belt that he might succour the widow and the fatherless, the wretched and the oppressed' (*Ep*. lx, 9, tr. Wright, 1933, 281). There seems to have been a sort of affinity between Christianity and good soldiers: one might draw attention to the prominence of centurions in the Gospels, of Cornelius in the Acts of the Apostles, and the later roll-call which included St George, St Martin, St Sebastian and St Ignatius Loyola, as well as less prominent examples.

7. This, and the previous citations, are from *Ep*. xiv (tr. Wright, 1933, 31, 49, 51).

8. Jerome, *Ep*. xxii, 34.

9. Ibid., 7 (tr. Wright, 1933, 67, 69).

10. Ibid. 11 (tr. Wright, 1933, 75, 77).

11. Jerome, *Ep*. xiv, 9 (tr. Wright, 1933, 49).

12. Much has been made of the effects of exalting virginity at the expense of marriage, e.g. Lecky (1905, II, 320f.) writes: 'The services rendered by the ascetics in imprinting on the minds of men a profound and enduring conviction of the importance of chastity, though extremely great, were seriously counterbalanced by their noxious influence on marriage.' Jerome is the arch-culprit (ctr. Tertullian's beautiful treatise addressed 'To my wife'),

but Jerome was an extremist who sometimes let his pen (as well as his tongue) run away with him. Sometimes his reasons are practical, as in the analogy: 'no soldier takes a wife with him when he is marching into battle' (*Ep.* xxii, 21), or the sapiential: 'there is a time to embrace and a time to refrain from embracing' (*Ep.* cvii, 13). In his book *Against Jovinian* (i, 3), he compares marriage, widowhood and virginity to the seeds in the parable of the Sower (Mark iv, 3ff.) which brought forth fruit: thirty, sixty and a hundredfold, respectively. Elsewhere, he describes marriage as 'a raft for the ship-wrecked, a remedy that may at least cure a bad beginning' (*Ep.* cxvii, 3) and says, 'I give praise to the marriage-bond only because it produces virgins for the religious life' (*Ep.* xxii). Besides taking account of Jerome's love of rhetoric, there are further considerations: the contemporary 'state of emergency' (cf. *infra*) and the low estate of marriage in Roman society of this time. According to Tertullian (*Apol.* vi) 'divorce is the fruit of marriage' and Jerome himself (*Ep.* ii) tells of a Roman woman who had married twenty-three husbands and was the twenty-first wife of her latest choice. There is similar evidence from earlier Roman authors (e.g. Martial, *Epigrams*, vi, 7; Juvenal, *Satires*, vi, 230). Against this, the Christians had expressed the ideal of a permanent union expressed in the 'one-fleshing' of the sexual union which they saw as a symbol of the faithful and eternal union between Christ and His Church. The notion of no second marriage after the death of a spouse and the institution of clerical celibacy were of a piece with the Christian ideal, though the antique Romans were accustomed 'to honour with the crown of modesty those who were content with one marriage, and to regard many marriages as a sign of illegitimate in-temperance' (Lecky, 1905, I, 324f.).

13. Jerome, *Ep.* xxii, 5 referring to Matt. v, 28; xxv, 1-13.

14. Jerome quotes with approval the 'pretty proverb of the Greeks, which perhaps in our [Latin] language loses some of its force: "A fat paunch never breeds fine thoughts."' (Ep. lii, 11.)

15. For Jerome's rejoinder to 'reasonable' Christians, see *Ep.* xxii, 13 (tr. Wright, 1933, 79). Similar principles could lie behind Jerome's rejection of Origenism which seems to have had some intellectual fascination for him. In his earlier life he had translated some of his works and strongly recom-mended these writings to his friend, Pope Damasus. See *Ep.* cxxvii, 9 and Wright, 1933, Appendix II.

16. Jerome, *Ep.* xxii, 38. It is important to see that the argument assumes that virginity arises from respect for the body not the contrary.

17. ibid. 39. The paradox of the Incarnation will be continually em-phasised in Christian writing and spirituality. One of these paradoxes was the inverted status of riches and poverty (cf. Magnificat in Luke i, 46–55). Jerome emphasises the poverty of Christ's family here and elsewhere e.g. 'This is the son of a working-man and a woman who served for wages.' (*Ep.* xiv, 11.)

18. Jerome, *Ep.* cxvii, 6. The previous quotation is from *Ep.* xxii, 40.

19. Jerome *Ep*. cvii, 11.

20. Jerome, *Ep*. lii, 2. All the letters cited are translated in Wright (1933).

21. This, as far as I know, is the first recorded public hospital. Such institutions were rapidly to become typically Christian foundations.

22. The four 'cardinal' or 'natural' virtues to which the Christians added the 'theological' virtues of Faith, Hope and Charity were the foundation of ethical theory. Their identification and enumeration as prudence, temperance, fortitude and justice were said to go back to Socrates and they are certainly found in Plato and Aristotle. Their assumption by Christian teachers is a mark of their willingness to recognise the good in paganism and, consequently, of the limited effects of the Fall. Jerome see the 'natural' virtues as the basis of practical religion whose manifestation should be carried 'in the heart, rather than on the body, to have God's approval rather than to please the eyes of men. Would you know, then, what kind of ornaments the Lord requires? Have prudence, justice, temperance, fortitude. Let these be your four cardinal points, let them be your four-in-hand to carry you, Christ's charioteer, at full speed to your goal.' (*Ep*. lii, 13.)

23. The new values created by this sensibility may manifest themselves in very different areas, e.g.:

(a) The priestly code of the Old Testament had barred the priesthood to the physically imperfect, but Jerome, arguing for the primacy of the spiritual, ironically suggests that the continuation of the old principles would require that 'Christ's priests take virgins as wives; and that a man should be deprived of his priesthood, however worthy, if he is scarred or disfigured in any way; that bodily leprosy be counted worse than spiritual faults' (*Ep*. lii, 10 written in A.D. 394). Canon 1 of the Council of Nicaea (A.D. 325) had enacted: 'If a man has suffered amputation by surgeons because of disease, or has been mutilated by barbarians, he is to remain among the clergy. But if a man in good health mutilates himself of his own accord and he is a member of the clergy, his ministry is to be terminated. In future, such self-mutilated are not to be presented for ordination. This regulation clearly concerns pre-meditation and those who voluntarily and presumptuously cut off their members, therefore if the mutilation is the work of barbarians or slave-masters and the victims are otherwise worthy, in respect to their manner of life, for admission to the priesthood, then they are canonically allowed to join the clergy.' (tr. in Howard, 1896, 4f.) These extracts show both respect for bodily perfection and overriding considerations.

(b) It tended towards the abolition of a double standard in sexual ethics and consequently towards the equality of women: 'A [divine] command that is given to men logically applies also to women. It cannot be that an adulterous wife should be repudiated and an unfaithful husband retained. If "he that is joined to an harlot is one body" (I Cor. vi, 16), she who is joined to a filthy whoremonger is one body as well. The laws of Caesar are different from the laws of Christ: Papinian (a famous Roman jurisconsult) commands one thing, our Paul requires another. Among the Romans, men's unchastity goes unchecked; seduction and adultery are condemned, but male lust is given free permission to range the brothels and to have slave girls, as though it were a person's rank and not the sensual pleasure that constituted the offence. With us, what is unlawful for women is equally unlawful for men: as both sexes serve the same God, they are bound by the same conditions.' (Jerome, *Ep.* lxxvii, 3.)

24. Cf. Jerome, *Ep.* cxxii: 'Time is short and now the axe is laid to the roots of the tree, the axe which cuts down the wood of legal marriage (*legis et nuptiarum*) by Gospel charity.' The phraseology is full of apocalyptic reminiscence – it is both the end of one age and the beginning of another in which the spiritual demands of the Gospel are set against human institutions (or in Pauline terms, the living spirit is to be preferred to the dead law).

25. St Ambrose mentions once-flourishing cities which in his time had become deserted ruins (cf. *Ep.* xxxix, 3, cited above, p. 67), and Jerome describes the recently made ruins of Vercellae in his *Ep.* i, 3.

26. *Ep.* lx, 16, 17, written in A.D. 396. The internal quotation is from the greatest Roman poet, Virgil. (*Aeneid*, II, 369).

27. Jerome, *Ep.* lxxvii, 8.

28. Jerome, *Introduction to Commentary on Ezekiel* (written A.D. 410–14). It is difficult for us to appreciate the effect of the fall of Rome on the contemporary world. Rome was more than a city, it was a symbol and living myth to Christian and pagan alike. It was regarded as eternal, there was a proverb/prophecy that when the city fell, the entire world would fall. It was believed by all to have a special destiny and to occupy a unique place in the divine ordering of things. To the pagan it was sanctified by tradition and history and the Christians owed it a special veneration as the seat of the chief bishop and the sanctified resting-place of innumerable martyrs, including Peter and Paul.

29. Jerome, *Ep.* cxxvii, 12.

30. The identification or union of the members of the Church, Christ's Body, with the Incarnate Lord Himself was conceived as a reality. Cf. e.g. Jerome's praise of Exuperius, the saintly bishop of Toulouse, who, in spite of his own continual fasting, was yet tormented by the hunger of his flock even though 'he has spent all his substance on those that are Christ's flesh'. (The last phrase is even more vivid in Latin *viscera Christi* – they are the empty belly of Christ.) Jerome makes a similar connection with the Eucharistic Body which the bishop conveys to the faithful.

31. Jerome, *Ep.* lx, 15, cf. Ambrose cited above p. 68. The previous quotation is from Jerome's *Letters* also, cxxviii, 5 – written in A.D. 413.

32. Jerome's *Letters*, cxxv, 20. Texts and translations of all passages cited from Jerome can be found in Wright, 1933. (See n. 1).

33. On this, see Pieper (1965), Eng. tr. 1952.

34. *Confessions*, viii, 7 (tr. Sheed, 1943).

35. Manichees were the adherents of Manicheism, an eclectic religion founded by Mani or Manes in Persia *c*. A.D. 240. Its basic tenet was belief in an infinite and eternal Dualism: the existence of two divine and equal Powers or Principles, one good and the other evil, which were locked in an everlasting struggle and involved mankind in their contest. See, e.g. *New Catholic Encyclopedia* s.v., and note in Sheed (1943, vii–ix).

36. Enrolment in the catechumenate was a preliminary step to becoming a Christian convert. It involved regular instruction (catechesis) and allowed the privilege of attendance at the first part of Mass: the service of psalms, readings and homilies which preceded the Eucharistic rite proper (*Missa fidelium*). When this instruction was satisfactorily completed, the catechumen could present himself for baptism which carried full membership and obligations and, in the early Church, was often postponed because of the strict moral discipline which was involved.

37. St Anthony (251–356), an Egyptian who founded the first monastery in A.D. 305. His wise government and supernatural gifts made him famous in both East and West. His life, written by St Athanasius, is a religious classic. The spirit of these 'Desert Fathers' can be gained from a perusal of Helen Waddell's *The Desert Fathers* (London 1936), the first part of her *Beasts and Saints* (London 1934) and E.A. Wallis Budge's translation of *The Paradise of the Fathers* (London 1907).

38. For a recent study of Augustine, see P. Brown, *Augustine the Bishop*. For an account of his 'system', see E. Gilson, *The Christian Philosophy of St Augustine* (Eng. tr. London 1961).

39. Cf. the oft-quoted words from the beginning of *The Confessions*: 'Thou has made us for Thyself and our hearts are restless till they rest in Thee.'

40. For his clarity in contrast to subsequnt sentimentality, cf. 'The innocence of children is in the helplessness of their bodies, rather than any quality in their minds. I have myself seen the jealousy of an infant: it was too young to speak, but it was livid with anger as it watched another small baby at the breast.' (*Confessions*, I, vii – written sixteen centuries before Freud.)

41. *The City of God*, henceforth referred to as *CG*, XXII, 22. There are many translations, perhaps the most accessible is that of M.Dods (Edinburgh 1934) 2 vols. The order in which the 'cruel ills' are enumerated, as well as their classification, is significant.

42. This objection is apparently anterior to, and more important than the later ones based on the 'natural law' that the prime end of sexual relations is procreation and, to the present writer at least, is more sympathetic in that it takes cognisance of an experienced fact. The essentially rationalistic St Thomas Aquinas seems to have shared Augustine's objection to swiving on the grounds that it brought a surcease of mental activity. One may question whether a temporary pause in ratiocination in favour of some

other form of 'knowing' is necessarily evil. Mystical writers of all traditions declare that mental activity is also surrendered in spiritual union with God. The best plastic expression of this is perhaps in Bernini's famous statue of St Theresa in Ecstasy, and perhaps not quite so obviously in Raphael's painting of sacred and profane love. Observers of both masterpieces have drawn attention to the close similarity of expression with those of sexual love. In spite of this analogy and the implications of the spiritual interpretation of the 'Song of Songs, the implications do not seem to have been explored in any depth by Christian thinkers, though this has been done in the Tantric forms of Hinduism and Buddhism. The problem has also been perceived from the other side, e.g. 'The most common metaphors for identifying erotic love are Paradise or Eden, the religious experience, the mystic trance, certain drug experiences (for which the term "altered states of consciousness" has been proposed), and death.' (Peckham, 1969, 188.) .

43. A century before Augustine, Lactantius, who is often described as 'the Christian Cicero', had seen an expression of the harmony of the universe in the wonderful way in which God had contrived men's nostrils 'so that the cavity of the nose should not deform the beauty of the face – which would certainly have been the case if one single aperture were left open' (*On the Workmanship of God*, x). Anyone who has seen a face from which the nose has been eaten away by syphilis might feel some sympathy with this argument.

44. *Coaptio* was a neologism, coined by Augustine, which also occurs in his *Book on the Trinity* (IV, 2). It is difficult to translate, but it contains the notions of harmony and concord, and implies a unified design which produces an integrated aptness for a common purpose contributed to by all the individual elements of the design.

45. Augustine's work is much derived from hard self-analysis as well as observed and recorded behaviour, and he is much concerned with the problem of will. Paul had wrestled with this problem in Romans where he summarises the problem: 'The good which I would, I do not; but the evil that I would not, that I do.' (Rom. vii, 19.) This is the fundamental mark of man's disintegration, and Augustine specifies its shattering manifestation in sexual activity. The manifest display of the sexual organs' independence of the will almost seems the crux (cf. *supra* pp. 87ff. esp. citation of *CG*, XIV, 16; also *De Genesi ad lit.* xi, 41; *De Corrept. et gratia*, xi, 31 and particularly *Contra Julianum*, iv, 52).

46. The basic meaning of the Greek work *gymnos* (from which gymnasium, etc. are derived) is 'naked' or 'exposed'. 'Gymnosophist' therefore literally means 'naked sage'.

47. It is remarkable that Augustine, with all his experience and psychological insight, does not seem able to have conceived any other purpose than propagation for physical sexual relations. This failure, on the part of one of the greatest teachers and thinkers of the Western Church, is probably the most important single source of subsequent Christian confusion on this matter (particularly in the Roman Catholic Church, though there may yet be clarification, cf. e.g. Blenkinsop, 1970).

48. It is important to recognise the distinction that Augustine is making in this passage. This act (of sexual congress) is not *intrinsically* shameful or sinful but, as a consequence of Original Sin (which was an act of disobedience which broke the order of creation), it is accompanied by visible evidence of that disorder which affects man's integrity in a fundamental and significant activity.

49. Augustine's ideas on order are much affected by the concept of the 'Great Chain of Being' which he inherited from Plato, modified, and then transmitted to the West where it was a seminal notion in European literature and thought for a further fifteen centuries (see Lovejoy, 1936) For an attempt to synthesise Augustine's 'order', see Przywara (1939).

50. One must remember that the Roman *familia* was, in the jargon of the sociologists, an 'extended' one and included many outside even a broad blood relationship, such as servants and clients. But, even in a 'natural' or 'nuclear' family, Augustine – like Paul before him – would believe that order involved some kind of hierarchy.

51. It cannot be too often emphasised that it was this fundamental Christian belief that made the development of science possible and part of the intellectual structure of Europe.

52. On the 'Desert Fathers' see Waddell (1934, 1937); Budge (1907); Smith and Wace (1877); *New Catholic Encyclopedia*, sv. Paul, Anthony etc. St Athanasius' *Life of St Anthony* rapidly became a spiritual classic, read in the drawing rooms of Rome as much as in the Egyptian desert.

53. St Augustine, *CG*, XXII, 4. For Augustine's views on the 'world of bodies' in general, see Bourke (1964, 98–120).

54. Cf. above p. 38f.

55. For a selection of passages from Augustine on the 'Three levels of reality' i.e. God, Spirit, Body, cf. Bourke, 1964, 43–66.

56. Augustine, *Questions for Simplicianus*, I, ii, 18 (tr. Bourke, 1964, 45).

57. See Przywara (1939, 169–97; 211–52).

58. Cf. n. 30. For the notion of this cosmic man, Irenaeus is important and the idea has been developed by more recent theologians, esp. Teilhard de Chardin, 1959.

Chapter 7

1. Edward Gibbon, *The Decline and Fall of the Roman Empire*, ch. xxxix, vol. III, p. 30 in ed. cit.

2. Apart from his judicial murder of Boethius, Theodoric was also responsible for reviving the gladiatorial shows in Rome.

3. There is much about rectitude and political incorruptibility in the *De Consolatione* and Boethius has been described by Gardner (1911, intro.) as a

'martyr for the liberty of Rome rather than for the faith of Christ'. Certainly the ideas in this extract owe at least as much to Seneca as to the Gospel, but we have already pointed out the assimilation between these two sources.

4. A similar point was made independently by the present writer in the *Loughborough Journal* (Loughborough, May 1964, No. 11, pp. 10–13).

5. Lyncaeus was one of the Argonauts, famous and proverbial for the keenness of his 'linx-like' sight. This attribution of a sort of X-ray quality seems peculiar to Boethius.

6. Alcibiades (c. 450–404 B.C.), Athenian political leader and con-temporary of Socrates, who was renowned both for the beauty of his physical appearance and the extravagance of his debaucheries.

7. Boethius' definition of a person was 'Persona est naturae rationabilis individua substantia' which might be roughly translated as 'A person is an individual entity which possesses a reasonable nature'. He described eternity as 'the possession of endless life whole at perfect at a single moment' (*De Consol.* V, vi).

8. St Pachomius was credited with the oversight of 7,000 monks (Palladius, *Lausiac History*, xxxviii); there was an alleged case of 5,000 monks living under a single abbot in the Nitrian desert in the fourth century (Cassian, *Institutes*, iv, 1); Rufinus tells us that the Egyptian city of Oxyrhincus contained 20,000 virgins and 10,000 monks (*Hist. Monach.* v) and St Serapion is said to have presided over 10,000 monks (Palladius; *Lausiac History*, lxxvi).

9. This passage and the even more famous one in Gibbon, ch. xxxvii (pp. 502ff. in vol. ii of ed. cit.) are exaggerated, emotive and much coloured by eighteenth-century prejudices. Many of the adjectives are subjective, St Jerome and others were hardly 'without knowledge' and there is plenty of evidence of affection, though it is perhaps beyond 'natural' if this word means 'normal'. The accusation that they lacked 'patriotism' might seem to some creditable rather than otherwise. For examples of their wisdom, see Waddell (1936, 189–223).

10. Examples of the hermits' and ascetics' friendly relations with animals are easily accessible in Waddell, 1934.

11. 'Benedict's monastery was Rome, Rome creatively withdrawn into herself. Benedict's monastery was a renewed and purified Rome. It was a Rome returned to manual labour, chastity, prayer and obedience.
'This daily round was a far more important thing for the intellectual constitution of Europe than many thousands of books written in the post-Benedictine age; far more important too, than the somewhat overrated intellectual activity of the Benedictines of the early Middle Ages. It is dif-ficult to overestimate the contribution of this orderly existence to the development of Western ideas. Its regularity and discipline fostered a rationalism which was confined within the multiple limits of this earth. The daily round fostered a matter-of-fact attitude which rejected spiritualist

enthusiasm and work for its own sake. Work was a means and not an end, as it later developed in Calvinist workhouses and poorhouses, the counter-monasteries of the modern world. We need only compare this apportionment of the day with our own: eight to sixteen hours of mechanised work, and the rest – an inorganic hodgepodge devoted to food, luxuries and the pursuit of pleasure. The crux of the changeover from the Benedictine culture of old Europe to what followed it was neatly expressed by Pascal in a famous sentence: "All the ills of man stem from his inability to be still in his own room." For the Benedictine it was possible to be still, still in spirit and in body, for his *stabilitas loci*, the ordering of his time and of his environment, gave him strength both for *otium* and *negotium*, for leisure and for work.' (Heer, 1966, 32, cf. Knowles, 1963, i–ii.)

12. 'The stability of the Church goes far to stabilise Europe; it is seen in so concrete an instance as the growing of the town round the episcopal palaces (or monsteries). King and Count live in and by perpetual progresses, so much of their revenues being in kind, and of the sort best consumed on the premises. But the bishop is bound by canon law to abide in his diocese, and industry first begins under the walls of the *évêche* or of the great abbey.' (Waddell, 1927, 162.)

It may be that the Benedictine differentia in the vow of *stabilitas* was a reaction to the unsettlement, the folk-wanderings, the physical disturbances of the time but it may be due more, as Clarke (1931, vii) suggests, to the insight that 'Mental and spiritual stability need to be secured by outward and physical stability, that we cannot bear fruit unless we stay long enough in one place for our roots to penetrate deep down into the surrounding soil'.

13. We have already drawn attention to the congruity of Christianity with the military life and Benedict's military imagery will be repeated in another cultural crisis which produced Ignatius Loyola, ex-soldier and founder of the Society of Jesus.

14. The Benedictines became the foremost farmers of Europe, as well as smiths, artists, architects (cf. Holt, 1957, I, 1ff., 8ff,) and brewers and distillers. For their intellectual culture, see Leclercq (1962).

15. Gregory had announced this conviction in his first sermon as Pope and it remained with him for the rest of his life.

16. On this, see e.g. Butler (1961), Leclercq (1962).

17. On Bede see e.g. Ker (1958, 95ff.), Knowles (1963), 12ff, Blair (1970) and on Alcuin: Duckett (1951), Crawford (1966, 104ff.), Boussard (1968, 134ff.).

18. As often, the monastic lead was extended and these practical expressions of neighbourly love became systematised under the name 'Corporal Works of Mercy' and taught in catechism, sermon and through visual aids (there is a window in All Saints', North Street, York which has survived the iconoclasm of Reformers and Parliamentarians as well as enemy bombs which depicts these acts: Feeding the Hungry, Giving Drink to the Thirsty, Entertaining the Stranger, Clothing the Naked, Visiting the Sick, Relieving

those in Prison. The seventh corporal work of mercy; Burying the Dead, is not illustrated. Opposite the normal representation of the donors of the window is the kneeling figure of a Benedictine monk). The attitude to the body which is implicit in these 'works of mercy' has not been adequately emphasised.

19. On the Carolingian Renaissance see e.g. Boussard (1968). The usage 'worthy' as a noun to mean a man of courage or noble character is late Middle English and 'The Nine Worthies' were a familiar group at the beginning of sixteenth century at the latest. They comprised nine famous persons from antiquity and the Middle Ages, having 'knightly virtue' as their common distinction. They included three Jews (Joshua, David and Judas Maccabaeus), three Gentiles (Hector, Alexander and Julius Caesar) and three Christians (Arthur, Charlemagne and Geoffrey of Bouillon).

20. This idea was portrayed in the mediaeval inn-sign of 'The Four Alls' which has survived in one or two places. It was also the subject of mediaeval preaching and literature, see Owst (1966, 544f.). The concept also underlies the structure of mediaeval education which included clerical, knightly, craft and legal divisions. The occasional transformation of the lewd and licentious soldiery into 'veray, parfit, gentle knights', however rare, must be one of the greatest triumphs of mediaeval or any other education. For stages in this process, see e.g. *The Song of Roland* and the knight and squire in Chaucer's *Canterbury Tales*.

21. English translations of both in Thorpe (1969).

22. Easter Saturday, Holy Saturday or Easter Eve, was one of the two great days for the mass baptism of those who had been under instruction in the Christian faith for the previous year or more (The other was the Eve of Whitsunday). It was customary for the newly baptised to wear a white robe or 'chrisom' in token of their new innocence and in reference to Rev. vi, 11; vii, 9, 13f. The custom continues in an attenuated form in the infant's christening-robe and shawl still in use at baptisms.

23. Described by Einhard as 'the most learned man anywhere to be found' (Thorpe, 1969, 79).

24. The magnitude of this task in the face of the universal chaos and destruction is almost unimaginable but its elements are well outlined in Southern (1959).

25. See Dawson (1946).

26. Canon 26 of the Council of Auxerre (A.D. 578).

27. Preserved in ninth-century MS. of Verona (tr. Waddell, 1929, 127f.).

28. Alcuin wrote a poem about the strife between winter and summer as well as a lament for his lost nightingale. Texts and translation in Waddell (1929, 83ff., 89f).

29. The decree is translated in Power (1939, 25). Servile work is the work characteristic of serfs or slaves, i.e. manual labour, drudgery. The transition

from holy days through holidays to the ultimate degradation of bank
holidays and national holidays is symbolically significant.

30. See e.g. Mason (1897), 88ff.

Chapter 8

1. 'Visual aids' were obviously more important when books were rare and
literacy a minority skill. Reliefs, sculptures, frescoes and stained glass offered the congregation and the clergy a bewildering gallery of subjects. The
higher orders of clergy and members of religious orders are caricatured
under a variety of animal guises. 'They could see, in stone, the familiar
burlesque actors of the day sticking out their tongues, showing their
backsides and genitals, letting farts, dropping their breeches and running
after women. There are plenty of sculptured nudes of both sexes being
punished for concupiscence by having their private parts devoured by snakes
and griffins. Here and there an actual whore could be seen in these groups,
recognisable by her special head-dress, a tall hat shaped like a sugar-loaf.'
(Cleugh, 1967, 21.) The same author mentions a fresco in 'the cathedral
apse of Alby in northern Savoy' with sodomites and Melville (1973, 14)
records 'an amazingly explicit carving showing a man performing cun-
nilingus' in the doorway of a church in St Martin de l'Isle Adam-sur-Oise.
Certainly the portrayal of copulation is not uncommon (e.g. Sonillac) and
there even appears to be a depiction of coprophagy on a misericord (a
frequent location of satirical carving) at Evreux Cathedral. The same kind
of subject-matter also occurs in mediaeval manuscripts. 'The frontispiece of
calendars at this period often displays a male citizen with a jester between his
legs, perhaps calling attention to the bestriding figure's private parts. The
depiction of acts of pederasty and masturbation, as well as ordinary sexual
congress, and of some very pleasing harlots, is not at all uncommon in other
documents.' (Cleugh, 1967, 25.) It should be mentioned that these examples
are comparatively rare, that the motivation is not erotic but edification and
that the bawdy and scatalogical were accepted as a natural part of life.
Cleugh (1967, 29), who does not appear to be entirely sympathetic with
mediaevalism, at least sees a contrast between Christian art and 'the
shameless brutality, combined with a cynical sophistication, of the pagan
style. It is this feature of mediaeval art in general, a kind of tender indulgence or charming sweetness that never approaches sentimentality, a
profound innocence, so to speak, or childish merriment, in dealing with
matters of terrifying or disgusting import, that renders the carving and
painting of the European Middle Ages absolutely unique.'

2. This is especially obvious in the great Cistercian houses of Yorkshire:
Kirkstall, Rievaulx and Fountains, especially.

3. It may be relevant at this point to summarise St Bernard's teaching on
the relationship between body and soul, united in two different senses:

(a) By a bond of natural necessity. Since the soul is obliged to serve the
body, it is inferior to the pure spirits (angels, etc.); but this is the normal
human condition and, in this sense, the body cannot be described as 'op-
pressing' the soul or detracting from its state which implicitly involves union

with a body. If the soul loves the body as it should, it will make the latter its auxiliary so that the two together, helping each other, will attain their *common* end which is heavenly glory.

(b) From another point of view, the soul is not so much 'united' as 'subjected' to the body by sin. This state is *not* natural but, on the contrary, is unnatural since the soul is superior to the body. In this sense, the body *can* be described as a 'burden' which 'weighs down' the soul and 'oppresses' it. (Gilson, 1940, 99ff. and nn.)

4. Taylor points out that 'Bernard adds when Paul says "flesh and blood shall not inherit the kingdom of God," it is not to be understood that the substance of flesh will not be there, but that every carnal necessity will have ceased; the love of flesh shall be absorbed in the love of the Spirit and our weak human affections transformed into divine energies.' The extract is from *Ep*.11 of St Bernard, written to his great friend Guigo, prior of the Grande Chartreuse – home of the famous liqueur, a proportion of the profits from which still support the Carthusians and thus allow the flesh to support the spirit, and vice-versa.

5. Perhaps the most famous writing of the sainted abbot of Rievaulx, Ailred (d. 1166), was his treatise *On Friendship*. One of the most interesting literary manifestations of the previous century was the (learned and amorous) correspondence of poets with learned women centring on the convent of Le Ronceray at Angers, discussed in Dronke (1968, i, 213ff). The notion of deep Christian friendship is as old as the faith – its archetype was Christ and St John and perhaps Christ and the Magdalene and in the fourth century St Ambrose had written: 'What is a friend if not a consort of love, to whom you can join and attach your spirit, mingling it so that the two of you would become one?' (*De Officiis*, iii, 22.) There are interesting potentialities in uniting this Ambrosian idea with the Pauline ideas of 'one flesh'. Perhaps it happened in the case of Abailard and Héloïse. Dronke (1968, i, 200) points out that 'it is precisely Christian monastic *amicitia* which provides the pretext [the only possible one] for the entire correspondence. It provides a cloak of form – yet even the form's highest individuality is not separable from this cloak.' What may be even more significant is the fact that St Hildegard of Bingen, a mystic who was born thirty years before this correspondence and who died about half a century after it in 1179, often repeats that in love each lover is the creation, the 'opus' of the other. They are conjoined in such a way that each is the other's 'work of art' and could not exist without the other. Each can become the perfected creation of God through the other's love – a process which is fulfilled in the love-union, 'whereby the whole earth should become like a single garden of love'. For, 'it is the power of Eternity itself that has created physical union and decreed that two human beings should become physically one' (*P.L.* 197, 885 b–c, cited Dronke, 1968, i, 68f.). For 'the garden of love' see Wilkins (1969, chs. 5 and 6) and especially: 'At a certain height of sophistication there is almost no dividing-line between the worldly and the other-worldly; both extremes are at least implicit, the garden that is earthly, sensual, even gross and the spiritual paradise. But all along the line from one extreme to the other the

garden is the scene of conjunction: the opposites conjoin in sexual or in mystical union or in both' (p. 128).

6. Cf. *supra*, p. 102.

7. Available in many translations including the one in the Temple Classics (1937), tr. by 'H.M.'. Helen Waddell has produced a scholarly and imaginative reconstruction of the *affaire* in her novel *Peter Abelard* (1933).

8. On Parsifal, see Taylor (1938, ii, 3–28).

9. The lovers had a son to whom was given the curious name of Astrolabe, an astronomical instrument.

10. On which see Waddell (1927).

11. In 1937 Carl Orff (who also set the *Catulli Carmina*) set twenty-four of these songs to music, available on record RCA, LSB 4006. His biographer tells us that when the composer discovered an edition of the *Carmina Burana* 'his theatrical imagination was fired by the very first page'. Orff himself has said: 'My entire interest is in the expression of spiritual realities. I write for the theatre in order to convey a spiritual attitude', and he dated his mature work from the première of *Carmina Burana* in 1937.

The *Carmina Burana* is a collection of more than 200 songs in several languages, preserved in the Benedictine Abbey of Beuren in Bavaria. Dronke (1968) firmly attributes the collection to the first third of thirteenth century.

12. In mediaeval literature the rose is the pervading symbol of love. It reaches its climax in Dante, *Paradiso*, cantos xxx–xxxiii in the vision of the celestial rose where Beatrice yields to St Bernard as guide. On this, see M. F. Rossetti; *A Shadow of Dante* (London 1901) 201ff.; C. Williams, *The Figure of Beatrice* (1943), esp. chp. xi. Paradise itself was (and is) a garden and therefore the rose-garden is a symbol of redoubled power. For some of the implications of the rose in the garden, see Wilkins (1969, 105–25).

13. For a splendid example of this attitude, see *Potatores exquisiti* in Waddell (1929, Penguin edn, 1952, p. 197). This book contains a representative selection of the *Carmina Burana* (nearly thirty) and an illuminating note, pp. 340f.

14. See the masterly *Apocalypse of Golias*, racily translated by F. X. Newman in Robertson (1970). This is a Latin poem from the turn of the twelfth and thirteenth centuries whose author is anonymous but probably English and abounding with mordant contempt for official hypocrisy and the corruption of institutional Christianity. Mocking of authority is recurrent, for a choice example see the 'Indulgence of Surianus' in Waddell (1927, Appendix C) and it could hover on the brink of blasphemy (if not beyond) as in the 'Credo au Ribaut' (op. cit. 192–4).

15. On which see Ziegler (1969).

16. Some of the goliards had enjoyed the protection of the highest church

dignitaries, from the Pope downwards, and it is perhaps not insignificant that the MS. of *Carmina Burana* was preserved, however surreptitiously (it was not entered in the library catalogue) of a Benedictine monastery.

17. The passage can be found in the English Dominicans' translation of the *Summa* (Gilby, 1964-6) in vol. XLVI, 15. On the 'hedonism' of contemplation, cf. 'spiritual delight is greater than carnal pleasure' (ibid. xlvi, 45) and see the discussion in vol. xx at 1a, 31, 5.

18. This was the teaching of the Franciscan school of theology, e.g. Bonaventura (II *Sent.* XX, i, 3); Alexander of Hales (*Summa Theol.* Ia, 2i, 496). The disagreement is a reminder that the idea of a mediaeval monolithic dogmatism is nonsense (see e.g. Heer, 1963, 213ff.).

19. St Augustine, *CG*, XIV, 26, cf. above, pp. 90f. In mediaeval thought, resulting from the notion of creation by a good and perfect God, there is an implicit, almost submerged, notion that all that is natural is good. Nature is simply God's intention in the world and human love, being natural, is a source of good and may even be itself divine (cf. n. 5 *supra*). This idea perhaps lies at the back of Capellanus' *De Amore sive de Deo amoris* (*c.* 1180) and more explicitly in Jean de Meung's *Roman de la Rose* (*c.* 1270). Certainly, related notions which tended towards heresy were condemned in 1270 and 1277 by Tempier, archbishop of Paris. Yet in this, as in most things, the mediaeval mind was not monolithic and attitudes to human love could extend from its conception as a quality of mind to a mere comedy of manners.

20. For easily accessible treatments of the relation of body and soul in Thomist thought see Copleston (1955, ch. iv) and Gilby (1964-6, XIII, 213, App. 5). Volume XI in the same edition is concerned with the powers of the soul, but provides a preliminary consideration of its union with the body (Ia, 75-83). St Thomas' original contribution in this area was 'the analysis of the conspiracy of flesh and spirit in man's yearning for God. Making use of the old terms, he taught that the 'soul' is the one and only 'form' in which the 'body' exists, so that it is improper to treat them separately' (XI, intro. xvi). His approach can be described as 'existentialist' in that his treatment 'is rooted in the original matrix of primitive sense-experience and immediate reflection' (ibid. xvii). Thomas is quite insistent that the human soul, in spite of its immortality and superiority, is not (as such) man. Other interesting points include:

'Sensuality consists of two drives: desire and aggression. All the aggressive passions start from and finish with the desirous passions (Ia, 81, 2), but both drives can respond to reason and will' (Ia, 81, 3).

'Man is said to be "after God's image" in virtue of his intelligent nature' (Ia, 83, 4.) 'God's image is found equally in men and women as regards that point in which the idea of "image" is principally realised, namely an intelligent nature.' (ibid. ctr. O'Faolain and Martinez, 1974.)

'It is man's nature to acquire understanding of things through his senses – that is why the soul is in union with the body, because it needs it for its own activity.' (Ia, 101, 1.)

On the body, St Thomas remarks, *inter alia*:

'It was proper for the human body to be made out of the four elements, in order to give man an affinity with lower bodies, as a sort of middle link between spiritual and bodily substances.' (Ia, 91, 1.)

'Man is called a little world or microcosm, because all parts of the created world are to be found in him in one way or another.' (ibid.)

To the argument that 'since man is the noblest of the animals, his body should have been the best suited for those activities that are proper to animals, namely sensation and movement', he replies that 'the immediate purpose of the human body is to serve a rational soul and its ac- tivities . . . and if there seems any fault in the human body's constitution, it must be taken that such a fault is a necessary consequence of the material used to give the body its required adaptation to the soul and the soul's ac- tivities' (Ia, 91, 3). (One would like to see these words prefacing any volume on 'the philosophy of physical education'.)

'Man has been given senses not only for obtaining the necessities of life Like other animals, but also for getting to know (for growing in conscious awareness). So while other animals take no pleasure in objects of sense except in so far as they can be referred to food or sex, man alone takes pleasure in the actual beauty of sense-objects for its own sake.' (ibid.)

'It is contrary to the whole notion of the perfection of the original establishment of things that God should have made either the body without the soul or the soul without the body, since each is part of human nature.' (Ia, 91, 4.)

'If God had removed everything from the world in which man has found an occasion of sin, the universe would have remained incomplete . . . nor should the general good be forgone to avoid a particular evil.' (Ia, 92, 1.)

21. See Wright (1960, chs. iii, iv). The hygienic engineering at Fountains Abbey is particularly spectacular.

22. Discussed in Wright (1960, 29). There is a similar contrivance at Shap Abbey in Cumbria, but this is thought to be concerned with some domestic industry.

23. Its most frequent occurrence is in the natural context of the primal Paradise – Adam and Eve in the Garden of Eden. It also occurs frequently in portrayals of the general resurrection and of the Last Judgment and, in a sub-category of the latter, in the representation of apt punishments for 'sins of the flesh'. Of course, 'mediaeval art' is not a monolithic concept, there are vast differences between Gothic and Romanesque, see e.g. Hauser (1962, i, 187, 212f.), and even between the spirit of earlyand late forms of one style (op. cit. 167–9, 170–2). Of Gothic art, Hauser (1962, i, 221f.) says: 'Its sensitivity, intimacy of experience and inwardness of feeling was unknown to the subtlest artist of the ancient world. Now this sensitivity is the peculiar effect of an interpenetration of Christian spiritualism and the awakening sensualism of the Gothic age.'

In this connection, it might be salutary to make distinctions (as mediaeval thinkers certainly would have done) between 'naked', 'unclothed' and 'nude'. For the background, one might follow through a Biblical concordance, s.v.

clothes, clothed; naked, garment, etc., and consider two sentences in descriptions of miracles: 'And he, casting away his garmènt, sprang up and came to Jesus' (blind man, Mark x, 50). 'And they found the man, from whom the devils were gone out, sitting, clothed and in his right mind, at the feet of Jesus' (Gadarene demoniac, Luke, viii, 35 and parallels).

24. And, perhaps one might add, his dignity. Hence the association of nakedness with destitution, madness and degradation, Hence, too, in relation to function and status, the frequent sumptuary laws of the mediaeval period which specifically related to clothes and even ornaments (for an example of this latter, see Wilkins, 1969, 48f.). The Church's injunctions on clerical dress fit within this same context.

25. A sculpture in the French church at Parthenay depicts a lady in her bath and in a number of others there are representations of mixed couples bathing in the same tub. See also Hauser (n. 31 *infra*.)

26. There was, of course, a close association between the practice of ablution (ceremonial and religious washing) and various kinds of physical washing. Before admission to the order of knighthood aspirants had to take a ritual bath before their vigil of arms and the name of the chivalric Order of the Bath reminds us of that custom. One wonders if the incidents mentioned in the text were an indication of a quasi-religious attitude to the act of physical love.

27. The setting up of these institutions may have been due to the influence of returning Crusaders who had met similar establishments on their travels, often survivals of Roman baths still maintained, in some places by the Turks and being given the false attribution of 'Turkish bath'. On mediaeval (and other) hygienic appliances, see Wright (1960). Roman baths had provided depillation, and the association of barbers with the mediaeval stews was natural. There were mediaeval guilds of barber-surgeons and the barber's pole (which dates from this time) is supposed to represent the white of bandages and the red of blood.

28. I have not come across a book devoted to mediaeval games, sports and recreations though the subject is touched on in general histories of these subjects, e.g. Wilson, P. *Sport Through the Ages* (London 1974), 14ff., 34ff., 40, 56ff., 76ff., 81. For documents, see e.g. Coulton (1938, vol. II, sect. 44).

As an example of possible sources, we might consider the misericords surviving in cathedrals and other churches. This physical aid to long prayers incorporated in stalls is itself not without significance for attitudes towards the body. Among the subjects portrayed in the carving beneath these tip-up seats are the following: hunting and coursing, hawking and tilting (including practice exercises) qhoits and football (including the foundations of both Association and Rugby codes), not to mention wrestling. There were a number of spectator sports – bear-dancing and bear-baiting, cock-fights and many shows exploiting the monkey's capacity to mimic. There was dancing and tumbling, contortionists and minstrelsy, juggling and jesting. Entertainment could extend from the deadly dangerous sport of jousting to the childish activities of arsey-versey, blind-man's buff and pulling grotesque faces. (See Bond F., *Wood-carving in English Churches* (O.U.P. 1914) and the more recent *Catalogue of Misericords in Great Britain*, G. L. Remant (O.U.P. 1969)).

Other sources show how mediaeval recreation was centred on the Church with its cycle of feasts and festivals and consequent holy days (holidays).. They all began with church services and continued with communal and individual celebration which naturally included sports, games and pastimes. Among those mentioned are such table-games as chess, backgammon, cards and dice; martial games including archery competitions, quarter-staff bouts, wrestling and fencing, slinging, throwing the javelin, contests between individuals armed with sword and buckler. The upper classes engaged in tilting, jousting and tournament and more elaborate competition such as 'the Troy game' and mock naval fights. Hunting extended from boars, through deer and foxes to rabbits, hares and other small game. A limited version of hunting was hawking and falconry which was strictly hierarchical and confined to the upper classes. Physical games included varieties of football and handball, the antecedents of hockey and tennis, bowls and skittles, closh and pell-mell (from which croquet is possibly derived). There were running and jumping competitions and a variety of spectator sports including bull-fighting, bear- and boar-baiting, and cock-fighting. There were performing animals, especially bears and monkeys, and a variety of human performers: fools and jesters, contortionists and jugglers, acrobats and buffoons. There were ice-sports in winter: skating, toboganning and 'tilting'. There was always a good deal of music: amateur and professional, instrumental and vocal, sacred and secular, and there was a wide variety of dance: ritualistic (as in the maypole) and social. There was an extensive provision of formal drama (as distinct from the informal drama of public events: cavalcades and processions, executions and trials) extending from the religious drama of mystery, morality and miracle plays to the secular drama of puppet and mime, masques and theatre-plays. There was a good deal of drinking and talking and adult involvement in what we might regard as children's games such as blind man's buff, tig, whip and top, girning, penny-pricke and arsey-versey.

Institutional attitudes are indicated by the introduction of medical faculties in the characteristic mediaeval foundation of the university and the founding of many varieties of hospitals.

Greek medicine first spread outside the monasteries at Salerno, under the influence of the Benedictine monks of Monte Cassino. St Benedict had said that 'the care of the sick is to be placed above and before every other duty, as if indeed Christ were being directly served by waiting upon them'. The humanist Cassiodorus (490–585) who founded the famous monastery of Vivarium (*c*. 540) not only similarly emphasised the care of the sick but advised his monks to 'read, above all, the translations of the herbarium of Dioscorides, which describes with surprising exactness the herbs of the field'. It is therefore something of a surprise to find St Bernard in the eleventh century telling his Cistercians that 'to buy drugs, to consult physicians, befits not religion'. In view of the persistence of the monastic herb-garden and the erection of 'infirmaries' with advanced amenities in Cistercian abbeys, it would seem that this precept is not to be interpreted too obviously: perhaps it simply indicates less faith in contemporary medical practitioners than in God and the brethren.

A very important source for the Church's attitudes to the body whose adequate consideration is prevented by space is the whole subject of religious practice and particularly the assumptions lying behind the liturgy. See n. 37.

29. See Owst (1966) and, for Italy in the early fifteenth century, Origo (1963). The following list taken from Owst's index may give some idea of homilectic subject-matter (an asterisk indicates that the topic occurs with some frequency): animals, amusements, anticlericalism*, art, avarice*, banquets, baths, boasting, bribes*, conscience, dances*, dice-playing*, drunkennes*, envy, gluttony*, knights, lechery*, marriage, morality-plays, pride*, prostitutes*, riches, sloth, taverns, vices and virtues*, women, women's dress (especially fantastic headgear).

The subject-matter of mediaeval art has been classified as mainly falling under the heads of Religion, Work, Order and Humour.

On mediaeval plays, see e.g. J. S. Purvis, *From Minster to Market-place* (York 1969) and his translation of *The York Cycle of Mystery-Plays* (London 1962).

For sculpture and stained glass, see E. Male, *L'Art religieux en France*, (Paris 1910), Eng. tr. *Religious Art in France of the Thirteenth Century* (London 1913), under the title of *The Gothic Image* (London 1961). The substance of mediaeval instruction is also reflected in iconography, the subjects of fresco, sculpture and stained glass and perhaps, most of all, in the miracle and morality plays which have not been adequately investigated from this point of view.

30. See Origo (1963, 43–75). The most frequent attacks on women centred on their alleged pride or vanity, their love of bedecking their bodies and their extravagant and fantastic head-dresses. The saintly Bernardino (1380–1444) had occasion to remark: 'I know some women who have more heads than the devil: each day they don a new one . . . I see some who wear them in the shape of tripe and some like a pancake, some like a trencher and some like a flap, some folded up and some turned down. O women, I bid you you take them off! . . . You have made a God of your head!' (Origo, 1955, 265.)

31. On courtly love see A. J. Denomy: *Fins Amors* (Toronto 1945); *Origins of Courtly Love* (Toronto 1944); and Bibliography: Heer (1963, 123ff.), Taylor (1965, 91ff.), Wilkins, (1969, 131, 137–41). This complex movement has been diversely interpreted:

C. S. Lewis (1936, 18ff.) claims that 'this erotic religion arises as a rival or parody of the real religion and emphasises the antagonism of the two ideals. . . . Where it is not a parody of the Church it may be, in a sense, her rival – a temporary escape, a truancy from the ardours of a religion that was believed into the delights of a religion that was merely imagined.'

Fr. A. J. Denomy saw it as 'an insidious and subtle influence . . . sinful and immoral' and even heretical 'in that it regarded man as a purely natural creature'. See his *Heresy of Courtly Love*, 1947 and arts. in *Mediaeval Studies* (Toronto 1944–53).

D. de Rougement described it as dualistic or Catharist in spirit and as setting a gulf between the human and the divine (*L'Amour et L'Occident*, Paris, 1939).

P. Dronke (1968, I, 6) stresses that 'to believe in the accord of human and divine love . . . characterises most of the poetry of our concern' (cf. I, 71, 75). A point also made by Wilkins, op. cit. See also Dronke, index III, s.v. 'Christ as the helper of lovers' and Saville, J., *The Mediaeval Erotic Alba* (N.Y. 1972).

A. Hauser (1962, I, 200) writes: 'Knightly love-poetry is, in spite of its sensualism, thoroughly mediaeval and Christian', and 'There is hardly an epoch of Western history whose literature so revels in descriptions of the beauty of the naked body, of dressing and undressing, bathing and washing of the heroes by men and women, of wedding nights and copulation, of visits and invitations into bed, as does the chivalric poetry of the rigidly moral Middle Ages. Even such a serious work, and one written with such a high purpose, as Wolfram's *Parzival* is full of descriptions that border upon the obscene.' (Cf. op. cit. 192f., 187f.)

32. By the fourteenth century some of these ideals had degenerated into conventions and then into 'romances' – an early form of escape literature of which modern romances are an even more degenerate manifestation. Popular moral treatises of the late mediaeval period take cognisance of this fact, see Pantin (1955, ch. x).

33. See n. 31 above. For possible connections between St Bernard and courtly love, see Gilson (1940, App.). Dronke (1968, 62) makes the point that 'the theologian like Bernard, who is unafraid to use the sensual imagery of the Song of Songs because it need not even for one moment be understood in its foul human sense, and the poet like Guinizelli, who sees this same imagery as reflecting the divine precisely because it shows human love with such fulness and splendour – these in one sense understand each other perfectly; the *language* they use is the same'. See also Hauser (1962, I, 187f. 192f.).

34. The absence of religious dance as a normal part of Christianity is a problem, if not a paradox. One feels that there is a deep affinity between the material expressionism of a sacramental religion and the art of dance and therefore the necessity of explaining its absence. There is, of course, its pagan associations, but the objection may be more to the Dionysiac element, the frenzy, the loss of rational control than to pagan associations (after all, the Church absorbed and developed many other practices which had pagan associations). Religious dance was not unknown to the Jews, though it was perhaps a little suspect (II Sam. vi, 12–23; I Chron. xvi, 28f.), and there is evidence that a ritual dance was associated with the Jewish Passover (Wilkins, 1969, 82, n. 3) and hence possibly with the Christian Mass whose movements (until recently) could resemble a slow and stately ballet. Its rejection could be explained by its adoption by the Gnostics who, in the Apocryphal Acts of John, portray Christ leading the apostles in dance after

the Last Supper (M. R. James, *Apocryphal New Testament*, 1955, 253f., cited Wilkins, 1969). On this subject, see van der Leeuw, (1963, 11–74).

Yet Christian dance is, at the most, only just beneath the surface: carols were originally dances, the stars dance in Dante's *Paradiso*, and in the Middle Ages dances accompanied the burial of venerated prelates, and followed a new priest's first Mass (Leeuw, 1963, 37). The very popular legend of Our Lady's Juggler (*c*. 1200) who could only offer his bodily skills is a powerful witness to an attitude which fortunately still persists: the consecration of the new Catholic Cathedral in Liverpool was followed by a dance-offering and I was present at a religious dance presentation in York Minster in the summer of 1976. Folk-custom and mystical poetry alike witness to this suppressed element which is explicit in the late mediaeval carol which begins:

> Tomorrow shall be my dancing day;
> I would my true love did so chance
> To see the legend of my play,
> To call my true love to my dance.
> Sing, oh! my love, my love, my love,
> This have I done for my true love.

> Then I was born of a Virgin pure,
> Of her I took fleshy substance;
> Then I was knit to man's nature,
> To call my true love to my dance.
> Sing, oh! my love. . . .

(*Oxford Book of Carols*, No. 71 discussed by G. R. S. Mead *in The Quest*, II (London 1910–11).

35. At Liège in 1374 a band of these fanatical balletomanes is said to have plotted to murder all the clergy (Cleugh, 1967, 37).

36. Flogging was a universal discipline (not only in schools) as well as a legal punishment which apparently gave a name to the shortest street in York (Whip-ma-whop-ma-gate). It was also an almost institutionalised part of ascetic training as 'the discipline'.

37. Richard Rolle, Water Hilton and the author of *The Cloud of Unknowing* represent the peak, but there are antecedents in the previous century as exemplified in the 'Ancren Riwle'. But mystics are not really representative and we ought to mention manifestations of a more general kind. Attitudes to the body (and Creation) are exemplified and implicitly or explicitly taught in religious activities, including liturgical and non-liturgical prayer, pious practices and customs (including the very popular pilgrimages), sacraments and sacramentals, the recitation of rosaries and psalters, processions, fastings, feasts, dances and tracing mazes. Much of this activity was either extremely physical in nature or concerned with physical reality: with the notion that places and things (including the body) could be sanctified or be the means of sanctification – as could time itself – and that redemption was a matter of body and soul and involved nature as well as supernature.

Any treatment of this theme which approached adequacy would require a book to itself, but because of its importance and paradoxical neglect it cannot be allowed to pass without at least a note since the nature of worship may be more indicative of attitudes to reality than almost any other pointer, especially in a 'religious' age. A beginning could be made with a study of Knowles' words which, though specifically concerning the prominent institution of monasticism, could be (with appropriate modifications) applied to religious activity in general: 'Those wholly unfamiliar with the monastic life are perhaps slow to allow for the moulding influence, upon minds and characters attuned to them, of the liturgical texts with their accompaniment of chant and ceremony, which brought to the thirteenth century, as they bring to those fortunate enough to know them at the present day, something of the purity, the austerity, the exquisite enjoyment of type, of symbol and of allusion, and the mingling of all that is best in the Hebrew and Roman genius, which was the supreme achievement of the age before the barbarians conquered Rome. Beauty of word and melody, beauty of architecture and ornament cannot create, and may even hinder, the purest spirituality, but pure spirituality is a rare treasure, and for men of more ordinary mould the liturgy in all its fullness may be a tonic nourishment, as well as an enobling discipline.' (D. Knowles; *The Religious Orders in England*, Cambridge 1962, vol. I, p. 318.)

Hints and ideas worth pursuing may be found e.g. in: Jungmann (1951, vol. I, p. 103–33 and pr. ii, *passim*), and Dix below, chp. xv.

For 'the sanctification of time' see: F. Cabrol, *The Year's Liturgy* (London 1938), vol. I, intro. pp. xii–xvi. F. Cabrol, *Liturgical Prayer* (London 1925), chs. xvi, xvii, xviii, G. Dix, *The Shape of the Liturgy* (London n.d.c. 1944), chap. xi.

For general ideas, see: F. Cabrol (1925) esp. parts v and vii; T. Wesseling, *Liturgy and Life* (London 1938) R. .Guardini, *The Spirit of the Liturgy* (London 1930); *Vom Geist der Liturgie* (Freiburg 1957); *Sacred Signs* (London 1930); C. C. Martindale, *The Words of the Missal* (London 1935, chaps. ii, vi.) Y. Hirn, *The Sacred Shrine* (London 1958); H. Rahner, *Greek Myths and Christian Mystery* (London 1963); Leeuw (1963); Wilkins (1969).

38. For the connection between Aquinas and Gothic architecture see e.g.: J. Maritain, *Art and Scholasticism* (Eng. tr. London 1942); E. Panowsky, *Gothic Architecture and Scolasticism* (N.Y. 1957). For the synthesis of philosophy and theology, e.g. G. Leff, *Mediaeval Thought* (London 1958) ch. 7; E. Gilson, *Elements of Christian Philosophy* (N.Y. 1963); *Reason and Revelation in the Middle Ages* (N.Y. 1939).
General: C. G. Crump, and E. F. Jacob, *The Legacy of the Middle Ages* (Oxford 1943); Heer (1963), Taylor (1938) and Dronke (1968, 69–75).

39. For the magnitude and difficulty of this achievement, see e.g. Southern (1959, ch. iv), S. Toulmin and J. Goodfield *The Fabric of the Heavens* (London 1961), p. 177.

40. Cf. Notes i, 23, 25, above. Of the artistic transformation of the eleventh century, Hauser (1962, I, 171f.) writes: 'The reference to the transcendent is now so predominant that the individual forms no longer

have any inherent value of their own; they are now pure symbols and signs. They express the transcendent world no longer merely in negative terms, that is to say, *they no longer hint at the reality of the supernatural by leaving gaps in the concatenation of the natural and by denying the independent character of the purely natural order; they now depict the irrational and supramundane in a thoroughly positive and direct manner.*' (Italics mine.)

With increased confidence and balance the assurance of the supernatural revalued the natural in a total celebration and one might see the culmination of this process in the appearance of the Gothic nude as an independent form at the beginning of the fifteenth century. It owes nothing to the classical Greek, but represents what Clark (1956, ch. viii) calls 'the Alternative Convention' not without analogies to Gothic architecture and ogival curves. For Melville (1973, 15), 'In general the Gothic nude is, in itself, more erotic than the Renaissance nude.' Whether this is true or not, the Gothic nude became a casualty of the Reformation and fashion and by the time of H. Baldung in the sixteenth century woman has become concomitant to lust and death.

41. Modern theologians are becoming aware of this loss, see e.g.: H.·Rahner, *Man at Play* (London, 1965); H. Cox, *Feast of Fools* (Cambridge, Mass. 1969); and from slightly different perspectives: J. Huizinga, *Homo Ludens* (London 1970 etc.); J. Pieper, *Leisure the Basis of Culture* (London 1965). Ancient philosophers admitted that it was pleasant to be less than rational at times, it may be a modern discovery that it is *essential* after losing the mediaeval practice.

42. Some of I. Illich's remarks in *Celebration of Awareness* (London 1973) are apposite here and perhaps it is not too far-fetched to relate our contemporary *Medical Nemesis* (Illich, 1975) to neglect of St Bernard's warning that 'to buy drugs, to consult physicians, befits not religion'.

43. See Ziegler (1969) especially chs. xv, xvi, xvii.

44. Among the many effects could be included the reorientation of mediaeval almsgiving, the institutions of chantries and bedesmen on a vast scale, the increasing dominance of the Requiem Mass with the tolling sequence 'Dies Irae'. The economic effects have received adequate attention, but too little attention has been given to the profound psychological effects of this catastrophe which may be discerned in surviving evidence from literate contemporaries. 'Those few discreet folk who remained alive expected many things, all of which, by reason of the corruption of sin, failed among mankind whose minds followed marvellously in the contrary direction. They believed that those whom God's grace had saved from death, having beheld the destruction of their neighbours . . . would become better conditioned, humble, virtuous and Catholic; that they would guard themselves from iniquity and sin and would be full of love and charity towards one another. But no sooner had the plague ceased than we saw the contrary: for since men were few and since, by hereditary succession, they abounded in earthly goods, they forgot the past as though it had never been and gave themselves up to a more disordered and shameful life than they

had led before. For, mouldering in ease, they dissolutely abandoned themselves to the sin of gluttony, with feasts and taverns and delight of delicate viands; and again to games of hazard and to unbridled lechery, inventing strange and unaccustomed fashions and indecent manners in their garments.' (Matteo Villani, Chronicler of Florence, cited Zeigler (1969, 270f.) Guy de Chauliac, a physician in the Papal household during the plague, described how 'the father did not visit the son nor the son the father. Charity was dead and hope abandoned . . .'.

45. '[Modern historians] see the beginning of the end of the mediaeval period in the disastrous pandemic (i.e. worldwide epidemic) of plague which devastated Europe in the middle of the fourteenth century and which is known as "the Black Death". Even the imagination of a modern novelist, nourished on the horrors of twentieth-century warfare, would find itself taxed by the effort to depict this historic event. Reasonable estimates suggest that about one-half of the population of Europe, including Britain, died in this outbreak.' F. N. L. Poynter and K. D. Keele, '*A Short History of Medicine*' (London, 1961), II, 88 which also contains the quotation from Guy de Chauliac, cited n. 44 above.

Chapter 9

1. On the 'Renaissance Problem', see e.g.: *The Renaissance: Mediaeval or Modern?* (Problems in European Civilisation) ed. K. H. Dannenfeldt (Boston 1965); *The Renaissance Debate* (European Problems Series) ed. D. Hay (N.Y. 1965); *The Renaissance* (Problems and Perspectives in History) P. Burke (London 1964); *The Twelfth Century Renaissance* (Major Issues in History) ed. C. Warren Hollister (N.Y. 1969).

2. The Florentine N. Machiavelli published *The Prince* in 1513. For an admiring treatment of this phenomenon, see the first chapter of Burckhardt (1944).

3. It might be argued that the cult of personality, initiated by the Renaissance, is itself a potent sign of decadence. Personality is no longer a 'natural' attribute growing from within but artificial, a construct, a 'work of art' like the State. The nadir of this process is with us today in the 'personalities' of TV and other mass-mediated and mass-media-produced artefacts.

4. Cited in Santillana (1956, 22).

5. See Baker (1961, 213).

6. G. Chaucer, 'The Parson's Tale', *Canterbury Tales*, 12. Lines 260ff. in W. W. Skeat's edition (Oxford n.d.).

7. See Lewis (1967a), esp. ch. vii.

8. Obviously a body which is only a temporary instrument and which can serve if it be a caterpillar's or a saint's or whatever has nothing like the significance of a specific entity for which a soul was peculiarly created and which together with that soul forms the full man.

9. See above, pp. 121f. and *Summa Theologica*, Ia, arts 2, 3 and especially 4.

10. For Leonardo da Vinci's ideas on the five senses and 'the common sense' see MacCurdy (1952, I, 106).

Popular mediaeval ideas can be seen in the Morality 'Everyman' where Five-Wits, who speaks of the sacraments, is the last friend to leave. There is a lively, original and extremely early graphic portrayal of this concept on the Fuller Brooch in the British Museum (on which see D. B. Harden, *Dark Age Britain* (London 1956), pp. 173–90). This dates from the middle of the ninth century and is the only Anglo-Saxon piece with representations of the human figure. It can be related to the subject-matter of Anglo-Saxon sermons and to a tradition that extends to Bernard Silvestris (mid twelfth century) and, with modifications, beyond. This first representation seems to refer to the wholeness (holiness) of man and his sensible knowledge of creation.

11. Hence our use of such expressions as being 'in good spirits', 'high spirits', etc.

12. On which see Tillyard (1943, 1966), Lovejoy 1936).

13. The most popular illustration of this attitude is Hamlet's speech beginning 'What a piece of work is man! . . .' (*Hamlet*, II, ii, lines 316ff.) For a general brief summary of Shakespeare's ideas on man, see R. M. Frye, *Shakespeare and Christian Doctrine* (Princton 1963), pp. 122–29, 199–205.

14. Tillyard (1966, 111f.).

15. Cf. Shakespeare, *Julius Caesar*, I, ii, lines 192ff. That the idea is not quite dead (or entirely erroneous) seems to be indicated by the recent work on 'somatatyping' by Sheldon and others.

16. Compare the 'modern discovery' of bio-rhythms.

17. Mentioned in J. Liggett, *The Human Face* (London 1974), p. 6.

18. 'With the sixteenth century England went into a dirty decline' (Wright, 1960, 68).

19. Illustrated in Wright (1960, 69).

20. Girolamo Romanino (1485/6–1566) of whom Berenson (1953, 189) remarks that his best qualities appear in fresco, notably the colonnades of the castle at Trent in northern Italy (the place of the reforming Church Council).

21. Wright (1960, 128) reproduces an engraving from one of these.

22. On their significance and interpretation, see e.g. Panofsky (1962), Wind (1967), and compare E. H. Gombrich's remark that the art of the Renaissance was 'an expression of ancient wisdom rather than of modern sexuality'. Naked is associated with truth, not only in words as in 'the naked truth' but also in images as in Botticelli's *Calumny of Appelles* or in Titian's

miscalled allegory *Sacred and Profane Love* on which see Panofsky (1962, 150–60). Most frequently, in the early Renaissance the nude is a symbol of ideal beauty, i.e. intelligible beauty. These figures are not portraits or representations of real women but the assemblage of general concepts of beauty 'for the individual parts of the body as well as for its proportions: concepts that were meant to rise above nature, being taken from a spiritual realm that existed only in the mind. In this way Raphael formed his *Galatea*. As he says in his letter to Count Castiglione, "Since beauty is rare among women, I follow a certain idea formed in my imagination."' (Winckelmann cited in Holt (1957, II, 341.) Clark puts the point another way when he says (1956, 28) that Raphael's *Galatea* 'leaves the realm of narrative and entertainment . . . and enters that of philosophy'.

23. Hauser (1962, i, 221f.) remarks that the novel element in Gothic art consists 'in an intimacy of expression whereby the artist makes any work of Gothic or post-Gothic art a sort of confession of his personal faith'. By the time of William Durandus (1220–96) every artistic detail of a church could represent some Catholic doctrine. See tr. of Durandus, *Rationale Divinorum Officiorum*, by J. M. Neale and B. Webb as *The Symbolism of Churches and Church Ornaments* (Leeds 1843), extracts in Holt (1957, 121–9).

24. St Augustine, *De pulchitudine simulacrorum*, cited Lovejoy (1936, 85).

25. Theophilus, *Essay upon Various Arts* tenth century tr. Holt (1957, 6ff.).

26. Extracts tr. in Holt (1957, 222–48). Panofsky (1955) has an interesting essay on Suger (ch. vii) which shows the part he played in the development of Gothic architecture, his anticipation of some aspects of Christian Platonism and the difference between him and a 'great man' of the Renaissance. This last passage is worth quoting: 'The great man of the Renaissance asserted his personality centripetally, so to speak: he swallowed up the world that surrounded him until his whole environment had been absorbed by his own self. Suger asserted his personality centrifugally: he projected his ego into the world that surrounded him until his whole self had been absorbed by his environment.' (p. 171.)

It is, of course the difference between the Benedictine monk and the egocentric, the balance and order of the individual in community as against 'aristocratic' self-importance. Even the austere Clumiac Peter the Venerable was impressed by the straitness and simplicity of Suger's personal cell, whatever the glories were of the abbey church – the shrine of God and His saints.

27. See Holt (1957, 9–17).

28. See Holt (1957, 88–91 and figs. 4–10). Panofsky (1955, 83–90) is also relevant.

29. See note 23 above.

30. Holt (1957, 141).

31. Mediaeval moral theology distinguished four symbolic meanings of nudity:

Nuditas naturalis – the natural state of man, conducive to humility like the words from the Ash Wednesday liturgy (following the Carnival) – 'Remember, O man, that dust thou art and unto dust thou shalt return.' This kind of nudity occurs in representations of Paradise, the Last Judgment, the Resurrection and in portrayals of savages, martyrdoms and (according to Panofsky) in scientific illustrations.

Nuditas temporalis which symbolises the lack of earthly goods due either to extraneous poverty or to voluntary abnegation as in the case of apostles, ascetics and members of religious orders. (One remembers the symbolic gesture of St Francis of Assisi and his hasty covering by a friendly bishop.)

Nuditas virtualis – the symbol of innocence, the soul denuded of its rags of guilt, the divesting of outward appearances. (One remembers the relationship in the Middle Ages between costume and status.) This state is often related to the sacrament of confession.

Nuditas criminalis – a sign of lust, bestiality, vanity and the absence of all virtues. (We might remember the association of irrationality – the loss of man's distinguishing attribute – with nakedness, in opposition to being 'clothed and in his right mind' (Luke viii, 35). This form of nudity explains the naked representations of pagan divinities, devils, personified vices and sinful humans.

The reader may see a connection between these distinctions and the significance of nakedness in the Old Testament considered on p. 25.

32. It was quite common for gargoyles to be designed so that water flowed from the mouths of grotesques or from where their urinary tracts might be conceived to be. There are representations of defecation and of normal and abnormal sexual intercourse (see notes 1, 23, 25 to Ch. i above) and there is a representation of bestiality: a woman copulating with a goat, but modern interpretations may miss the mark, e.g. a goat is a normal metamorphosis of the devil on the one hand, and thus the carving could for instance symbolise heresy or sin, and on the other hand, since in mediaeval symbolism the goat represent lust, the group could signify one of the deadly sins.

33. Melville (1973, 15) writes: 'Realism is the key to provoking a physical as opposed to an intellectual response, and obviously the more clearly a painting of the nude evokes an actual human being the more physically erotic it will be. In this respect another crucial aspect of the Gothic nude is that both sexes are often shown with pubic hair and women sometimes have the vulva indicated as well, whereas the Renaissance nude almost without exception adheres strictly to the convention of a bland and hairless pubic region.'

One might wonder how 'realistic' the ogival, small-breasted woman of mediaeval art was and how far she related to their 'ideal' woman whose facial proportions were reckoned in term of the mystical number seven: 1/7 hair, 2/7 forehead, 2/7 nose, 1/7 nose to mouth, 1/7 mouth to chin. It may be relevant to reconstruct the female physical ideal of the Middle Ages whose attributes would include blonde hair like gold wire, bright blue sparkling eyes, lily-white or rose-pink cheeks, white teeth evenly set, long white slender fingers, small and willowy waist and a skin that everywhere was dazzling white and soft as silk.

34. The 'Milky Way' was conceived as an outpouring from the breasts of the sidereal Venus.

35. Bernard Silvestris was an influential writer of the mid-twelfth-century. These words of his are cited in D. W. Robentson, *Literature of Mediaeval England* (N.Y. 1970), p. 288.

36. Cited Robertson, op. cit. p. 289. This distinction is roughly equivalent to that between the Heavenly and Natural Venus, on which see Clark (1956, chs. iii, iv). With it might be compared the distinction between Eros and Agape.

37. For Ficino's ideas on the 'two Venuses' see Panofsky (1962, 141-4).

38. Ficino defined man as 'a rational soul, participating in the divine Mind, employing a body'. His was a unique and temerarious endeavour to unify developed Christianity with a developed Plantonism and, according to him, the position of man was 'both exalted and problematic. With his sensual impulses vacillating between submission and revolt, his Reason facing alternate failure and success, and even his imperilled Mind often diverted from its proper task, man's "immortal soul is always miserable in the body"; it "sleeps, dreams, raves and ails" in it, and is filled with an unending nostalgia to be satisfied only when it "returns whence it came".' (Panofsky, 1962, 137f.)

39. Cited Clark (1956, 92), cf. the quotations from Pico de Mirandola, ibid. '[Venus] has as her companions and her maidens the Graces, whose names, in the vulgar tongue, are Verdure, Gladness and Splendour; and these Graces are nothing but the three properties pertaining to Ideal Beauty.' Both quotations show the aristocratic nature of art whose message is no longer for the common people (as it was in the Middle Ages.) It is no coincidence that the attributes of 'Humanitas' are the qualities of an ideal Renaissance prince. The norm of education is moving from the edification of a Christian to the production of a gentleman.

40. For an extreme example: an edition of Ovid was published in Paris in 1515 indicating the 'real meaning' of his stories and, according to this, Ganymede, whose beauty had so inflamed Jove that he snatched him to heaven, was to be interpreted as a prefiguration or ante-type of St John the divine in which Jove's eagle symblised Christ, or the sublime vision which revealed the secrets of heaven. Following this tradition, Landino in his indispensable commentary for the sixteenth-century student of Dante described the ascent of the mind to God in terms of this Christianised myth: 'It leaves behind its companions – i.e. the vegetative and sensitive souls and being removed, or as Plato says divorced, from the body and forgetting corporeal things, it concentrates entirely on contemplating the secrets of heaven.' (Panofsky, 1962, 215.)

41. For the elegance and sophistication of this mutation, see Wind (1967) and for a modern expression of similar ideas, Rahner (1963).

42. The so-called 'Areopagite' who was for a time identified with the man mentioned in Acts, xviii, 34, but probably flourished in the fifth or sixth century. He was the author of a very influential treatise *On the Celestial Hierarchies* which was an earlier attempt to fuse neo-Platonism with Christianity. He taught that however wide the gap between the world of God and that of matter, it is never unbridgeable. There are hierarchies, but no dichotomies. Even the lowliest things partake of the divine qualities of goodness, beauty and truth and thus the process by which the emanations of the Divine Light flow down until they are nearly lost in matter can always be reversed into an ascent from pollution and multiplicity into purity and oneness. Hence man, 'the immortal soul who makes use of a body' need have no shame in depending on his sensory perceptions and sense-controlled imagination. Instead of turning his back on the physical world, he can hope to transcend it by absorbing it (see Panofsky 1955, 159ff.). This teaching was transmitted and expanded by John Scotus Eriguena who flourished in the middle of the ninth century until, according to legend, his pupils in an English monastery stabbed him to death with their pens (the proto-martyr of education?). His major work *On the Distinctions in Nature* was known to Suger who put these ideas into architectural and artistic practice, commenting in his long poem about his work:

> Bright is that which is brightly coupled with the bright,
> And bright is the noble edifice which is pervaded by the new light . . .
> Bright is the noble work; but being nobly bright, the work
> Should brighten the minds so that they may travel, through the true lights
> To the True Light where Christ is the true Door.
> In what manner it be inherent in this world the golden door defines:
> The dull mind rises to truth, through that which is material
> And, seeing this light, is resurrected from its former submersion
> In mere materiality (Panofsky, 1955, 163f.).

This metaphysical approach to the phenomenon of light probably also inspired the research into optics of Robert Grosseteste, bishop of Lincoln (1235–53) and first Chancellor of the University of Oxford.

The point that we wish to make is that the Middle Ages were at least as much concerned as the Renaissance with light and the mediatory function of material creation.

43. Wind (1967, 13).

44. Geometry (along with arithmetic, music and astronomy) was a basic undergraduate study in the Middle Ages. God himself was sometimes portrayed as a geometer and geometry affected architecture and the plastic arts (see e.g. fig. 6–9 in Holt, 1957, I, and Panofsky, 1955, ch. ii). This point seems to have been missed by W. M. Ivins in his very interesting *Art and Geometry* (N.Y. 1964).

45. But there were, of course, shifts between mediaeval and Renaissance attitudes and some of them may be indicated by the following antitheses.

Mediaeval art was (naturally) concerned with the eye, but much more with the response of the soul (the interior reflection); the Renaissance artist, significantly disassociating himself from the craftsman, was more concerned with physical vision (reflection from material surfaces). This change was reflected in a shift in the typical art form of the period. In the Middle Ages it was sculpture – particularly that total structuring of space exemplified in the cathedral or great church. In the Renaissance it was painting – the best medium for representing surfaces and possessing the additional attributes of being portable and the possession of an individual (on this, cf. Berger, 1972).

Ruskin, cited with approval by Clark (1969, 1) thought architecture was the most revealing form of the spirit of an age: the Renaissance shows several shifts – an external one from ecclesiastical to civil architecture and an internal one in the transition from vertical to horizontal emphasis and a change in the principles of design. Renaissance building seem to grow from the outside in, design and proportion are dominant and they are given (in the books of the ancients), so the result is only a building, a construct.

Mediaeval buildings grow from within as an external manifestation of something interior and hidden, the result is a shrine or symbol, seeking beyond the here and now, but firmly based on external verities and human experience and experiment. Expressed another way: Gothic art is geometrical, based on the circle (symbol of eternity); Renaissance art is arithmetical or proportional, based on counting, on the accumulation of individual units whose origins are in time (the classical world).

Renaissance art is static, backward-looking; mediaeval art is dynamic and apocalyptic. Ivins (1964, 61ff.) points out that the mediaeval artist early lost interest in the shape of the naked human body and was much more interested in the portrayal of motion and gesture. Mediaeval art is dramatic – concerned with communication – and it is an interesting paradox that scenes from mediaeval drama seem to have provided the subject-matter of Renaissance painting.

In every sense, the Renaissance produced 'a point of view', self-centred and limited. It became obsessed with 'perspective' in art and it could detach itself from the flow of time and discover 'history' in the sense of periods different from and discontinuous with the contemporary. As Adam at the request of God named the animals, Renaissance man confidently nominated periods of history and divided it into ancient and modern with an unimportant intervening interlude which they disparagingly called 'the Middle Ages'. 'No mediaeval man could see the civilisation of antiquity as a phenomenon complete in itself and detached from the contemporary world.' (Panofsky, 1962, 26.)

Mediaeval art was concerned with the symbolisation of an eternal and total order centred on the Incarnation of the beginning and end (the Alpha and Omega). Renaissance man was interested in the representation of the world of man, limited in time and space: the world 'sub specie *hominis*' replaced the world 'sub specie *aeternitatis*'.

46. Panofsky (1955, 119).

47. See, e.g. Wind (1967, App. I).

48. Cf. Wind (1967, ch. v).

49. Cf. Wind (1967, ch. ix).

50. Perhaps the appearance of pornography might be taken as a significant event. Its appearance (as distinguished from 'earthiness' or whatever) can be dated fairly precisely in the second decade of the sixteenth century. The occasion was the publication (c. 1524) of some rather brutal engravings depicting sixteen copulatory positions which stimulated Aretino to write an appropriate sonnet for each. He describes the occasion in a letter of 1538 to his friend Battista Zacchi, a surgeon of Brescia: 'After I had persuaded Pope Clement to release Marcantonio Bolognese, who was in prison for having engraved the *Sedici Modi*, I felt a desire to see the pictures which set off Ghiberti's complaints that this brilliant artist ought to be crucified, and when I had seen them I felt the same spirit which moved Giulio Romano to draw them. And since poets and sculptors both ancient and modern have from time to time written or carved erotic things . . . I rattled off the Sonnets which you see at the foot of each page. Their wanton memory I dedicate to you, *pace* all hypocrites, for I renounce the bad judgment and dirty habit which forbids the eyes to see what pleases them most. What harm is there in seeing a man on top of a woman? Must the animals have more freedom than we? It seems to me that the you-know-what given us by nature for the preservation of the species should be worn as a pendant round our necks or as a badge in our caps. It has created you, one of the first living surgeons; it has made me who am better than bread. It has brought forth the Bembos, the Molzis, the Fortinis, the Franchis, the Varchis, the Ugolin Martinis, the Lorenzo Lenzis, the Docis, the Titians, the Michelangelos; and after them the Peopes, Emperors and kings; it has produced the pretty children and the beautiful women with their *sancta sanctorum*, and for this reason we should decree holy days and dedicate festivals in its honour, not hide it away in scraps of cloth and silk!' (Rawson, 1973a, 9.)

The letter reveals the 'cultural shift' very clearly. Beauty (*id quod visum placet* in the mediaeval definition) has been reduced to voyeurism, animal sexuality is the model for human, the coyness of 'you-know-what' hand in hand with a permissive bravado, the numerous illogicalities, the procreative emphasis, the aristocratic tone (one is reminded of the aristocratic lady who was alleged to have said, after her first sexual experience, that it was too good for the working class), the new direction of male chauvinism. Above all there is the mechanism, the reductionism which is the critical element in pornography, the element of violence, the lack of love and tenderness which makes physical conjunction an end in itself rather than a sacrament of unity. These elements are evident in both the poems and Romano's engravings (illustrated in Melville 1973, nos. 26–45).

51. It is interesting that psychological theories tend to become self-fulfilling diagnoses. Just as patients under a Freudian or Jungian analyst

have, respectively, Freudian or Jungian dreams, so Renaissance figures seem to have alternated between tempestuous wrath and melancholia. Following a statement of Aristotle, it was a Renaissance belief that all 'great men' were melancholics, an idea that dominated the Romantic age and is not without influence on present-day popular concepts of genius. Dürer's powerful images of this 'humour' are very relevant, Michelangelo was very conscious of the soul's struggles in this 'vale of tears' though modern psychologists (with different presuppositions) might refer his state to latent bisexuality.

52. The four rivers of the underworld in classical mythology.

53. From the contemporary 'Jests' of F. Berni, cited Tolnay (1966, II, 519).

54. E. Garin in Tolnay (1966, II, 529).

55. It will be noted that the 'scenario' of Michelangelo is identical with that of the mediaeval mystery plays.

56. On Michelangelo' inner tensions Hauser (1962, II, 115) comments: 'Michelangelo's way out of the conflict was also merely an escape. What mediaeval artist would have felt induced by his experience of God to give up his artistic work as he did? The deeper the religious feelings of the mediaeval artist, the deeper was the source from which he was able to draw his artistic inspiration. And not merely because he was completely a believing Christian, but also because he was completely a creative artist. The moment he stopped being artistically productive, he ceased to be anything at all; Michelangelo, on the other hand, remained, even after he had finished his work as an artist, a very interesting person both in the eyes of the world and in his own eyes.' Hauser (1962, II, 125) makes Tintoretto the real heir to Michelangelo as 'the only artist in Italy in whom the religious rebirth of the age found just as deep expression as in Michelangelo, though it was of a different kind', and he identified El Greco as Tintoretto's only real successor: the most deeply religious artist since the Middle Ages (Hauser 1962, II, 127).

57. For a Renaissance view of man, see e.g. Burckhardt (1944, 81–103 which concludes with an assessment of Aretino), Panofsky (1955, 24f.), Baker (1961). Its essence might be seen as pride and its idea as the progenitor of the Nietzchean 'superman'.

58. Though Melville, (1973, 266) thinks that his drawing of the vulva of a female carcase was 'made in a spirit of denigration and . . . reflects an aversion to woman little short of horrow and disgust' (ill. op. cit. 186). Anatomy and dissection were traditionally repugnant to Christians whose respect for the human body, even when dead, made them regard its ill-treatment as a kind of sacrilege. They recognised the need for dissection, but the operation required special dispensation. See Walker (1954, 180f. and Plate 4). For a short appreciation of Da Vinci's anatomical activities, see Poynter and Keele (1961, ii, 28–30).

59. For the traditional and less critical appreciation of Leonardo, see e.g. Vallentin (1939) esp. ch. vii.

60. On mediaeval symbolism through art and architecture, see e.g. my own *Church Explorer's Guide* (1978).

Chapter 10

1. More's hedonism has many interesting characteristics. Worthy of mention is the repeated emphasis on balance or equilibrium, characteristically late mediaeval and Aristotelian. There is also a passive or contemplative quality about his categorisation. His first set centres on the removal of pain due to deficiency or irritation while the second emphasises health as itself the source of tranquillity, a good in itself and the source or foundation of all other pleasure. The admission of the minor pleasures of scratching and evacuation is pleasing, though whether all would be happy in the association of orgasm with these is another matter.

The acceptance of bodily pleasures (great and small) alongside the pleasures of the soul is noteworthy.

2. Erasmus of Rotterdam (*c.* 1466–1536), humanist, wit, scholar and Catholic reformer. His most famous work is the *Praise of Folly* dedicated to his friend Sir Thomas More, easily accessible in Dolan (1964). He wrote that reason had been confined to a narrow corner of the brain, leaving the rest of the body to our passions, especially anger and lust. Erasmus thought that without the article on 'the resurrection of the flesh' we should believe all the rest of the Creed to no purpose and defined 'the flesh' as 'a human body animated by a human soul'. See his *Enquiry concerning Faith*, in Dolan (1964,219).

3. As in the work of Leonardo da Vinci, on which see Vallentin (1939,427–45).

4. Nor could Luther discover anything praiseworthy in the fine arts. He condemned every kind of artistic externalisation of religious feeling, identifying it with the 'idolatry' which he discerned even in the adorning of churches with pictures. His attitude represented a sort of tradition in that all mediaeval heresies contained an iconoclastic element. But Luther was a moderate compared with Karlstadt, Zwingli, Calvin and the Anabaptists in whose minds doubts about art grow into a raging iconophobia whose roots might be better sought in the unconscious than in their rationalisations.

5. Maritain (1941) makes an implicit statement about his own psychosomatic theories by illustrating the section on Luther by a series of pictures progressing from an engraving of Luther as an ascetic friar (opp. p. 32) to a reproduction of the gross face of Luther dead (opp. p. 37).

6. 'Not long after [the Renaissance which transformed the functional cod-piece into a work of art that by stiffening devices simulating a permanent erection] followed Luther's disengagement from the policing-evasion function of the Church, the deliberate violation of his vows, and his marriage to a nun. . . . Thus the Renaissance and the Reformation directed Europe's attention to the body and the personality as man's environment inside-the-skin. . . . . Nor was the Renaissance alone in its creation of

pornography, for the rhetoric of Luther and the Reformers was often Rabelaisian and very close to pornography . . . and in the Reformation tradition Foxe's *Book of Martyrs* achieved a new and higher level of sado-masochism than the old saints' legends had ever accomplished.' (Peckham 1969,289f.)

7. This neologism is an adjectival form from what the psychologists call 'patrism' – a world-view caused by a dominating father-figure. There is such an element in Christianity, derived largely from the Old Testament, but it is balanced by, for example, the personification of Wisdom as feminine, the cult of Our Lady, etc. See also the article by S.M.A., 'God is our Mother', in *Life of the Spirit* (Blackfriars, Oxford, May 1945) reprinted in C. Hastings and B. Nicholl, *Selection I* (London 1953).

8. The powerful efflorescence of witchcraft after the Reformation may have been partly due to an attempt to fill the vacuum created by the abolition of Catholic 'superstitions'. Most of our newspapers have their tame astrologers and many people still hang horseshoes over their doors. For a fascinating general survey, see K. Thomas, *Religion and the Decline of Magic* (London 1971), esp. chs. 2 and 3.

9. For the association between sacramentalism and art and the converse, one might notice the Puritan objection to music, the most immaterial of the arts. At the beginning of Elizabeth's reign over 100 church organs had been dismantled in deference to Protestant philistinism.

10. Cf. note 37 to Ch. 8 above.

11. For the connection between Protestantism and Capitalism see e.g. H. Tawney, *Religion and the Rise of Capitalism*; A. Fanfani, *Catholicism, Protestantism and Capitalism*; M. Weber, *The Protestant Ethic and the Spirit of Capitalism*; and ctr. R. Tribe, *The Christian Social Tradition*; W. Shewring, *Rich and Poor in Christian Tradition*. I believe it is still a crime in England to be 'without visible means of support', i.e. without cash in pocket.

12. Erasmus saw greed as the overriding contemporary sin and a Freudian might see all the signs of a regression from the genital stage (love) to the anal stage (possession).

13. The Reformation began in a theological objection to justification by works (of piety, almsgiving, etc.) and ended in an economic asseveration of justification through work (business). The tradition had made *negotium* (business) a merely negative thing – the absence of *otium* (leisure) which was the desirable state for a free man. Benedict had felt the need to sanctify necessary work, while Calvin (or at least his followers) seem to have believed that work as such was good and regarded the alternatives of 'leisure', 'playing the fool' and 'recreation' (a significant word) with the deepest suspicion.

14. There is a paradox in the austere Calvin objecting to a traditional and minor form of asceticism in the abstaining from meat on the day of the Crucifixion, but fish-eating took on a distorted importance in Reformation

controversy, see e.g. Erasmus' colloquy *On the Eating of Fish* (Dolan, 1964,271ff.).

15. The Catholic tradition was of a sanctified place not of a sanctifying person (other than Christ), see Cabrol (1925,203ff.).

16. The Crown attempted to protect its subjects from the 'godly' as in James I's declaration of 24 May 1618: 'Whereas we did justly, in our progresse through Lancashire, rebuke some puritans and precise people, in prohibiting and unlawfully punishing of our good people for using their lawfull recreations and honest exercises on Sundayes and other holy days, after the afternoone sermon or service; it is our will that, after the end of divine service, our good people be not disturbed, letted or discouraged from any lawful recreation, such as dauncing, either for men or women; archery for men, leaping, vaulting, or any other such harmless recreation. . . . But withall, we doe here account still as prohibited all unlawfull games to be used upon Sundayes onely, as bear and bull-baitings, interludes, and at all times in the meaner sort of people by law prohibitted, bowling.'

Charles I continued the tradition, but after his execution the rigorists had full control and Harris (1975,36) comments, 'Probably at no time in human history has the effect of religion on sport been so decisive or so deadly.'

17. It was about this time that the word 'gossip' changed its meaning from 'a woman friend' to 'a tattler'. The churchyard was the traditional recreation area in the Middle Ages (though not with the Church's approval of some of the activities that took place there).

18. 'Idleness' covers not merely non-activity but non-productive (in the sense of material end-product) activity. The Reformation objected to contemplation, celebration and play. It is from this epoch that the proverb 'The Devil finds work for idle hands' seems to date together with the somewhat Freudian 'Cleanliness is next to godliness'.

19. This movement is associated with the Restoration in England, but it was paralleled on the Continent where there had not been an equivalent Puritanical dictatorship.

20. 'Pornography as we know it today in our culture emerged during the Renaissance' (Peckham 1969,288). 'Erotic art' means 'erotic for men': 'There really is no erotic art in the nineteenth century which does *not* involve the image of women and precious little before or after.' Erotic art is created about women for men by men on the principle that the customer is always right and that he who pays the piper calls the tune. See Hess and Nochlin (1973, 9, 17).

21. Morse Peckham (1969,235) has a lengthy attempt at definition, but his approach is not convincing when it leads to conclusions like 'Erotic love is the model and classic case of a nonsexual interest which can, under certain cultural conditions, be introduced into the sexual role.'

22. Chp.1 of *The Nude*. See also n. 31 to Chp.9 above. Because of the many meanings of 'erotic', some critics have preferred to distinguish bet-

ween 'good' and 'bad' erotic art. See e.g. Johnson, (1949,173ff.) who makes the criterion 'the nature of the impulse and the manner of its expression'. V. Kahmen (1972,7) defines eroticism as 'the aesthetic elements which can restrict or modify our total experience of sexual or sensual desire' and glosses it as referring to the sensual impulses which are at work in the mind.

23. Unfortunately we do not seem to have established the concept of 'agapaic art' which seems a necessary distinction in view of the close relationship between physical and spiritual love. This dialectical interrelationship is most clearly expressed in Mannerist art which attempts to maintain the natural and supernatural in vital tension. These new formal ideas involving intellect, self-consciousness and spiritualist and sensualist trends 'do not in any way imply a renunciation of the charms of physical beauty, but they portray the body struggling to give expression to the mind and they show it, as it were, turning and twisting, bending and writhing under the pressure of the mind and hurled aloft by an excitement reminiscent of the ecstacies of Gothic art' (Hauser, 1962,II,96). Clark (1956,286) makes a similar point: 'The line between sacred ecstasy and profane, fine-drawn at all periods of true religious fervour, was at its finest in the anxious years of the early sixteenth century.'

24. 'About a third of the way through the sixteenth century pornography as we know it emerged in the form of the *Ragionamenti* and the *Sonnette Lussoriosi* of Aretino and of Giulio Romano's *Pozizioni* – engravings of sexual positions with stimulated genitals fully displayed in coital activity and behaviour preparatory to it. But even before that, something of the greatest significance had happened to costume; and modern pornography first appeared in the new styles for women, which by tightening the waist, emphasised the sexual cues of large and nearly naked breasts and of buttocks; the hooped skirt made its first appearance.' (Peckham,1969,289.)

25. '[Marcus] agrees with David Foxon that pornography as we know it today began to appear in seventeenth century England' (Peckham,1969,28).

26. For the effect of commercialism and mechanical reproduction see Berger (1972), especially pp. 32f. 'The rise of commercialised pornography as we know it today began in the seventeenth century and emerged in recognisable form in the eighteenth. In the nineteenth and twentieth centuries it developed with great rapidity and would appear now to be at flood stage in Europe and America, were it not for the fact that it continues to rise.' (Peckham,1969,256,cf. Freeman,1967,3 and n.)

27. Romano's *Pozizioni* are reproduced in Melville (1973), illustrations 26–45. For the relationship between theological and artistic conflicts cf. Clark (1956,286f.): 'Lorenzo Lotti, more concerned with Lutheran ideas, could not admit Corregio's easy catholic acceptance of the flesh. . . . Just as the mediaeval sculptors had understood the transports of the sea-Thiasos in a spiritual sense, and used the Nereids as souls on their way to heaven, so Lotto (in the *Triumph of Chastity*) has turned them the other way, the Puritan way as it was shortly to become, in which all that is expressed through the body is fundamentally evil.'

28. See Bloch (1965, ch.xix). Berger (1972,32ff.) has drawn attention to the relationship between capitalism and the corruption of art (see n. 26 above). Davis (1976,41) makes the analogous point that the centrality of money is a clear development of the abuse of the body resulting from the demands of the mind and represents a descent from true materialism through the introduction of symbolic counters which are an intellectual invention: 'And the mind invented money. Money is material wealth made abstract, made immaterial. The pursuit of money is a mental, not a material pursuit. A man in touch with the sensuous rhythms of his body would undoubtedly be a disabled contender in the race to accumulate money.'

29. See n.26 above.

30. See e.g. Bloch (1965,ch.xvii), Marcus (1966), Pearsall (1971) and Freeman (1967).

31. Cf. Taylor (1965, ch.ix), though he prefers to see events in terms of alternating 'patrist' and 'matrist' attitudes.

32. There is plenty of evidence of an unconcealed and violent hatred of Christian beliefs, institutions and symbols. The latter were not only removed or destroyed with malevolent precision (cf.Lady Chapel at Ely) but, where possible, deliberately profaned as in making sanctified altar-stones into paving flags. Iconoclasm, which included smashing windows, breaking down statues and woodwork with axes and hammers and ripping out the illuminations from manuscripts, was an obvious and universal feature of the Protestant revolt. But there were even more violent manifestations of antipathy to venerable traditions: 'While von Urslingen declared himself the enemy of God, Malvezzi consciously befriended heretics and prided himself upon violating nuns. Braccio so detested the Church that he had monks thrown down from their own church tower.' (Taylor,1965,144.)

33. With his usual awareness, Shakespeare exemplifies this contemporary attitude in a number of his characters, e.g. Edgar in *Lear*, Iago in *Othello*.

34. Cf. Bloch (1965, chs.xiii–xv).

35. In the violent Middle Ages there was usually the formal excuse or justification from social or religious order, but the Renaissance seems to have introduced a violence (that was almost an accepted character-trait as 'Black Wrath') that was incidental to a personal development which was adequate justification if justification was thought necessary. (Consider the motive of revenge which almost provides a literary genre.) This violence was apparently not held to indicate a breakdown of social order or exemplify some kind of inhuman behaviour, for it was performed within a framework of set rules and acted out at every level of society. Burckhardt (1944,278) writes of Sigismondo Malatesta: 'It is not only the court of Rome but the verdict of history which convicts him of murder, rape, adultery, incest, sacrilege, perjury and treason, committed not once but often.' The situation within the institutional Church seems no better as we range from the Borgia

Pope Alexander VI and his nephew Cesare who were alleged to arrange for the nightly murder of four or five dignitaries, 'bishops, prelates and others', to the simple priest Niccolo de' Pelegati who was executed for his misdeeds in 1495: 'He had twice celebrated his first Mass: the first time he had committed murder the same day, but afterwards received absolution at Rome; he then killed four people and married two wives with whom he travelled about. He afterwards took part in many assassinations, violated women, carried others away by force, plundered far and wide, and infested the territory of Ferrara with a band of followers in uniform, extorting food and shelter by every kind of violence'. (Burckhardt 1944,275.)

At the close of the Middle Ages there was a single example of this type of privileged monster in the person of Gilles de Rais who was executed in 1440, apparently sincerely repentant of his abominable crimes (Cleugh, 1967,194–205). There are certain features of the trial of de Rais which raise questions about the whole proceedings: the irregularities in procedure, the fact that his alleged accomplices went unpunished, and the financial interest in his ruin of the Head of State. Later ages were to produce Sacher-Masoch and De Sade, but a modern writer (Freeman,1967) warns us that 'in fact Sacher-Masoch is poor stuff, in terms of violence, compared to (contemporary) male magazines. De Sade, too, hides his acts of pain in pages of common-place narrative. Far more accessible to the semi-literate is the pornographic brutality in *Man's True Danger*.'

36. Bloch (1965,233). In C. de Laclos' *Les Liaisons dangereuses* (1782), the body of the human quarry has become the 'enemy', the emotional factor in a male–female relationship has been entirely eliminated and 'love' has been reduced to the intellectual satisfaction of the planning and execution of a successful chase and the sensual pleasure that accompanies the preliminary skirmishes and final victory.

37. See Bloch (1965,157–71), Taylor (1965,186), Pearsall (1971,360ff.).

38. As was the first pornography. Perversion, in all its fullness, was originally a perquisite of the idle rich such as the Marquis de Sade and the Chevalier Leopold von Sacher-Masoch, each of whom enriched the vocabulary of psychopathology. With the spread of egalitarianism and schooling, such pleasures could be brought within the more democratic milieu of Brady and the clients of the 'fladge-world'. Similarly, in England, initiation to flagellation was chiefly through the discipline of public schools (Pearsall 1971,404ff.) and then, by a process of imitation, throughout the education system. It is a sad irony that with the practical disappearance of corporal punishment it is still sought in fantasy in children's comics (and other reading) see Freeman (1967,71ff.,184f. and illus. 15).

39. Hauser (1962,III,31).

40. Is there a significant difference in objectively watching an animal suffering through 'An experiment with an air-pump' and Madame de Noirceuill's experiment with another element in de Sade's *Juliette* (cited Freeman 1967,86)?

41. Extract from *The Lustful Turk* (1828) quoted in Marcus (1966,217). The same mechanism penetrated into theology and Christian apologetics (as in Paley's *Watchmaker*) requiring the genius of Newman to restore personalism.

42. 'Descartes finally reversed the order of human cognition and made Metaphysics an introduction to Mechanics, Medicine and Ethics' (Maritain, 1941,82).

43. Maritain (1941,89).

44. Mechanism has been responsible for mass-production, mass destruction and the subordination of man to machine not only in his life, work and play but also in his concepts, images and values.
For sexual-organ = man = machine, see Marcus (1966,215f.).

45. See e.g. Open University Correspondence Texts; *Renaissance and Reformation*, Units 20,21.

46. As, for example, by Possevinus, the influential Counter-Reformation theorist in his *De Poesi et Pictura* on which see Janelle (1972,161ff.).

47. In its twenty-fifth session on 3 and 4 December, 1563. The important decree may be found in Janelle (1972,160) abbreviated, and in Holt (1958,II,63–5). Hauser (1962,II,113f.) comments: 'The Counter-reformation, which allowed art to play the greatest conceivable part in divine worship, desired not merely to remain true to the Christian tradition of the Middle Ages and the Renaissance, in order thereby to emphasise its antagonism to the Reformation – to be friendly to art whereas the heretics were hostile, but it desired, above all, to use art as a weapon against the doctrines of heterodoxy.'

48. One might compare this assessment of 'Catholic Puritanism' with the Protestant one of which Peckham (1969,74) says: 'In the evangelical tradition, art is not merely devalued; it is trivial.'

49. Reason was regarded as the organ of morality by almost all moralists up to the eighteenth century. The moral conflict was seen as lying between passion and reason, not between passion and conscience nor between duty and kindness. It was assumed that all moral maxims were grasped by the intellect as self-evident first principles. (In mediaeval language, morality was concerned with 'intellectus' rather than with 'ratio' see p. 131).
From the eighteenth-century morality is connected with 'reflection' or 'conscience', then related to a 'moral sentiment', 'good taste' or 'good feeling'. By Wordsworth's time the 'heart' can be favourably contrasted with the 'head' and the heart of morality reduced to 'domestic affection'. The original concept of a 'rational soul' has shrunk to a kind of 'logical ability'.
Before the eighteenth-century (and as far back as classical antiquity) there had been the idea that to recognise a duty was to perceive a truth because man was conceived as an intellectual being, not the possessor of a 'good heart' (though St Paul's 'heart' is nearly equivalent to 'mind'). In terms of images, reason descends from being a goddess to being a sort of computer.

Deficient notions of 'soul' are related to deficient notions of 'body' and there is evidence that both were affected by a reductionism after the Renaissance.

50. M. Ficino, the celebrated humanist teacher, once advised a colleague: 'Don't talk about virtue (to your male pupils), present her as an attractive girl and they will fall for it.'

51. See, for example, Reeves (1958,112,282ff.) and cf. comment in Walker (1954,279): 'Not only had man been cloven in twain by Descartes but, worse still, the two halves had been handed over for study to different kinds of experts.' The whole of Walker's ch. xviii is relevant.

52. Neuroses were regarded in the same terms as the breakdown of a piece of machinery (cf. Walker, 1954, 277).

53. Maritain deals with Descartes' 'angelism' – the idea that the 'real' man is spirit – on pp.53–89, but he claims that it is to Rousseau 'that we owe that corpse of Christian ideas whose immense putrefaction poisons the universe today' (1941,147). Rousseau's disastrous influence on education is beginning to be recognised, but most would not connect him with the 'drug culture' and the world of 'happenings' which would be included in a Pelagian mysticism of sensation.

54. See Wilkins (1969,ch.iv).

55. Simone de Beauvoir; *La Deuxième Sexe* (1961,i.183 Eng. tr.).

56. Hess and Nochlin (1973).

57. 'The essence of art is sensuality . . . . eroticism is sensuality in action.' (Eduard Fuchs, cited Kahmen, 1972,10).

58. Here and elsewhere where it is used by itself the word 'man' refers to the human species and not to the male sex (*pace* O'Faolain and Martinez,1974,etc.).

59. L. Nochlin in Hess and Nochlin (1973,15).

60. See Kahmen (1972) *passim*, but especially pp.13–24.

61. M. Allentuck in Hess and Nochlin (1973,33). The version exhibited at the Royal Academy in 1782 has the mediaeval trappings of the incubus (*Malleus Maleficiarum*, Pt.II, Q.1, ch.4,tr.Summers,1968,72–81) and both the nightmare itself with protruding eyes ('the lust of the eyes') and the incubus snugly ensconced on the woman's belly, sneer posessively at the spectator.

62. J. L. Connolly in Hess and Nochlin (1973,17–31).

63. Declaration in TV interview, broadcast on BBC 2 on 28.11./1975.

64. Cf. Melville (1973,263) 'Picasso, whose art makes Freud's view that civilisation has no permanent defence against a vigorous barbarism something to be thankful for.'

Chapter 11

1. Leeuw (1963,169). It is worthwhile pointing out that the bodies given to the gods were 'idealised' human forms and Voltaire remarked that if God made man in His own image, man was not slow in returning the compliment.

2. Hauser (1962,I,64f.) points out that classical Greek art was determined by 'the ethics of nobility and the aristocratic ideal of bodily and spiritual beauty . . . the same manly ideal based on the concept of life as a contest (*agon*), the same typical produce of aristocratic breeding and all-round athletic training'. Before State subsidies and 'shamateurism' only the nobility could partake in the Olympic Games because they alone had the financial resources and leisure to meet the requirements of the competition and the preliminary training.

The honorific statues of Olympic victors did not aim to be individual likenesses but were 'idealised portraits whose sole purpose, it seems, was to preserve the memory of a particular victory and to make propaganda for the games' (Hauser,1962,I,64).

Mass-production of 'ideal' bodies to which more or less 'personalised' heads could be added explains the existence of the multitude of headless classical statuary to some extent.

3. Alexander the Great (336–323 B.C.) pupil of Aristotle and conqueror of empires. He dreamed of a world state unified on the basis of Greek language and culture and, though his empire fell apart at his early death, the idea of the trans-national culture of Hellenism was largely realised. He more than exemplified the achievements of the mythical heroes of Greek antiquity and 'the cult of personality which developed out of the new hero-worship redounded to the advantage of the artist both as a bestower and recipient of fame' (Hauser,1962,I,105).

4. Plotinus (A.D.205–70) a completely Hellenised Egyptian who was converted to philosophy by a lapsed Christian and also had Origen as one of his pupils. Plotinus is the founder of Neo-Platonism, an attempt to reconcile the teachings of Plato and Aristotle. He saw the Beautiful as an essential attribute of the Divine Nature and the artist as, in some sort, a creator himself (cf. *Enneads*,Book V, chs.8,9).

5. See Hauser (1962,I,112f.).

6. Faith affected liturgical worship and even bodily postures therein, cf. above.

7. See Matt., vi, 16.

8. The matter is considered in some of the earliest canons of the Christian Church and remains in modern canon law. It is notable that the Jesuits regard bodily beauty as an attribute in a postulant.

The Council of Braga (561) condemned the followers of Priscillian (d. 385) and other Manichees and anathematised those who condemned marriage and procreation (Canon 11), those who said that the body was a demonic fabrication, that conception was due to the activity of evil spirits or who denied the resurrection of the body (Canon 12) and those who denied that the creation of all flesh is the work of God (Canon 13). 'In these Canons it should be noted that the Church intervened from the beginning against the decrying of matter, and especially against denigration of the human body.' (Rahner,1967,106f.)

Similarly, the Church formally asserted the goodness of all matter, of corporeal as well as of spiritual creation, against Waldensian and Albigensian heresies in 1208 and 1215 (Fourth Lateran Council) as well as against such suspected tendencies within the Eastern Orthodox Church (General Council of Florence,1442). (Translation of these canons in Rahner,1967,108f.,110). The principles were reasserted at the First Vatican Council (1870) in Canons 1, 5.

The idea of metempsychosis (transmigration of the soul) is logically a denigration of the body and consequently is frequently condemned, e.g. Constantinople (543), Braga (561), Canons 6, 9.

Insistence on the unity and integrity of man as a psychosomatic entity led to the condemnation of the 'spiritualist' Franciscan Olieu at the General Council of Vienne (1311–12) which declared that the intellectual soul was the 'form' of the body, a principle re-emphasised at the Fifth Lateran General Council (1513).

The consistency and continuity of the Church's teaching in this area is exemplified in the Provincial Council of Carthage's anathematisation in 418 of 'whoever shall say that Adam the first man was made mortal so that he would die in the body whether he sinned or did not sin; that is, that he would quit the body not as punishment for sin but by necessity of nature'. Rahner (1967,127) adds the following note: 'In the language of the first centuries of Christianity the word "nature" did not mean the purely natural powers of man independently of his supernatural or preternatural gifts, but his original state before the first sin, which included natural capabilities, supernatural elevation and preternatural gifts.' The Provincial Council of Cologne (1860) uses 'nature' in its later and narrower sense when it says: 'Also supernatural and gratuitous was the complete subordination of concupiscence to understanding; that is, the great gift of integrity whereby God so ordered the emotions and desires of man's soul that they always obeyed the commands of reason. Since, namely, that man consists of a rational soul and a body, it can in itself happen that he allows himself to seek the good of the body more than that of the soul and that concupiscence would be rebellious were it not kept in check.'

9. Notably in *De Incarnatione Verbi Dei* (c. A.D. 336?).

10. It is however possible in, for example, the scholarly and irascible Jerome, the tender Francis who described his body as 'Brother Ass' and even in the Desert Fathers (Waddell,1936) remarkable for their wisdom and animal friends (Waddell,1934).

11. *Poems*,XXIII,307–427. In Sidonius' writings we may see the beginning of the Christianisation of 'knightly virtues' as exemplified in his admiring description of Theodoric's physique (*Letters*,I,ii,pp.335f. in Loeb,II,1963),

Germanicus' appearance (*Letters*,IV,xiii,p.115 in Loeb,II) and that of Sigismer (*Letters*,IV,xx,p.137 in Loeb,II). He has an impressive description of a private swimming bath (*Letters*,II,ii,8) and is clearly fond of sports himself (*Letters*,II,ix,4;V,xvii,7,cf.VIII,xi,8). There is a well-developed Christian humanism in his frank description (*Letters*,II,ix) of his enjoyable holiday with its good food and wine, variety of games and sports and its libraries well stocked with both Christian and pagan authors: 'To sum up, our entertainment was moral, elegant and profuse.' (Loeb,II,457.) He admires lavish architecture as a fitting honour to Christian saints (*Letters*,IV,xviii,5) and uses as a natural simile of a small imperfection adding to beauty that of 'a black mole on a fair body' (ibid.). Most interesting is his description (*Letters*,V,xvii,3–8) of a 'breather' between the vigil and the 'morrow-mass' of a church festival. The entire congregation relaxes outside the church in conversation and story-telling until 'those who felt sluggish for want of exertion, resolved to do something energetic' (Loeb,II,231). The choice was apparently between very active dice-playing or a vigorous ball-game involving a good deal of body-contact 'until limbs deadened by inactive sedentary work could be reinvigorated by the healthful exercise' (ibid.). The description of the ball-game is inflated but very interesting (see Loeb,II,231–5 and note). Yet man's body is as nothing compared with his mind. Animal bodies often excel that of man – it is his soul that gives him pre-eminence (*Letters*,VII,xiv,4–6). Man is essentially a twofold entity who approaches God through both mind and body, declares Sidonius in an orotund letter (VIII, xiv) to the saintly Bishop Principius who is told that 'as often as anyone, on your admonition, seeking to reduce his grossness, grills in the fire of frequent fasting his obese body with its load of fat heaving on his swollen belly, it is clear to all that you will then be in a manner consecrating an offering of fine flower baked in a pan of self-denial' (Loeb,II,489).

12. Zarnecki (1972,18).

13. It may well be that the Christian attitude to the body is best exemplified in its attitude to death which naturally and inevitably means the end of the 'body of this flesh', but this, like many other sources, has had to be ommitted for reasons of space. For mediaeval attitudes, see T. R. S. Boase, *Death in the Middle Ages* (London 1972).

14. The cathedral at Bamberg in Bavaria (rebuilt early thirteenth century) possesses sculptures which are among the greatest achievements of German art. The *Bamberger Ritter* is justly renowned as expressing the quintessence of the mediaeval knightly ideal – power in the service of order (One might compare the slightly later sculptures of Naumberg where those of the founders, Uta and Eckhart, perfectly express the associated notion of 'nobless oblige'.) Bamberg also contains the first life-size independent nude figures of mediaeval art in the representations of Adam and Eve. The sculptures, almost architectural in quality, make no concession whatever to sensuousness, but according to Clark (1956,303) they 'have a gaunt nobility and an architectural completeness which makes them nudes and not naked people'.

15. The chief subjects of mediaeval art have been identified as religion, work, order, humour, nature and, perhaps above all love which even in its human form is 'a sovereign principle of education, an ethical power and channel of the deepest experience of life' (Hauser,1962,I,191, cf. Dronke,1968; Peckham,1969,188–92; Wilkins,1969,126ff.)

The developing language of love in the Middle Ages drew from mystical, noetic and sapiential vocabularies. At its pinnacle Dante, poet, politician, theologian and lover, unites all three (cf. his *Convivio*,III,ii). Clark (1956,301) can make the remarkable statement that 'the whole of mediaeval art is a proof of how completely Christian dogma had eradicated the image of bodily beauty'. He is, however, somewhat nearer the truth when he says (1956,303) that 'in general, the unclothed figures of the early Middle Ages are more shamefully naked and are undergoing humiliations, martyrdoms or tortures. Above all, it was in this condition that man suffered his cardinal misfortune, the Expulsion from Paradise and this was the moment in Christian story of his first consciousness of the body, "they knew that they were naked". While the Greek nude began with the heroic body proudly displaying itself on the palaestra, the Christian nude began with the huddled body cowering in the consciousness of sin.' Though even here truth may be regarded as subordinate to rhetoric. On the other hand, Hauser (1962,I,212f.) draws attention to the increasing mediaeval interest and joy in nature, including the human form. 'In this field we meet everywhere a thoroughly new conception of art, and one radically opposed to the stereotyping abstraction of Romanesque. Interest is now completely centred upon the individual and the characteristic – even before the time of the statues of the kings at Rheims and the portraits of the founders at Naum-berg; the freshness, vitality and directness of these portraits is already to be found to some extent in the figures on the West portal at Chartres . . . the kind old man with the look of a peasant, high cheek bones, broad splayed nose and somewhat slanting eyes must have been personally known to the artist. The remarkable fact is that these figures . . . are so surprisingly full of character. Feeling for the individual is evidently one of the first symptoms of the new dynamic. . . . Nature is no longer characterised by absence of Spirit but rather by her spiritual transparency, her power of expressing the spiritual. . . .'

The face is traditionally that bodily part which expresses character, i.e. the manifestation of the inward element in man. Greek bodies had replaceable heads, while in Gothic statuary the head is the summation of the psychosomatic entity which is man.

16. Peckham (1969,192) says: 'The gradual imposition of Christian sexual morality upon the populace of Europe led irresistibly to the in-troduction of love, the yearning for and attainment of suspension of cognitive tension, into the sexual role.' Dronke (1968,I,ch.ii) shows how in the Middle Ages the concept of love was linked with the concept of knowledge. This junction is expressed in an attenuated form in the idealisation of the beloved as an 'angel' (i.e. a pure intellect), it also exists in the double use of the Hebrew verb 'to know' which means 'to have sexual union' and 'to comprehend'. It is developed in the liturgical identification of

Holy Wisdom and the Madonna and the Sapiential Books of the Old Testament where the love of Wisdom is expressed in erotic terms (hence the 'double meaning' of the Song of Songs.) This unification of the highest activities of body and soul is perhaps the highest possible tribute to the significance of the body in Christian thought. The mediaeval synthesis provided a fertile ground for mysticism and for the development of the love-lyric as well as for a yet undeveloped theology of sex (but cf. Lilar,1965, and Brown,1966).

17. This is the notion of 'the great chain of being'. For the ideas of Albert the Great, Thomas Aquinas and Nicholas of Cusa on the subject see Lovejoy (1936, 70ff.) For St Thomas Aquinas, the heart of this 'connection of things' lay in the relationship of mind to body in man: whose constitution was 'aequaliter complexionatum, having in equal degree the character of both classes of being [corporeal and spiritual], . . . and is therefore said to be the horizon and boundary line of things corporeal and incorporeal' (Summa c.Gentes,II,68). This principle, so long as it survived, modiked the sharp dualism of body and spirit.

18. For the expression of this in art da Silva (1968,32–5 and 41–6). For the rediscovery and modern expression of the mediaeval idea see Lilar (1965), especially pp. 153ff. and n. 93. The theological source of this idea is, of course Eph., v,22–32, but not enough emphasis has been given to the liturgical support of the marriage rite and its teaching (along with the mediaeval elevation of marriage to a sacrament). There were no Jewish antecedents to the marriage ceremony which, from the outset, was a Christian 'invention'. Though it had no Jewish elements it retained 'pagan' elements (Duchesne,1931,428f.) It apparently spoke so deeply that at the Reformation, the Church of England retained the mediaeval rite almost unchanged. The concluding words of the bridegroom at the actual moment of marriage are remarkable – 'With my body I thee worship', and they were always uttered in the vernacular even in the Latin liturgy.

Much could be derived about Christian attitudes to the body in particular and creation in general from a close study of liturgical texts and an attempt to estimate their influence. We will content ourselves with two quotations referring to situations eleven centuries apart: 'To oppose the repudiation of matter, which was a doctrine of the growing Hellenistic Gnosis, it was necessary to stress the value of the earthly creation, even in divine worship. The peril then [near the end of the second century] no longer lay in the materialism of heathen sacrificial practices, but in the spiritualism of a doctrine that hovered just on the borderline of Christianity.' (Jungmann,1951,II,1f.)

'Those wholly unfamiliar with the monastic life are perhaps slow to allow for the moulding influence, upon minds and characters attuned to them, of the liturgical texts with their accompaniment of chant and ceremony, which brought to the thirteenth century, as they bring to those fortunate enough to know them at the present day, something of the purity, the austerity, the exquisite employment of type, of symbol and of allusion, and the mingling of all that is best in the Hebrew and Roman genius, which was the supreme achievement of the age before the barbarians conquered Rome. Beauty of word and melody, beauty of architecture and ornament cannot create, and may even hinder, the purest spirituality, but pure spirituality is a rare treasure, and for men of more ordinary mould the liturgy in all its fullness may be a tonic nourishment, as well as an ennobling discipline.' (Knowles,1961,I,318.)

19. The relationship of science to Christendom has not been adequately appreciated. 'Science begins with the concepts of order and regularity and the belief that the universe is not arbitrary, but governed. . . . r Western civilisation has its roots not only in the Hebraic vision of a unified world but also in the . . . Greek emphasis on rationality. It is now generally recognised that these two influences were fused in the Western world in the Middle Ages by the theologians who went under the name of scholastics. Of these, the best known is St Thomas Aquinas (1225–1274).' (Schneer,1960,13,19f.)

20. Berger (1972) makes the point that the 'framed picture' destroyed the relation between the image and its location (between the icon and its sacral setting) and Gombrich (1972) draws attention to an associated fact that there was an 'opening up to secular art of emotional spheres which hitherto had been the preserve of religious worship'.

21. For evidence of this revaluation, compare the earliest documents in Holt (1957) with later ones.

22. On this, see Berger (1972,45–64). Naked is associated with truth, not only in words as in 'the naked truth' but also in images as in Botticelli's *Calumny of Appelles* or in Titian's miscalled allegory *Sacred and Profane Love* on which see Panofsky (1962,150–60). Most frequently, in the early Renaissance the nude is a symbol of ideal beauty, i.e. intelligible beauty. These figures are not portraits or representations of real women but the assemblage of general concepts of beauty 'for the individual parts of the body as well as for its proportions: concepts that were meant to rise above nature, being taken from a spiritual realm that existed only in the mind. In this way Raphael formed his *Galatea*. As he says in his letter to Count Castiglione, "Since beauty is rare among women, I follow a certain idea formed in my imagination".' (Winckelmann, cited in Holt, 1958,II,341.) Clark puts the point another way when he says (1956,28) that Raphael's *Galatea* 'leaves the realm of narrative and entertainment . . . and enters that of philosophy.'

23. Cf. above, p. 124. Doubtless, Chaucer's 'Wyf of Bath' represented a well-known contemporary type and we know of Margery Kempe and the female Pastons.

24. As, for example, in Botticelli's *Venus and Mars* which could be taken as an extremely sophisticated version of the contemporary, 'Make love, not war.' In this connection it is worth asking whether the male or the female is dominant in the famous Arnolfini wedding portrait (J. van Eyck) and what is the significance of the clothed bodies and other corporeal objects in the picture. Mediaeval artists were as predominately male as those of the

Renaissance, but their mocking or denigration included both sexes, as in their frequent depictions of 'foolish lovers' or were predominately male – popes, friars, bishops, knights. Apollo is, of course, the truer counterpart of Venus and ch.ii of Clark (1956) is so entitled. It should be pointed out that the Renaissance Venus is merely a continuation of the mediaeval Venus who was a guide to the complex notion of temporal perfection denoted in *cortesia* which influences mediaeval Christian mysticism as much as the proper conduct in and of the courts of love. For Botticelli's *Mythologies*, see Gombrich (1972,31–81). For the mediaeval Venus, see Robertson (1970,288ff.)

25. Even after it had become an 'art object', the human body carried with it slowly vanishing metaphysical and theological ideas.

Melville (1973,260) classifies Titian's *Magdalen* as an erotic painting, but when Cardinal· (subsequently Saint) Charles Borromeo presented a workshop facsimile of it to the Ambrosiana in 1618 he declared that Titian knew how to maintain the honesty of the nude. 'Greco sits behind curtained windows in broad daylight to see things which an artist of the Renaissance would probably not have been able to see at all, but which an artist of the Middle Ages would have been able to see, if at all, even in daylight.' (Hauser, 1962,II,116.)

26. The divorce between body and soul is related both to the recrudescence of Neo-Platonism and to the exigencies of the new statecraft which reified the body politic. Passions such as anger and revenge receive social approval during the Renaissance and 'virtu' acquires a new connotation. 'Self-expression' is invented and Hauser remarks (loc. cit.) 'from now on the number of cranks, eccentrics and psychopaths among artists increases from day to day'.

27. *Praise of Folly*. To the scholarly Erasmus 'lust' means 'inordinate desire' of any kind.

28. 'In the evangelical tradition, art is not merely devalued; it is trivial.' (Peckham, 1969,74.) Cf. above, Ch.10, n.4.

29. For brutishness, see Taylor (1965, ch.vii). To the list of alternative 'ideologies' we ought to add 'nationalism': 'The religion of nationalism was beginning to grow out of the despairing loneliness of the individual.' (Heer, 1966,213.)

30. The works of P. P. Rubens (1577–1640), as an approved and extensively used ecclesiastical painter, may be taken as a culminating statement of the Church's attitude to the body. The struggle between soul and body which inspired the greatest achievements of Mannerism is reconciled and the artificiality of the Baroque swept aside in Rubens' glorious confidence in the body. 'Rubens is the noblest refutation of Puritanism and . . . I have tried to show how his religious and his pagan painting are the fruit of a single well-grown tree . . . a true son of the Catholic reformation.' (Clark, 1956,287,cf.254–7.) His art, like that of the Middle Ages and early Renaissance, is public, democratic, symbolic and

metaphysical. Such a painting as the 1610 self-portrait with his wife in the honeysuckle arbour represents the union of eros and amicitia in a sanctified physical coupling. It also expresses a unification of symbolism and realism, of naturalistic and emblematic art. (For reproduction and comment, see da Silva, 1968,41–4.)

31. The aristocratic individualism fostered in the Renaissance had combined with new notions of nationalism and 'empire' to produce the 'enlightened despot' – the ruler who personified the reified state and whose values were derived from the 'philosophes'. The body politic had replaced the Body of Christ as the supreme social organisation. 'Enthusiasm' was anti-social, religion virtually ceased to be a factor in international affairs which were conducted on Machiavellian principles supported by the arbitration of mass armies. Military strength replaced religious loyalty and the suppression of the Jesuits by secular rulers is highly significant (beginning in Portugal,1759). 'Parallel to this decay of ecclesiastical influence was a corresponding corruption of political morality.' (Cragg, 1960,217.) In this respect as in most others, the eighteenth century heralded in the 'modern world'. Ideas of magnitude and movement replaced those of essence and form and there was a return to a new Gnosticism, a secret key to truth confined to aristocratic adepts, set against the democratic wisdom of the Church, preserving a 'Secret Doctrine' or 'Great Tradition'. The 'philosophes' spawned both freemasonry and the scientism which reduces all knowledge and wisdom to physics.

32. The magnificent achievement of Pascal (1623–62) was marred by an Augustinianist pessimism which doubtless was an element in his quarrel with the Jesuits. The citations are from H. F. Stewart's (1950, trans. 25, 29, 21, 29) to which we might add: 'This internal war of reason against the passions has divided lovers of peace into two camps. Some have wished to renounce the passions and become gods; others have wished to renounce reason and become brute beasts. But neither lot has been able to do so. Reason is ever present to condemn the baseness and injustice of the passions, and to trouble the repose of whose who yield to them; and the passions are always alive in those who would renounce them.'

33. On Descartes (1596–1650) see Maritain (1941, 53–89), and a significant extract from *Meditations of First Philosophy* in Gerber (1972, 133ff.).

34. La Mettrie was the author of the significantly titled *L'Homme Machine* (Eng. tr. Chigago 1912) which was written in Holland in 1748 and publicly burnt there. 'Its author being a doctor, of whom Voltaire said that he was a madman who only wrote when he was drunk.' (J. A. Farrer *Books Condemned to be Burnt*, London 1904, p. 14.) The Abbé(!) de Condillac lived from 1715 to 1780.

On this process Walker (1954, 277, 279) comments 'the symptoms exhibited by a neurotic patient resemble far more closely possession by an alien and hostile mind than they do a breakage in a piece of machinery, the terms in which doctors of a later age attempted to explain all illnesses . . . not only had man been cloven in twain by Descartes, but, worse still, the two halves had been handed over for study to different kinds of experts.'

35. 'What distinguishes oil painting from any other form of painting is its special ability to render the tangibility, the texture, the lustre, the solidity of what it depicts. *It defines the real as that which you can put your hands on.* Its potential of illusion is far greater than that of sculpture, for it can suggest objects possessing colour, texture and temperature, filling a space and, by implication, *filling the entire world.*' (Berger, 1972, 88f – my italics.) This is part of Talleyrand's 'sweetness of life', known only to those who lived before 1789.

36. Either in the increased commercialisation and devaluation (to male trophy-hunting) of sex, in the inhuman slave trade of the eighteenth century or the kindred reduction of human beings to hands for the nineteenth century industrial expansion (D. H. Lawrence rightly saw industrialisation as a spreading source of exploitation, even into human relations which were measured in terms of quantity rather than quality, e.g. his essay 'Return to Bestwood'), but the evil had been seen much earlier and more vividly by the poet Blake who prayed for God to keep us from 'single vision and Newton's sleep'.

Though it was not his total view and only sometimes his predominant one, Leonardo seems to have been the first to view the human body as a machine and, from this point of view, he concluded that it was inferior to that of the animals: 'I have found that in the composition of the human body, as compared with the bodies of animals, the organs of sense are much duller and coarser. Thus it is composed of less ingenious instruments and of less capacious surfaces for sense-impressions.' (Anatomic MS. B in Windsor Castle Library, 13 – published Turin 1901. This extract cited from Vallentin, 1939, 443f.)

37. See Clark. (1966).

38. For Rousseau (*Emile*, 1762, *Confessions*, 1765) see Maritain (1941, 93 – 164).

39. Wordsworth retired to the 'desert' of the Lake District and opposed the railways that would bring the masses there. Blake was aware of the 'dark, satanic mills', but even more aware of his world of angelic visions. Constable lost himself in the picturing of a landscape in which there were no signs of the contemporary Industrial Revolution and idealised a world which was already lost.

40. An earlier age had seen woman as the intermediary between man and the world and even between man and God. She incarnated the marvellous flowering of life and simultaneously concealed its obscure mysteries. (For a somewhat unbalanced collection of historical documents depreciating woman, see O'Faolain and Martinez, 1974.)

41. If woman is destined (by man) to be possessed (by man), her body must present the inert and passive qualities of an object. See Beauvoir,

(1961) cited p. 154 above. The ultimate degradation of the female body is its reduction to a mere slit or orifice as in the novels of Henry Miller and lesser pornographers.

42. Especially cars which have become the transferred sex symbol. If one has the 'right' car, cigarette or deodorant the women will come.

43. Contempt for the human body seems proportionately related to the reification of metaphorical bodies and corporations. In this connection one might also consider the developments of such concepts as social, biological and genetic 'engineering'.

44. Another interesting linguistic development is the use of the word 'cannibalisation' to describe the use of parts of one machine to repair another.

45. Not to mention the 'sexologists' with their laboratories, experiments and statistical tables.

46. Novelty is a necessary element in sensationalism and its pursuit may be seen as a recurring indication of decadence.

47. Melville (1973, 263) revealingly speaks of 'Picasso, whose art makes Freud's view that civilisation has no permanent defence against a vigorous barbarism something to be thankful for.' There is an abiding connection between art and geometry. A building unit based on square lines (which are not found in nature) seems to mark a significant development from the mediaeval and Renaissance concern with curves.

48. Some of the stages are reproduced in Clark (1956, ill. 291, opp. p.353).

49. Kahmen (1972, 72).

50. But notice that he uses some words, e.g. 'image' in a very ambiguous or ambivalent sense.

51. Lucie-Smith (1972, 53f.). He is talking specifically about Picasso, but his words are capable of a more general application.

52. Cited in Lucie-Smith (1972, 90).

53. To some extent, modern artists are reacting against the detachment and irrelevance of 'academic' art. An attitude which, significantly, seems to have originated in the eighteenth century, e.g. the influential J. J. Winckelmann in his *'Thoughts on the 'Imitation' of Greek Art'* (1755) was mainly concerned with 'good taste' and not with the communication of meaning. J. L. David, the epitome of 'classicism', justifies the nudity of his heroes on the grounds that such nudity was 'the practice in ancient art'. He accompanied his culminating work *The Sabines* with an explanatory brochure (1799) – a procedure which is adequate commentary on communicative dissonance – which contains a lengthy note on nudity, explaining that poses are harder to execute than clothed figures and summarising his ambition as 'to represent the customs of antiquity with such

exactitude that the Greeks and Romans . . . would not have found me a stranger to their customs.' (Extracts in Holt, 1958, III, 3, 12.) By the nineteenth century the production of enormous canvases containing a multitude of nude figures inspired by antique statuary had become boring so that a contemporary critic could remark: 'The Greeks liked the nude; we, we never see it, and I will go further and say it disgusts us.' (Holt, 1957, III, 40.)

54. For philosphical insights, see Peursen (1966, ch. x) on 'Bodiliness'. There are also interesting extracts and a bibliography in Gerber (1972, 127 – 188).

55. For some very challenging psychological syntheses see Brown (1959 and 1966).

56. The traffic is not merely one-way: witness the work of Berger and Greeley in sociology or of Allport and Frankl in psychology (the essay by Wren-Lewis 1966) raises some interesting questions). Teilhard de Chardin should receive honourable mention in any discussion of modern attempts at a resynthesis. An important aspect of his contribution is mentioned in Lilar (1965, 228ff. and nn.).

57. R. N. Bellah, discussing Brown (1966) in *Beyond Belief* (N.Y. 1970, 232).

58. There is more in Lilar (1965) and Brown (1966) than in most 'theologians'. Christians have not yet met the psychologists' objection to God as a projected father-figure (though Jung offers possibilities for development). Theologians should consider Rawson's words (1973a, 14f.). 'Hinduism has assimilated both goddess worship, which is commonly, though not always, orgiastic and paternalism, which is puritan. This is something which, with rare exceptions among heretics, Christianity has never managed to do: its goddess worship and its family trinity (father, son, mother) being solidly rooted in a paternal and largely prohibitive God; so that its excursions into sexual mysticism all start with a piacular rejection of the physical – the goddess is a virgin, the love of Christ for the Bride can only be acted out in human relations against a continual background of abstinence and expiation, embodied in the two chief icons, the child at the breast of the virgin-mother, and the same child dying to placate the father: love is expressed as death. This is an icon which, for our culture, is out of date as well as unedifying.'
This may not do full justice to the Christian position, but it reflects some of the unbalance of some Christian presentations. For balance, see Brown (1966) and 'God is our Mother' in *Life of the Spirit* (Oxford, May 1945). See also Davis (1976).

59. For example, there is no entry under 'Body' in the *New Catholic Encyclopaedia* (1976) but on the other hand, we have: 'If the dance of the body belongs to the integral act of human worship, the intuition of the intellect is no less an essential part of the human being and must also be assumed by worship.' (Pannikar, 1973, 87, cf. 45.) Cf. Clarke (1940, 45.)
'It was God who made our body, equipped it with wonderful powers and

made it live by means of our soul. The Son of God took to Himself a human body. The Holy Ghost sanctified our body in baptism and made it His temple where He dwells. On the Last Day God will raise our bodies in glory from the dead. Therefore we should always treat our body and its life as sacred.

'We must take care of our body, and of its life and health . . . keep our body clean . . . feed and clothe it properly . . . exercise, develop and train it and give to it both reasonable health and recreation.

To neglect our health or to put it into danger without a serious reason is sin.' *(Catholic Catechism* – international edition, Freiburg 1957, pp. 361ff.)

It is also significant that Williamson (1955 108f.), in the course of a commentary on the Canon of the Roman Mass, remarks: 'Christian asceticism has nothing in common with the self-denying creeds which, regarding the flesh as something evil, attempt by mortifications to 'escape from the body'. On the contrary, the discipline imposed by the Christian is rather that of the athlete who cares for his body precisely because it is the instrument of his triumph. The nature of the Resurrection-body we cannot know, except that it will be in some way related to the earthly body; and the implications of this relationship have been well expressed by Coventry Patmore in a verse of his *The Victories of Love*, where he speaks of the body with its five senses under the image of a 'five-stringed lyre'.

> 'Beware: for fiends in triumph laugh
> O'er him who learns the truth by half!
> Beware; for God will not endure
> For men to make their hope more pure
> Than His good promise, or require
> Another than the five-stringed lyre
> Which He has vowed again to the hands
> Devout of him who understands
> To tune it justly here.'

60. I. Illich (1971), cf. E. Goffman, *Asylums* (N.Y. 1961, Eng edn. 1968).

Chapter 12

1. C. Davis, *Body as Spirit* (London 1976).

2. Op. cit. pp. 38f.

3. On which see F. Bottomley, *The Church Explorers' Guide* (London 1978).

4. Davis (1976, 40).

5. Ibid. pp. 41f.

6. Ibid. p. 43.

7. Ibid. p. 44

BIBLIOGRAPHY

Achilles, Tatius, *Adventures of Leucippe and Clitophon*, tr. S. Goulee in Loeb Classical Library (London 1967).

Ambrose, *Sancti Ambrosii Mediolanensis Episcopi Opera*, 2 vols. (Paris 1686).

— —, *Letters*, in *Library of the Fathers*, vol. 45 (Oxford 1881).

Appian, *Roman History*, tr. H. White, in Loeb Library, 4 vols. (London 1961).

Arendzen, J. P., *Men and Manners in the Days of Christ* (London 1928).

Augustine, *City of God*, tr. M. Dods, 2 vols. (Edinburgh 1934).

— —, *The Confessions*, tr. F. J. Sheed (London 1943).

— —, *Tractates on St John*, vi, tr. H. Browne (London 1897).

Athanasius, *The Life of St Anthony*, in Library of Nicene and Post-Nicene Fathers (Oxford *c.* 1898).

— —, *Contra Gentes* and *De Incarnation* . . ., tr. R. W. Thomson (Oxford 1971).

Bainton, H. *Here I stand* (London 1950).

Baker, H., *The Image of Man* (N.Y. 1961).

Bamm, P., *The Kingdoms of Christ* (London 1961).

Barr, R., *Main Currents in Early Christian Thought* (Glen Rock 1966).

Beauvoir, S. de, *La Deuxième Sexe* (Paris 1949). Eng. tr. 1953, PB, Vol I – *History of Sex* (London 1961).

'— —, *The Second Sex*, Vol II (London 1960).

Bellah, R. N., *Beyond Belief* (New York 1970).

Benthall, J. and Polhemus, T. (ed), *The Body as a Medium of Expression* (London 1975).

Berenson, B., *The Italian Painters of the Renaissance* (London 1953).

Berger, J., *Ways of Seeing* (London 1972).

Blenkinsop, J., *Sexuality and the Christian Tradition* (London 1970).

Blair, P. H., *The World of Bede* (London 1970).

Bloch, I., *Sexual Life in England* (London 1965).

Boethius, *Consolations of Philosophy*, tr. H. R. James (London n.d.).

Bottomley, F., *The Church Explorers' Guide* (London 1978).

Bourke, V. J., *The Essential St Augustine* (N.Y. 1964).

Boussard, J., *The Civilisation of Charlemagne*, Eng tr. (London 1968).

Bouyer, L., *Woman and Man with God*, Eng. tr. (London 1960).

Bowie, T. and Christienson, C., *Studies in Erotic Art* (N.Y. 1970).

Bright, J., *History of Israel* (London 1960).

Brophy, J., *Body and Soul* (London 1948).

Brown, B. F., 'Natural law', in *New Catholic Encyclopedia* (Washington 1967).

Brown, N.O. *Love's Body* (New York 1966).

— — *Life against Death* (Middletown, Connecticut 1959).

Buchanan, S., *Rediscovering Natural Law* (Santa Barbara 1962).

Budge, E. A. Wallis (tr.), *The Paradise of the Fathers* (London 1907).

Burckhardt, J., *The Civilisation of the Renaissance in Italy* (London 1944).

Butler, C., *Benedictine Monachism* (Cambridge ed. 1961).

Cabrol, F., *Liturgical Prayer: Its History and Spirit* (London 1925).

Calder, R., *Leonardo and the Age of the Eye* (London 1970).

Callus, D. A. (ed.), *Robert Grosseteste: Scholar and Bishop* (Oxford 1969).

Carcopino, J., *Daily Life in Ancient Rome* (Penguin 1956).

Cary, M. J. and Haarhoff, T. J., *Life and Thought in the Greek and Roman World* (London 1961).

Catullus, Tibullus, *Pervigilium Veneris*, in Loeb Library (London 1935).
Cave, S., *The Christian Estimate of Man* (London 1957).
Celsus, *De Medicina* tr. W. G. Spencer, in Leob Library, 3 vols. (London 1960).
Chambers, F. W., *The Mediaeval Stage*, 2 vols. (London 1913).
Cicero, *De Republica*, tr. C. W. Keyes, in Loeb Library (London 1966).
— — *Tusculan Disputations*, tr. J. E. King, in Loeb Library (London 1946).
Clark, K., *The Nude* (London 1956).
— —, *Landscape into Art* (London 1966).
— —, *Civilisation* (London 1969).
Clarke, K. W. Lowther, *The Rule of St Benedict* (London 1931).
— —, *Liturgy and Worship* (London 1940).
Cleugh, J., *Love Locked Out* (London 1967).
Cochrane, C. N., *Christianity and Classical Culture* (N.Y. 1957).
Coplestone, F., *Aquinas* (London 1955).
Coulton, G. G., *Mediaeval Panorama* (Cambridge 1938).
— —, *Life in the Middle Ages*, 4 vols (Cambridge 1928).
Cox, H., *The Feast of Fools* (Harvard 1969).
Cragg, G. R., *The Church and the Age of Reason* (London 1960).
Crawford, S. J., *Anglo-Saxon Influence on Western Christendom* (Cambridge 1966).
Crawley, E. *The Mystic Rose* (London 1932).
Cruden, A., *Complete Concordance to the Old and New Testaments and Apocrypha* (London n.d.).
Cyprian, *Writings*, in Ante-Nicene Christian Library, 2 vols. (Edinburgh 1868–9).
Dalby, J., *The Catholic Conception of the Law of Nature* (London 1943).
D'Arcy, M. C., *The Mind and Heart of Love* (London 1946).
Davis, C., *Body as Spirit* (London 1976).
Dawson, C., *Christianity and Sex* (London 1930).
— —, *Making of Europe* (London 1946).
Dods, M. (tr.), *The City of God* – Augustine, 2 vols. (Edinburgh 1934).
Dolan, J. P., *The Essential Erasmus* (New York 1964).
Doms, H., *The Meaning of Marriage*, Eng. tr. (London 1939).
Douglas, M., *Purity and Danger* (London 1966).
Dronke, P., *Mediaeval Latin and Rise of European Love-lyric*, 2 vols. (Oxford 1968).
Duchesne, L., *Christian Worship* (London 1931).
Duckett, E. S. *Alcuin, friend of Charlemagne* (New York 1951).
Dudden, F. Homes, *The Life and Times of St Ambrose*, 2 vols. (Oxford 1935).
Eliade, M., *Myths, Dreams and Mysteries* (London 1968).
Ferguson, G., *Signs and Symbols in Christian Art* (Oxford 1961).
Fill, J. H., *The Mental Breakdown of a Nation* (N.Y. 1974).
Fortescue, A., *The Mass, A Study of the Roman Liturgy* (London 1937).
Fowler, W. Warde, *The Religious Experience of the Roman People* (N.Y. 1974).
Freeman, G., *The Undergrowth of Literature* (London 1967).
Freemantle, A., *The Papal Encyclicals in their Historical Context* (N.Y. 1956).
Frye, R. M., *Shakespeare and Christian doctrine* (Princeton 1963).
Gardner, E. G., *The Dialogues of St Gregory* (London 1911).
Garland, M., *The Changing Face of Beauty* (London 1960).
Gerber, E. W., *Sport and the Body* (Philadelphia 1972).
Gelin, A., *Concept of Man in the Bible* (London 1968).
Gibbon, E., *The Decline and Fall of the Roman Empire*, 4 vols. (London n.d.).
Gilby, T., et al. (trs.), *St Thomas Aquinas*, 60 vols. (London 1964–6).
Gilson, E., *The Christian Philosophy of St Augustine* (London 1961).
— —, *The Mystical Theology of St Bernard* (London 1940).
Gombrich, E. H., *Symbolic Images* (London 1972).
Gorer, G., et. al. (eds.), *Psychoanalysis Observed* (London 1968).

Grant, M., *The Climax of Rome* (London 1968).
— —, *The World of Rome* (London 1962).
Greeley, A. M., *The Persistence of Religion* (London 1973).
Greene, J. J. and Dolan, J.P., *The Essential Thomas More* (N.Y. 1967).
Harris, H. A., *Sport in Britain* (London 1975).
Hauser, A., *The Social History of Art*, 4 vol edn. (London 1962).
Hay, D., *The Italian Renaissance* (Cambridge 1961).
Heer, F., *The Intellectual History of Europe*, Eng. trs. (London 1966).
— —, *The Mediaeval World*, Eng. tr. (London 1963).
Hendy, P., *The National Gallery, London* (London 1955).
Hess, T. B. and Nochlin, L., *Woman as Sex Object* (London 1973).
'H.M.' (ed.), *The Love Letters of Abélard and Heloïse* (London 1901).
Holt, E. G., *A Documentary History of Art*, 3 vols. (N.Y. 1958).
Horace, *Odes and Epodes*, tr. C. E. Bennett (London 1964).
Howard, G. B., *Canons of the Primitive Church* (London 1896).
Huizinga, J., *The Waning of the Middle Ages* (London 1924).
Illich, I. D., *Medical Nemesis* (London 1975).
— —, *Celebration of Awareness* (London 1973).
— — *Deschooling Society* (London 1971).
Ivins, W. M., *Art and Geometry* (London 1964).
Jacob, E., *Theology of the Old Testament* (N.Y. 1958).
Janelle, P., *The Catholic Reformation* (London 1972).
Jerome, *Select Letters*, tr. F. A. Wright, in Loeb (London 1933).
Johnson, C., *The Language of Painting* (Cambridge 1949).
Josphus, *Life Against Apion*, tr. H. St J. Thackeray, in Loeb (London 1966).
Jowett, B., (trs.), *The Four Socratic Dialogues of Plato* (Oxford 1928).
Jungmann, J. A., *The Mass of the Roman Rite*, 2 vols. (N.Y. 1951).
Juvenal, *Satires*, tr. E. G. Ramsay, in Loeb Classical Library (London 1965).
Kahmen, V., *Eroticism in Contemporary Art* (London 1972).
Ker, W. P., *The Dark Ages* (N.Y. 1958).
Kiefer, O., *Sexual Life in Ancient Rome* (London 1969).
Knowles, B., *Saints and Scholars* (Cambridge 1963).
— —, *The Religious Orders in England*, 3 vols. (Cambridge 1961).
Lake, K. (trs.), *The Apostolic Fathers*, 2 vols., in Loeb (London 1930).
Landau, R., *Sex, Life and Faith* (London 1946).
Larousse, *Encyclopedia of Mythology* (London 1961).
Lebreton, J. and Zeiller, J., *History of the Primitive Church*, 4 vols. (London 1944).
Leclercq, J., *The Love of Learning and the Desire for God* (N.Y. 1962).
Lecky, W. E. H., *History of European Morals*, 2 vols. (London 1905).
Leeuw, Gerardus van der *Sacred and Profane Beauty* (N.Y. 1963).
Le Trocquer, R., *What is Man?* (London 1961).
Lewis, C. S., *The Abolition of Man* (London 1946).
— —, *The Allegory of Love* (Oxford 1936).
— —, *Till They Have Faces* (London 1956).
— —, *The Discarded Image* (Cambridge 1967a).
— —, *Studies in Words* (Cambridge 1967b).
Lewis, N. and Reinhold, M., *Roman Civilisation*, 2 vols. (N.Y. 1966).
Licht, H., *Sexual Life in Ancient Greece* (London 1969).
Lilar, S., *Aspects of Love in Western Society* (London 1965).
Livy, *History*, tr. E. T. Sage, 14 vols in Loeb (London 1965).
Lovejoy, A. O., *The Great Chain of Being* (Cambridge, Mass. 1936).
— —, *Essays in the History of Ideas* (Baltimore 1948).
Lucie-Smith, E., *Eroticism in Western Art* (London 1972).
Male, E., *The Gothic Image* (London 1961).

MacCurdy, E., *The Notebooks of Leonardo da Vinci*, 2 vols. (London 1952).
Marcus, S., *The Other Victorians* (London 1966).
Maritain, J., *Three Reformers* (London 1941).
Marshall, D. S. and Suggs, R. C. (eds.), *Human Sexual Behaviour* (N.Y. 1971).
Mascall, E. L., *Christ, the Christian and the Church* (London 1946).
Mason, A. J., *The Mission of St Augustine* (Cambridge 1897).
McCabe, H., *The New Creation* (London 1964).
McDonald, W. J. (ed.), *The New Catholic Encyclopedia* (Washington 1967).
Meer, van der F. and Mohrmann, C., *Atlas of Early Christian World* (London 1958).
Melville, R., *Erotic Art of the West* (London 1973).
Mersch, E. tr. J. R. Kelly, *The Whole Christ* (Milwaukee 1938).
Mitchell, R. J. and Leys, M. D. R., *A History of the English People* (London 1967).
Mode, H., *The Woman in Indian Art* (Leipzig 1970).
Molesworth, H. D., *Sculpture in England* (Mediaeval) (London 1951).
— —, *Sculpture in England* (Renaissance) (London 1951).
— —, *Sculpture in England* (Baroque) (London 1954).
Morey, C. R., *Christian Art* (London 1935).
Murdoch, I., *The Fire and the Sun* (Oxford 1977).
Murray, P. and L., *The Art of the Renaissance* (London 1963).
Neuner, J. and Dupuis, J., *The Christian Faith* (Bangalore 1973).
Newman, J. H., *The Mission of the Benedictine Order* (London 1908).
O'Faolain, J. and Martinez L., *Not in God's Image* (London 1974).
O'Connor, D. J., *Aquinas and Natural Law* (London 1967).
Oesterreicher, J. M., *The Bridge* (IV) (N.Y. 1962).
Orchard, B. et al. (ed.), *A Catholic Commentary on Holy Scripture* (London 1953).
Origo, I., *The Merchant of Prato* (London 1955).
— —, *The World of San Bernardino* (London 1963).
Ovid, *Metamorphoses*, tr. F. J. Miller, 2 vols. in Loeb Library (London 1966).
—, *Ars Amatoria*, tr. J. H. Mozley, in Loeb Library (London 1962).
—'—, *Fasti*, tr. J. G. Frazer, in Loeb Library (London 1967).
Owst, G. R., *Literature and Pulpit in Mediaeval England* (Oxford 1966).
Pannikar, R., *Worship and Secular Man* (London 1973).
Panofsky, E., *Gothic Architecture and Scholasticism* (N.Y. 1957).
— —, *Studies in Iconology* (N.Y. 1962).
— —, *Meaning in the Visual Arts* (London 1955).
Pantin, W. A., *The English Church in the Fourteenth Century* (Cambridge 1955).
Patai, R., *Man and Temple* (London 1947).
Pearsall, R., *The Worm in the Bud* (London 1971).
Peckham, M., *Art and Pornography* (N.Y. 1969).
Perowne, S., *Roman Mythology* (London 1969).
Petronius, *Satyricon*, tr. M. Heselton in Loeb (London 1961).
Peursen, van C. A., *Body, Soul and Spirit* (London 1966).
Phillips, J. B., *Letters to Young Churches* (London 1955).
Pieper, J., *Leisure, the Basis of Culture* (London 1965).
Pignatorre, T., *The Ancient Monuments of Rome* (London n.d.).
Piper, O. A., *The Christian Interpretation of Sex*(London 1942).
Plautus, *Plays*, tr. P. Nixon, 5 vols. in Loeb (London 1963–6).
Pliny the Elder, *Natural History*, tr. H. Rackham, (10 vols. in Loeb) (London 1958–62).
Pliny the Younger, *Letters*, tr. Melmoth, 2 vols. in Loeb (London 1963).
Plotinus, *Enneads*, tr. H. Armstrong, 3 vols. in Loeb (London 1966).
Poynter, F. N. L. and Keele, K. D., *A Short History of Medicine* (London 1961).
Power, E., *Mediaeval People* (London 1939).
Propertius, *Poems*, tr. H. E. Butler, Loeb Library (London 1967).

Przwara, E., *An Augustine Synthesis* (London 1939).

Purvis, J. S., *From Minster to Market Place* (York 1969).

— —, *The York Cycle of Mystery Plays* (London 1962).

Ramsay, A. M., *The Gospel and the Catholic Church* London 1956).

Rahner, H., *Greek Myths and Christian Mystery* (London 1963).

— —, *Man at Play* (London 1965).

Rahner, K. (ed.), *The Teaching of the Catholic Church*, Eng. Edn. (Cork 1967).

Radhakrishnan, S., *Eastern Religions and Western Thought* (Oxford 1969).

Rawson, P., *Erotic Art of the East* (London 1973a).

— —, *Tantra* (London 1973b).

Reeves, J. W., *Body and Mind in Western Thought* (London 1958).

Rhymer, J. (ed.), *The Bible in Order* (London 1975).

Richardson, A., *A Theological Word-book of the Bible* (London 1950).

Robertson, D. M., *Literature of Mediaeval England* (N.Y. 1970).

Robinson, J. A. T., *The Body: A Study in Pauline Theology* (London 1952).

Romestin, H. et al. (trs.), *Some of the Principal Works of St Ambrose* (Oxford 1896).

Rycroft, C. et al., *Psychoanalysis Observed* (London 1968).

Sacred Congregation for the Doctrine of the Faith, *Declaration on Certain Questions Concerning Sexual Ethics* (Rome 1976).

Salu, M. B. (tr.), *The Ancrene Riwle* (London 1955).

Santillana, G. de, *The Age of Adventure* (N.Y. 1956).

Schneer, C. J., *The Search for Order* (London 1960).

Seneca, *Moral Epistles*, tr. R. M. Gunmere, 3 vols. in Loeb (London 1967).

Sidonius Apollinaris, *Poems and Letters*, tr. W. B. Anderson, 2 vols. in Loeb Classical Library (London 1963, 1965).

Silva, de A. et al. (ed.), *Love and Marriage in 'Man through his Art'* (London 1968).

Smith, W. and Wace, H., *Dictionary of Christian Biography*, 4 vols. (London 1877).

Steinberg, S. H., *Historical Tables* (London 1966).

Steward, H. F. (tr. ed.), *Pascal's Pensées* (London 1950).

Summers, M. (tr.), *Malleus Maleficiarum* (London 1968).

Southern, R. W., *The Making of the Middle Ages* (London 1959).

Sylvester, D., *Interviews with Francis Bacon* (London 1975).

Taylor, G. Rattray, *Sex in History* (London 1965).

Taylor, H. O., *The Mediaeval Mind*, 2 vols. (London 1938).

Teilhard de Chardin, P., *The Phenomenon of Man* (London 1959).

Tertullian, *The Writings of Tertullian*, in the Ante-Nicene Christian Library (Edinburgh 1868–70).

Thorpe, L. (ed.), *Two Lives of Charlemagne* (London 1969).

Tillyard, E. M., *The Elizabethan World-Picture* (London 1943, 1966).

Thornton, L. S., *The Common Life in the Body of Christ* (London 1942).

Tolnay, C. de et al., *The Complete Works of Michelangelo*, 2 vols. (London 1966).

Turnbull, G. H., *The Essence of Plotinus* (N.Y. 1934).

Ulanov, B., The Song of Songs, in *The Bridge* (N.Y. 1962).

Vallentin, A., *Leonardo da Vinci* (London 1939).

Vasari, G., *Lives of the Great Painters*, var. edn., tr. G. Bull, *Life of Michelangelo Buonarroti* (London 1971).

Voegelin, A., *The Ecumenical Age*, vol. IV in *Order and History* (Baton Rouge 1975).

Waddell, H., *Beasts and Saints* (London 1934).

— —, *The Desert Fathers* (London 1936).

— —, *The Wandering Scholars* (London 1937).

— —, *Mediaeval Latin Lyrics* (London 1929).

— —, *Peter Abélard* (London 1933).

Walker, K., *The Story of Medicine* (London 1954).

Warner, M. *Alone of All Her Sex* (London 1976).

Wassmer, T. A., 'Natural law', in *New Catholic Encyclopedia* (Washington 1967).
Watkin, E. I., *Catholic Art and Culture* (London 1947).
Wendel, F., *Calvin* (London 1973).
Westow, T., *The Variety of Catholic Attitudes* (London 1963).
Williams, C., *The Figure of Beatrice* (London 1943).
Williamson, H. R. *The Great Prayer* (London 1955).
Wilkins, E., *The Rose Garden Game* (London 1969).
Wilson, W., *Christian Art since the Romantic Movement* (London 1965).
Wind, E., *Pagan Mysteries in the Renaissance* (London 1967).
Wolff, H. W., *Anthropology of the Old Testament* (London 1975).
Wren-Lewis, J., 'Love's coming of age', in *Psychoanalysis Observed* (London 1966).
Wright, L., *Clean and Decent* (London 1960).
Wu, J. C. H., 'Natural law', in *New Catholic Encyclopedia* (Washington 1967).
Zarnecki, G., *The Monastic Achievement* (London 1972).
Ziegler, P., *The Black Death* (London 1969).

INDEX